Praise for *Member of the Family*

"Dianne Lake met Charles Manson in 1967, when she was just 14. She didn't participate in the horrific murders carried out by Manson and his followers in August 1969, but she was the youngest member of the Manson Family. And at 17, she was a key witness at the trial that resulted in his conviction, a death sentence that was commuted to life in prison. . . . Lake is a rarity—someone who escaped and survived a cult."

—*Newsweek*

"Part memoir, part compelling true-crime narrative, Lake's new book, *Member of the Family: My Story of Charles Manson, Life Inside His Cult, and the Darkness That Ended the Sixties,* is a painfully relevant account of manipulation, abuse and masculinity so toxic it ended in murder. . . . Lake offers a detailed, heartfelt and strangely relatable telling of how a teenage girl fell in love with one of the most notorious criminals of the 20th century, and how she ultimately fought her way out."

—*Rolling Stone*

"Lake breaks 47 years of silence on her infamy as the youngest of 'Charlie's Girls,' the women who lived under the cult leader's sway on his two California ranches. She did not participate in the Manson family's slaughtering of seven people on two horrifying nights in 1969, crimes that would come to be known as the Tate-LaBianca murders—but at age 17, she testified against the killers."

—*People*

"Fans of Emma Cline's novel *The Girls* will enjoy this nonfiction account of a teenager living under Charles Manson's cult leadership in the '60s and her eventual aid in his arrest and imprisonment."

—*AM New York*

"In this disturbing, courageous memoir, Lake, a former special education teacher, recounts her dark journey as the youngest member of Charles Manson's 'family.' . . . Her testimony, at age 17, helped convict Manson. This is a moving, intense insider's view of the cult of Manson."   —*Publishers Weekly*

"Compelling. . . . Without sacrificing scintillating details about the family's birthing rituals or underage prostitution, Lake offers both a human portrait of her notorious colleagues and a thoughtful take on counterculture sexism."   —*Booklist*

"The book is a horror story, but the real horror comes late in the game . . . The book's highlights include Lake's firsthand memories of day-to-day Family rivalries, and her own response to the surrounding descent into madness. If you've ever wondered what the innocent Mansonites thought about the guilty ones, then read this book."   —*LA Weekly*

"[Lake's] tale of emotional and sexual manipulation at the hands of an older, sociopathic man is all too prescient in this moment in time, in which we're finally bringing abusive and manipulative men the reckoning that they deserve. But beyond the book's modern day relevance, it's also just a good memoir—especially for those of us who have an interest in gripping true crime and nefarious cults. You'll get your fill of both from this young woman's terrifying search for a 'family' to call her own."   —*Shondaland*

MEMBER OF THE FAMILY

MEMBER OF THE FAMILY

MY STORY OF CHARLES MANSON, LIFE INSIDE HIS CULT, AND THE DARKNESS THAT ENDED THE SIXTIES

DIANNE LAKE

AND DEBORAH HERMAN

WM
WILLIAM MORROW
An Imprint of *HarperCollins*Publishers

HarperCollins books may be purchased for educational, business,
or sales promotional use. For information, please email the
Special Markets Department at SPsales@harpercollins.com.

A hardcover edition of this book was published in 2017 by William Morrow,
an imprint of HarperCollins Publishers.

FIRST WILLIAM MORROW PAPERBACK EDITION PUBLISHED 2018.

Designed by William Ruoto

Library of Congress Cataloging-in-Publication Data has been applied for.

ISBN 978-0-06-269558-1

18 19 20 21 22   DIX/LSC   10 9 8 7 6 5 4 3 2   1

*To the victims and their families; those who needlessly
lost their lives and those who continue to suffer because of
the madness of this dark time in our shared history. May
God's grace prevail and heal the pain that remains.*

CONTENTS

AUTHOR'S NOTE

IT IS TIME FOR ME TO EXORCISE MY OWN DEMONS AND TO FACE THE truth as much as I can remember it. In this book, I have shared what I can re-create through straining my memory muscle, research, corroboration from people who knew me, and my own words from trial and interrogation transcripts. They tell only my piece of the story from personal experience and perception. I was with the Manson Family from the age of fourteen until my arrest at Barker Ranch at the age of sixteen. My memories by necessity reflect the mind of a teenager. Everything in this book is true. Some of the names and identifying details have been changed to protect people's privacy. Some conversations are re-created to the best of my ability, as no memory is perfect. This is my perspective. This is my story and this is my confessional.

PROLOGUE

IT BEGAN, AS THESE STORIES OFTEN DO, WITH A PHONE CALL, ONE THAT I had been dreading for decades.

"Are you Dianne Lake?" the voice asked.

The question stopped me in my tracks. I hadn't heard that name for years. This could be about only one thing.

"Uh-huh," I said hesitantly. "What do you want?"

Immediately after the words left my mouth, I regretted saying them. I'd done nothing wrong, committed no crimes, but I had a reason to hide. So many people out there had looked for me over the years—reporters writing about the crimes, journalists seeking sources for books about the Family—and of course the worst were the crazies obsessed with Charles Manson. For the most part, I'd been able to evade them all—flying under the radar all these years, hiding in plain sight with my husband's last name. I immediately wished I had hung up the phone right at that moment, but it happened too fast, my answer a reflex. Even after all these years, I still wasn't prepared.

I had buried my history so well I'd almost forgotten that once I was someone else: a young girl named Dianne Lake who was only fourteen when Charles Manson had inducted her into his Family of followers. A girl who had spent almost two years being manipulated by him before a moment of clarity broke the spell, and who then went on to testify against him on November 3, 1970, helping to put him in prison forever. Over the course of the eight years that followed, I'd been in and out of the courtroom through the Manson trial and two retrials of fellow Family member Leslie Van Houten, coming of age on the witness stand and telling my story to the juries and the judges, as well as to the gawkers who obsessed over the gruesome acts that were committed by Charles Manson and members of his Family on two nights in August 1969. I'd told stories of life with the Family, of the things we'd done and the drugs we'd taken, of how I'd joined with the blessing of my parents, hippies themselves, thinking that I was in control of my life, only to discover a reality darker than I ever could have imagined.

And in 1978, after my final appearance on the witness stand for Leslie Van Houten's retrial, I put away these stories of Charles Manson and the Family and left them behind for good. In a case that had captured the attention of people around the world, where spectators waited all night for one of the fifteen seats in the courtroom, I was the last witness.

From then on, Charles Manson and his Family were a part of my past—they had nothing to do with my present or my future. By that point, I was already being courted by my husband, with whom I spent the next thirty-five years. He knew about my past, but we decided to create a life without ties to that former identity. We never told his family or the three children we went on to have together about what I'd been through. Even when my daughter brought in a stray cat and named it Charlie, I never acknowledged why I suggested she call him something else.

Over time, my memories of the Manson Family became watercolors, the lines soft and blurry without clear definition. Whenever I was reminded of the Family, either because of events in the news or anniversary retrospectives, I disconnected, all too willing to forget the events of my own life. Until the phone rang.

"I am Paul Dostie," the voice said. "I am a detective and my partner is a cadaver dog named Buster."

"What is this about?" I asked.

"I know that you told investigator Jack Gardiner that you thought there were more bodies buried up by Barker Ranch."

Barker Ranch. It was where we'd hidden out after the murders, in Death Valley, the middle of nowhere and as far away as Charlie could take us. A place where they weren't supposed to find us. Only they did. Two months after the killings, with a warrant for an unrelated charge of vandalism, the police raided Barker Ranch, rounding up all of us. In the interim it was Family member Susan Atkins, one of the killers, then in jail on another charge, who made the connection between these crimes and Charlie. I kept my identity secret as I shared a cell with the other girls in the Family. When it came time to testify before the grand jury, I admitted my real age of only sixteen and gave them my true name. Confessing my true age made me a ward of the court and landed me in a mental institution, an interesting twist for a teenage girl who'd experienced all that the counterculture of the 1960s had to offer.

Jack Gardiner, the cop who'd been my arresting officer, must have seen something in me worth saving, because when I was institutionalized he began visiting me there. When it was time for me to be released, he and his wife took me in as a foster child. They were the first people who helped me feel safe enough to speak about what I'd been through, what I'd seen and heard. I lived securely with them until I testified.

As I cradled the phone in my hand, I strained to recall what I might have said to Jack all those years ago. Maybe I had told him there were other bodies. There could have been. People would often come and go from the Barker Ranch, disappearing at random. Maybe they were passing through or maybe something more sinister happened to them; Charlie and the others were obviously capable of murder.

"Dianne, there are people who may never have been brought to justice. My dog has alerted to some possible human remains."

I didn't respond. While in the moment I couldn't be sure if he was telling the truth, I'd later learn this was indeed the case. In February of 2008, a team of investigators including former Inyo County detective John Little, who had worked for Jack in the early 1970s, went with Dostie and others to see if they could find anything at the old Barker Ranch.

"Do you know that undersheriff Jack Gardiner back in 1974 sent Detective Little to Barker to investigate possible human remains buried there? He was your foster father during the trial. Now why would he do that if he had nothing to base it upon?"

My hands began to sweat. For the first time in many years, Charlie's face appeared in my mind, along with the words: "Don't talk to no one in authority." I felt as though I was going into a tunnel and could hear the small voice of my sixteen-year-old self somewhere in the distance.

"What do you want with me, Mr. Dostie? I don't remember anything I might have said to Jack back then."

"I am calling you out of courtesy. We are going back there to dig. And we are going to tape it and show it on television. If anything is discovered out there, we are going to have to trace it back to tip-offs you likely gave to Jack Gardiner."

"Please, I am not that person anymore," I said. "I have a family and children. I go to church. I sing in the choir. I teach autistic children, for heaven's sake. My children don't know anything about my past."

"That is why I am giving you a heads up," he said coolly. "I know you were not a killer, but you were part of something bigger than you are. And it is news and it is history. I think we are going to find things out there that are going to be gruesome. It is up to you how you want to handle this with your family."

"Can't you just keep me out of this?"

"I am sorry, Dianne, but from what I have read, you became a part of it the second you got on that bus with Charles Manson."

That night I told my husband about the call. We both knew this day would come—it had to. It was a terrible secret to keep from my children, but I knew that I couldn't bring myself to tell them any other way; I'd buried the past too carefully. Nothing about their upbringing would suggest what I'd hidden. For most of my children's lives, I enjoyed the privilege of being home with them, taking care of them. We lived modestly but well, and I made sure the house was clean, dinner was on the table, and I was in the front row at their every school function. My children never spent a day thinking I was not there for them. But now the front was going to collapse under the weight of my former life and the shame I'd concealed for years. Now I would have to tell my children what had really happened during those two treacherous years in California.

But first I myself would have to face the truth. Memories fade, but trauma remembers. It is stored in your body, your senses, your synapses and cells. It would take strength to tell my story, but more importantly, it would take strength to tell myself, and to remember.

PART I

TURN ON

I

A MINNESOTA CHILDHOOD

THIS IS HOW MY REAL STORY BEGINS. NOT WITH SUNNY SOUTHERN CAL-
ifornia, hippies, and drugs, but as white-bread and middle class as it
gets: 1950s Minnesota.

Born in 1953, I was my parents' first child. My father, Clarence,
was a sturdy man with a wide, crooked smile. He'd followed his father's footsteps into the house painting trade to put the food on the
table, but art was his passion. He began art school after his marriage,
using painting as an outlet for his creativity—house painter by day,
artist by night. My mom, Shirley, was a housewife who made every
effort to look her best each day and keep a lovely home. As a little
girl, I would follow her around the house and try to imitate everything she did. If she was washing a dish in the sink, I would beg to
be picked up. "I do it!" I would squeal until she gave me my own
sponge to wash with. I was her little shadow and became a "mini
momma" when my brother, Danny, and then later my sister, Kathy,
were born.

When I was in first grade, my parents must have felt prosper-
ous enough to buy a sizable house outside Minneapolis with a
huge backyard. Our neighbors had a greenhouse, in which they
grew all kinds of fragrant flowers. When you opened the door, you
were greeted with the smell of potted perennials, herbs, and colorful annual flowers for every season. I kept an eye on my younger
brother and sister while my father worked and my mother took
care of the house. Kathy was a baby, so I would wheel her in her

stroller across the lawn or carry her in my arms so she could smell the blooms.

My mother continued to let me help around the house, and in many ways, the housework was exciting to me. There were new household gadgets available and we had a top-of-the-line Hoover Constellation, a round, space-age-looking vacuum that was supposed to float on its own exhaust. You almost wanted to throw dirt on the floor just so you could see how it worked. Our home was always clean, but sometimes I vacuumed just to have something to do.

My mom taught me how to sew on the toy sewing machine I got one year for Christmas, setting me up at a table next to her Singer sewing machine, showing me how to thread the needle and guide the fabric to make the stitches stay straight. In the weeks that followed, she gave me scraps of fabric so I could create outfits for my dolls and little quilts. Eventually I got so good at this that she got me a pattern so I could sew clothes for myself.

From the outside, ours was a traditional family, but there was a restlessness beneath the surface. Before I was born, my father had served in the Korean conflict, and although I wouldn't have known the difference, my mother always said it had changed him. A father's dissatisfaction is not always expressed out loud, but it is certainly felt. Over time I came to understand how the currents of his behavior affected our family life. After coming home from work, he would disappear into the corner of the living room that he had set aside for painting, and we weren't allowed to go near him when he was working. We had our own playroom, and whenever Danny and Kathy tried to bother him, I would catch them so he wouldn't be disturbed. Even at that age, I understood that he needed room to create.

Even young as I was, I sensed that there was a distance to him, a detachment that made him different. When he smiled, the sun would shine, and my earliest memories are of him laughing and playing with me. But when he was depressed, it was as if the air had been sucked out of the room; he was sullen unless he was working on a project. On those sad days, he would sit quietly in a dark room staring off into space smoking cigarette after cigarette, the smoke thick in the air around him.

I must have taken my cues from my mother because she largely allowed him the space to indulge his whims. Despite his moodiness, he could do no wrong in her eyes. She interacted with him in a manner that bordered on worship and defined much of our domestic lives. She watched him closely, gauging his expressions before she would interact with him. When he got home from work she would wait until he settled in before beginning any conversation. She wouldn't present him with our misdeeds the minute he walked in the door. Instead we were instructed to greet him cheerfully. He was the stoic king of our castle and we learned to wait until he addressed us before sharing too much with him. I wanted him to notice me, and if he did, I held on to the moment in my heart and in my memory. My remembrances of the times he would grumble and tease me about something that would make me feel bad or tell me "I'll give you something to cry about" would be countered by his moments of playfulness even if they were not directed at me.

Perhaps because of my father's unpredictability, my mother controlled the money in the house, as she was the more responsible person. At the end of the week my father handed her whatever money he'd earned painting houses, and I would watch as she paid all the bills. Each month my mom would make sure that the mortgage on the house was paid along with every other bill, spreading the envelopes on the table, writing out checks, and asking me to lick the stamps. Then she would take them to the post office in town to mail them.

Each week she would give my father an allowance in cash and set aside our money for our food. She did all the shopping for us and prepared all our meals. She would pack his lunch in the morning, sometimes putting a little note in his brown bag. She also made dinner every night. Though my dad always seemed busy, he did take time to have dinner with us. This was my favorite time of day because he led the discussion and included me just as if I were a grown-up.

"Dianne, what are you learning in school?" he'd ask me.

"Be right back," I'd reply, running off to gather a stack of papers. "Look, Daddy, I got good grades on these." I'd spread out my spelling tests, writing practice books, and math papers, showing him my schoolwork and my achievements and trying to impress him.

"That's great. Keep up the good work."

At dinner, my father would often bring up the books he was reading, eager to discuss them with my mother, and always somehow disappointed that she didn't share his interest in them. For my part, I was excited in anything that interested him.

"I am reading a great book, Shirley. I think you should read it too," he said one night while we were eating.

"You know I don't have that much time to read," my mother responded.

"What is it about, Daddy?" I asked. "I can read now." I was in the top reading group in my class.

"Oh, honey, I think this is a little too old for you," he said. "But I will tell you about it. It's by this guy named Jack Kerouac, and it's about two friends who go on this road trip to find out more about themselves."

"Read it to me." I liked hearing my father's voice whether he was reading me *Horton Hatches the Egg*, which I could now read myself, or if he read to me from his own books that I didn't really understand.

"Well, actually, I just got another book by Jack Kerouac," he said, getting up from the table and reaching into the pocket of his jacket, which was hanging on a hook by the door. The book cover had funny writing and a man with a woman riding on him piggyback.

"This book is called *The Dharma Bums*," he informed me. "Here is something he says in the book: 'One man practicing kindness in the wilderness is worth all the temples this world pulls.'"

"I like that, Daddy." I had no idea what it meant, but I liked that it had the word *kindness* in it. It must have been something good. I gave my daddy a hug, and he left the table to continue working on a painting.

Another night after dinner, he had retreated to the living room to paint when he noticed I was sitting outside the room. I didn't want to disturb him but wanted to watch him work.

"Hey, little girl, do you like this music?" he asked suddenly. We had a small record player, and while he painted, he usually would play something from his collection.

"What is that?" I had never heard sounds like the ones coming from the record. There wasn't really any singing, just music.

"It's jazz," he replied. "Isn't it cool?"

My dad showed me the album cover. It was wild. Then he took out another record and showed me how to carefully clamp an album between my hands by the edges so it wouldn't get scratched. He used a black brush on the record's surface before he put it on the record player, placing the needle delicately on the first groove and inviting me to sit down with him.

We sat on a love seat next to his easel. I watched as the smoke rose from his cigarette, curling its way toward the ceiling. Every so often he would blow a smoke ring just to get me to laugh.

"Listen to this part—*bah bah bah*," he sang along with the trumpet. After a while we were both bobbing our heads up and down in time to the beat. The music changed with each instrument. I liked the timpani and the cymbals; I had never heard anything like them.

"Dianne, that is Buddy Rich. He is arguably the best drummer in history."

Now I was rocking back and forth.

After a while my eyelids got heavy. The last thing I remembered were the sands of a trumpet. In the morning, I woke up in my bed, the beat still ringing in my ears.

ONE MORNING DURING THE EARLY MONTHS OF MY SECOND-GRADE year, I was in the kitchen with my mother when my father walked in.

"Do you want some coffee? I brewed a fresh pot," my mom said, apron tied around her waist.

"Sure, honey," he replied, and then, as if it was part of an ongoing discussion, he said, "Too bad we don't live in California. Do you know they get to listen to jazz all the time?"

"I thought if you want to talk about jazz, the scene is in New York?" she asked.

"There is a happening scene for artists and poets in Venice Beach, California. I read about this place called the Gas House. Everyone goes there, including Jack Kerouac. They opened it last year, and it is an exciting place for artists to get started. I could get my master's degree out there and get somewhere."

I could see my mother's body tense as she went about making breakfast for him. Her fingers tightly gripped the handle of the pan as she scraped his eggs onto his plate. "Look, we have a nice house here and the kids are all settled," my mother said. "It is hard enough to take care of three kids, a house, and a husband. Can't you do your master's here?"

My dad relented and the conversation petered out. He continued working as a house painter during the day, keeping his desire for a change of scenery mostly to himself. While I never knew exactly what he was thinking, it was clear there were things about our life, about his life, that were not satisfying him. Still, beyond my mother, he really had no one he could talk to about this desire to break from the mold of his life that was gradually hardening around him. He couldn't tell his father about how he felt. Grandpa's reply would have been "house painting kept food in your mouth and kept you alive. Do you think you are better than me?"

My father remained largely silent on the matter, but none of this eased his malaise. It's hard to say exactly what impact his reading had on him, but there's no doubt that it influenced him and enhanced his impatience. The Beats. Jazz music. These were the first sounds of the underground reverberating out from the coasts toward Middle America and making men like my father question the choices they'd made.

The tipping point came from something that seemed innocent enough. Somewhat impulsively, my father ordered a hi-fi, a high-fidelity stereo system, by mail. He couldn't wait to get the thing—he thought it was going to fill the entire house with sound, in contrast to the little phonograph, music from which barely carried into the next room. But when the hi-fi arrived, he looked at the bill, apparently for the first time, and freaked out at the cost. Shortly after that, he broke from their usual pattern of letting my mother handle the finances and instead sat down with her while she was writing out the bills. He turned them over and read them one at a time, eventually stopping at the mortgage bill. As he stared at it, he figured out the interest on the mortgage, becoming more and more upset. Perhaps the mortgage became a symbol of his frustration with our situation. The perpetual responsibility, the way it tied us down in Minnesota, and the fact that our house and family would apparently be his life's work—all of it seemed to weigh on him.

"How the hell are we going to keep up with these payments?" he shouted at my mother, who was surprised that he had suddenly started caring about the money they spent. His response might also have had something to do with the books he was reading, because he was telling her that they were being pulled into, as he put it, "the establishment trap of materialism."

"This house and this stuff is going to steal our soul!" He slammed the bill on the table and knocked the other papers on the floor.

"It was *your* idea to get the hi-fi," Mom shouted back. It was not really a shout, so much as a mix of utter surprise and confusion. She never raised her voice to him, because to her, he was always right. But his reaction was puzzling, even for her. She had never wanted the hi-fi in the first place. He'd wanted to play his music as well as records by people he had been reading about like Timothy Leary and Allen Ginsberg. He wanted her to spend time with him listening to them, but she always had her hands full and only feigned interest.

This debate over our mortgage and our "stuff" went on. My father held fast to the idea that the house was a problem for us, refusing to let it go. And in the end, he impressed my mother with what she believed was his sincerity about materialism. What my father really wanted, and which we'd seen glimpses of already, was to move to Berkeley, get his master's degree, teach art, and paint. California was where it was happening, and that was where he wanted to be.

My parents put the house on the market, and instead of a Realtor or an actual buyer, one of the neighbors approached them about the house. My father was being very impulsive and wanted to get out from under the stress of the mortgage, so when they offered their travel house trailer as a trade, he and my mother agreed it was a clever idea. That was that. It wasn't even considered a down payment. They simply traded this lovely home with the big lawn, room to play, and a greenhouse next door, on a handshake and a whim.

Like many decisions made during those years my parents just did it and that was that. It all happened quickly, and before the end of a year that had started out calmly enough, before Christmas of the year I was in second grade, we gave away most of our things, took what we could, like my toy sewing machine, and packed the trailer. We didn't even have anyone to tell that we were leaving. We didn't have family in the area and I just had my teachers and friends from school. My mom even had to leave her own sewing machine behind. On the day we moved, they hitched up the trailer to our car and we all got in, resigned to the fact that we would be headed west to California and to the new life my father craved, setting out for the promised land of California, like pioneers in a wagon train.

Except that's not what happened. As we drove away, the car kept stalling. My father finally pulled over to the side of the road and got out. We stayed in the car, huddled together against the Minnesota wind, which penetrated fiercely through the windows. In the back seat I held baby Kathy close to my chest to keep her calm as I watched my father jiggle things under the hood of the car.

My mother was already sobbing and mumbling about how she would miss her sewing machine. She vested all her regrets on the one thing she couldn't bear to leave behind. My father was cursing and stomping around, chain-smoking. I didn't typically see my father this angry. Usually he would withdraw rather than yell. There were times when he was drunk when he would lose his temper, and I saw him hit my mother a few times. But this felt different. It was scary to watch as he unraveled. Clearly he was upset about more than an aborted trip to California. With this useless trailer came a useless dream and more disappointment than he was ready to accept.

As my mother continued to cry, I wished that I could calm her, but I had the baby asleep in my arms. Meanwhile Danny was surprisingly relaxed considering the histrionics happening all around us. My father saw her crying and yelled at her to stop blubbering, which only made her cry even louder. At this point I think she was just exasperated. Everything was happening so fast and she hated to be so out of control.

My parents eventually figured out that we weren't going to be taking this trailer to California and found someone to tow us to the nearest trailer park, which was in a suburb south of Minneapolis called Burnside. Mostly dirt and mud, the trailer park was not really set up for permanent living, but we stayed where we landed, next to a few other trailers that must have met the same fate.

About twenty-three feet long and without many amenities, our trailer was not set up for such permanent living either. The five of us learned to squeeze into the small space, my father still chain-smoking in our tin-can home. The trailer had a galley kitchen and a living room, where we put the baby's crib. Danny and I had bunk beds in the back of the trailer and my mom and dad had their own little room. We had a small living room area where we could play games at night and do homework. We had a potbelly stove at the entrance to the trailer, on which I could easily iron my hair ribbons. All I had to do was run them along the heated top and they came out wrinkle free.

We all did our best to settle into Burnside. My brother and I were enrolled at a funky little country school and had to take a bus, where I spent the second half of second grade and the first half of third grade. I got used to the situation, but my mom still missed her sewing machine. She never mentioned the house and her stove, but we all knew that she missed them as well. The impulsive trading of our house had been done with a handshake, and since we were not that far away, one day my parents went back for some of the belongings they'd left behind. But when they arrived, no one was home. The new owners were not just out for the day—it appeared they hadn't been living there for a while. There were no belongings to reclaim, no house to trade back, and my parents had no one to blame but themselves. It wouldn't be the last time my parents' idealism was betrayed by reality, or the placing of trust in the wrong people. But that didn't mean they'd learn from it.

We lived in the trailer park until my father found a patron of the arts to support his painting. He had been searching for someone to believe in his art for quite a while, so meeting this wealthy art-loving couple was the break he had been waiting for. They owned a gallery and asked my father to provide them with some paintings. When they found out about our living situation, they invited him to become a regular artist for them. They loved his style and couldn't stand that my father was an artist without a studio or a proper home.

The arrangement would be that he would provide them a certain number of canvases for the gallery to sell and he could work on other projects if they did not conflict.

Even more generously, this new couple set my father up with his own studio where he could paint and create, and placed us in a small house with a nice yard where we could live more comfortably. Kind as these actions were, they were also part of the patron's role. Gallery owners were supposed to take diligent care of their artists. When word spread of their generosity, other artists would be enticed into joining their stable.

All of us loved our new little house, and once again it felt like home, but more important, it felt like home to my father, a place where he could pursue his art to his content. Gradually his fixation with moving to California abated, and life returned to some sort of normal. At least for a time.

2

FAMILY MATTERS

WITH MY DAD OCCUPIED PAINTING FOR HIS PATRONS, OUR FAMILY SET-
tled into a routine of sorts, and he threw himself into his work. He
spent the days in his studio, which was filled with supplies, canvases,
and a drafting table. It smelled like a combination of linseed oil,
India ink, cigarette smoke, and creativity. He smiled and listened to
jazz records while he worked

Christmas Day during my third-grade year, when we lived in
this little house, was the best time I can remember ever having with
my entire family. That morning I awoke to the smell of fresh cinna-
mon buns that my mother had made from scratch and raced Danny
downstairs to see what was under the tree. Beside the presents from
Grandma, Grandpa, and my parents that had been under the tree
the night before, there was a new one. There it was in all its glory,
the Barbie Dreamhouse I had wanted—a gift from Santa Claus.

I ripped through my other presents, opening gifts from my
father's parents from Milwaukee. Our only close family, they would
be visiting us in the summer now that we were settled into a proper
home. Finally, I got to a present that was marked *To Dianne, from
Dad*. I tore into the package and couldn't believe what was in it. My
father had made a bed for my Barbie to fit into the house that Santa
had sent me. On the verge of tears with excitement, I went to hug
my dad; always a bit awkward at affection, he turned away, giving
me a sideways hug.

Later that day, we had a Christmas dinner with some of my

parents' friends. My parents had settled into our new home, our new life, and had added new people. My father had collected a new crowd matching the life he was creating and his new persona as a professional artist. Around the table this year was an Ethiopian artist who wore a dashiki. The dark-skinned man chewed on toothpicks made of orange sticks and used them to clean his teeth. He told us about how in his country they did not use forks and knives when they ate. Instead, he explained, they used a special bread to scoop food into their mouths and into the mouths of others sharing the table. This Christmas meal would be strictly American, and he was looking forward to our traditions. My parents were also friends with a Ukrainian couple who joined us. They brought us pysanky as a gift and explained that they were typically for Easter. These were eggs decorated with Ukrainian folk designs. The wife promised to show me how the eggs were created during the holiday.

It was a remarkably special day, but sadly it was also one of the last of its kind. We never were that happy and secure again in Minnesota. Things always had a way of changing, especially in a family like mine.

MY PARENTS SEEMED CONTENT WITH THEIR FRIENDS, BUT MY MOTHER encouraged us to keep in touch with my father's parents as well. Sometimes I would hear them arguing about having them come visit us, with my mother insisting it was good for children to know their family and my father saying he didn't need to see his parents. During the summer between first and second grade my grandparents had come out to visit us back in our big old house. It was a fun visit, and I'd enjoyed having them around, eating meals together and going places. I was proud when during dinnertime one evening, my father hung a portrait he had painted of me on the wall for everyone to see. My dad and grandpa worked on the car together and we all seemed to get along.

Still, in the aftermath of the visit, there seemed to be some residual tension between Grandpa and my father. It was obvious that my grandparents didn't share my father's interests, and that Grandpa in particular never liked my father's desire to be an artist, looking down on him for it. The following summer we didn't see my grandparents, and I don't think my parents ever let them know that we had been living in a trailer park. But now that we were back in a real house and my father was becoming successful, my mother began encouraging him to contact them again.

"The children miss their grandparents, Clarence, we should invite them out."

"I'm too busy to take the time with them. Besides, I am finally enjoying myself," he said. Father and son exasperated each other, which made it difficult for the two wives, who made it their mission to keep their husbands happy. Any tension that could not be relieved by copious amounts of beer would have repercussions for both women after dark.

"Your mother called and really wants to see Dianne. She said she will be all grown up before you know it. Your father agrees."

"Well then, maybe she could go to see them," he suggested.

"By herself?" Mom asked, not so sure she should allow my unsupervised independence. She had grown to love her mother-in-law, who had become something of a Rosetta stone to help her understand her son, but she still had reservations about sending her daughter so far away on the train.

"She'll be fine, and we can have a break from at least one child for a few weeks. And it will get them off our backs for a while."

And so, in the summer of 1962, when I was nine years old, my parents made plans for my visit to Wisconsin. When my parents told me I would be visiting my grandparents in Milwaukee, I wasn't even scared of being by myself, just excited to have all the attention without my brother and sister being around all the time. I planned everything out. The first things I carefully packed were my Barbie and Ken dolls, along with the clothing I had sewn for them. I didn't want to go on this adventure without them. Like me, my Barbie had red hair that she wore in a bouffant hairdo. I wrapped her hair in tissue so it wouldn't get mussed during the long train ride. I dressed Ken in a makeshift suit so he would be properly attired for the visit. I also packed some of my favorite books, *National Velvet* and Nancy Drew, my hairbrush, and some Max Factor lip gloss my mom let me buy. It was shiny but tasteless, and it made me feel beautiful. Mom helped me carefully fold my clothes, as well as some pink clip curlers for my hair, a robe, and a pair of pink fluffy slippers.

When I got to Milwaukee, my grandma and grandpa met me at the station.

"You've gotten so big," Grandma said. "You look so grown up since we saw you last." It had been two years and I had been more like a baby during their last visit. Grandma pulled me into a hug against her soft chest; she smelled of a combination of lilac powder and beer.

Grandpa patted me on the head and grabbed my bag. He was about the same height and size as Grandma, but his arms were much stronger. The years of house painting had preserved a muscularity more common in a younger man. Now they owned an apartment building together and he did all the maintenance while Grandma collected the rent and kept the tenants happy.

When we got to the building, they gave me my own room across from theirs and Grandma helped me unpack. We put my Barbie, Ken, and books on the oak highboy next to the bed that they said used to belong to my dad. Then we carefully placed my folded clothes in the now-empty drawers. I thought about my dad's clothes in those same drawers when he was a little boy. Sitting on the highboy was a framed picture of Grandpa and me taken during their last visit.

When we got settled, Grandpa and Grandma took me right across the street to a bar.

"Hey, Dutch," Grandpa said, "two brews for us and a Shirley

Temple for our little Shirley Temple." I liked that they were showing me off. This would not be the only time that they took me to the local bars. They liked their beer and I liked my Shirley Temples. The room was smoky and dark, but I liked that they let me be in there with the grown-ups. The later it got, the louder they got. Then we walked home and Grandma helped Grandpa into bed.

That first night after I had gone to bed I heard Grandpa rustling around in the kitchen. I found him by himself at the small dinette with a glass of milk and a box of graham crackers. He crumbled the graham crackers into the milk until it was thick as pudding.

"You want some, little girl?" It looked lumpy, but I was happy he was offering me some of his snack.

"Sure."

"Get a glass and I will show you how it is done."

I poured some milk from the bottle in the Frigidaire and grabbed two graham crackers. "You got to have just the right number of crackers to make it good," he explained. It seemed like a delicate operation, but I got it right the first time.

"You're a natural," he said. We spent the next twenty minutes in silence as we slurped down our graham cracker mush. "You ought to get back to bed. We are taking you to the zoo tomorrow." I was so excited to go that I didn't even plead to stay up later with him. I shuffled away in my pink shag slippers and went right to sleep.

The zoo was everything I'd hoped it would be, and I spent the next few days after that with Grandma, going to an elderly neighbor's apartment to check on her and taking a trip to the salon, where I got a rather unfortunate perm. One morning at breakfast, Grandma told me that this day would be a bit different.

"You're going to spend the day with Grandpa today," she said, giving me a hug. "Be good and do what he says. I have some shopping and errands to do. I will be back for supper."

I was eager to spend the day with my grandpa—watching TV, reading the funny papers, and crumbling graham crackers into our milk. We sat together on the couch for a while and I leaned my head on his shoulder. We were watching a Western. It was such a treat to watch a television that I didn't mind that it turned out to be old Zorro reruns. Grandpa smelled like green grass. He wore a kind of aftershave called something like old bay rum. I could have stayed like that for hours.

"I have an idea for what we can do together." Grandpa broke the silence.

"What's that, Grandpa?" I replied excitedly. "Do you want to play Parcheesi?" We had been having a running competition.

"Let's take a bath together."

"A bath?" The idea seemed kind of strange. I had never taken a bath with my father or even my brother except when we were little.

"It will be great," he added. "It is a natural thing to do and you will like it. It is how I like to relax."

He turned on the faucet while I went to my room to put on my bathing suit.

"You won't need a bathing suit in a bath. You can take off your clothes in here," he added, gesturing for me to come into the bathroom with him.

When the bathtub was full, he took off his clothes and got in. Then he told me to take off my clothes and join him. I took off my shorts and top and folded them. I put them on the floor in the corner by the sink. The last thing I took off were my panties. I got in the warm water facing him and it felt good.

"See how relaxing this is." He sat in the water with his eyes closed for a few minutes with his hands along the tub rim. I closed my eyes too but peeked out of one open eye. I watched him put his hands under the water. His breathing changed. It became deeper and faster. Then he opened his eyes and grabbed my hand. I barely moved.

"You know, Dianne, you are old enough now to know where babies come from."

"I do know where they come from, Grandpa," I proudly answered. "God puts a seed into the mom's belly and the baby grows in there." I thought I was clever to know this fact already. Grandpa laughed and held my hand more tightly.

"That is not how the seed is put into the mom, Dianne. There is more to it and I need to tell you the truth." He stood up and his body looked different than what little I had seen when he got into the bath. His boy-part was big and he touched it with both his hand and mine. The skin felt warm and soft. When he began to move our hands over what he explained was what the man used to plant his seed in the woman, I pulled my hand away. I couldn't picture that what he was saying was true. How could that go into what I believed was a very small hole?

He explained how the man and the woman would make the seed come out and then demonstrated with his hand. "It is just like blowing on a dandelion." Then this milky liquid dripped out from between his fingers as he made a heavy sigh. It landed in the tub, so I didn't move. I didn't want to be near the seeds. He got out of the bathwater and wrapped himself in a towel. When he left the bathroom, I gathered up my clothes and quickly got dressed. I couldn't wait to tell my best friend back home what I had learned.

Grandpa did tell me not to mention my lesson to Grandma. He said they disagreed on when a girl should learn the important facts of life. I promised.

THE TRAIN RIDE HOME FELT DIFFERENT THAN THE TRIP THERE. I LEFT Barbie and Ken in their box, but now they faced each other in case they wanted to make a baby.

My mother picked me up from the train, and as soon as we got home I asked if I could go to see my best friend, Emily. She lived down the street, and since she was a late-in-life child with much older siblings, she had the best of everything, including a playroom that was just for her.

When I arrived, Emily hugged me as if I had been gone forever and we went into the playroom. We took out all the dolls and clothes and set out to create their lives in miniature.

"I know how babies are made," I told Emily matter-of-factly.

"I do too," she bragged. She explained the same "God planting the seed" story that we both must have heard at church, and so I decided to show her with our dolls.

"That can't be true." She seemed shocked.

"No, it is true. My grandpa took a bath with me and showed me how the man makes the seeds in his penis that are planted inside the woman. He said it was time for me to learn the right way."

"Did you see his penis?" Emily asked with her eyes opened wide.

"Of course, I did, silly. How else would he have shown me how it all worked?" Emily disappeared for a few minutes, and I continued to pretend that Barbie was cooking a casserole in the Barbie kitchen. After a while Emily returned with her mother, a stylish woman who wore her hair piled up on top of her head like a movie star.

"Dianne, come join us for a snack," she said, guiding us up to the kitchen. She had made peanut butter and jelly sandwiches on Wonder Bread and added Bosco to our milk. We chewed on our sandwiches as we had many times, but Emily's mother kept staring at me.

"Dianne, Emily told me about what happened at your grandfather's house. You do know that grown men are not supposed to take baths with little girls and tell them about where babies come from?"

I knew it felt weird when it happened, but it was my grandpa, and if he thought it was time for me to know the truth, then it must have been time.

"Dianne, you need to tell your mother what happened at your grandpa's house. She needs to know."

I had not thought about telling my mom. Even though I didn't think much of what had happened, I had a feeling that telling my mother would be embarrassing.

"If you don't tell her, I will," Emily's mother insisted. I knew that she would too, because she and my mother were friends who often went to each other's houses for coffee.

"Okay, I will tell her," I promised.

When I got home my mother was in the kitchen by herself. She was making soup and asked me if I would like to stir the pot.

"Can I talk to you, Mom," I said softly. She turned off the stove and we went into the dining room.

"If it is about your hair, I already told Grandma she should not have permed it without asking me first." She reached for my hair. I started to cry. "It will grow back soon enough," she reassured me. This only made me sob more.

I told her about Grandpa and the bath and watched her expression change. Tears streamed down her cheeks and she held me close. We both cried.

"That wasn't your fault," she reassured me. I didn't understand what she meant. But I knew by her reaction that something bad had happened, something that could never be taken back.

Later that night I overheard my parents arguing. I knew it had to do with my grandpa telling me about where babies come from. I was very confused. Why was it wrong for my grandpa to tell me the truth? He didn't make it sound like it was wrong. Maybe I did something wrong to make everyone so upset. I wished I had never said anything to Emily.

The next day I overheard my father calling my grandpa on the phone. I wasn't even trying to listen, but he was yelling for most of the call. I could hear only his side of the conversation, but he seemed very angry. "It's me. You know why I am calling. You expect me to believe you over my own child? I know what a sick old bastard you are!"

I wasn't used to hearing my father curse since the car broke down, and especially not at Grandpa. But I knew my father meant what he said. I felt awful about Grandpa and somehow felt sad for Grandma. If I hadn't gone to see them, no one would have been upset. I ran into my room before my dad could see that I had been eavesdropping on his phone call.

Like most kids who have been sexually abused, I didn't understand at the time what was going on or how I'd just been violated. Still something felt off, and I felt different—about my grandpa, about myself. Something had changed, I knew that much, even if I didn't fully understand what it was. Thankfully, unlike what happens in many situations of sexual abuse, they didn't blame me, but they didn't know how to talk to me about the abuse either, so they avoided it. And without more reassurance from them, I fully blamed myself and dealt with the consequences of that guilt for years.

But guilt was just one piece of my emotional chaos. Though I wouldn't understand it fully until much later, this upsetting and disturbing encounter enabled years of sexual confusion to come, as a part of me would spend the rest of my youth seeking a level of safety in the wrong people and for the wrong reasons. Sexual abuse creates an emptiness in the darkest places within. From now on, things would never be the same for me.

3

ONE STRAY ASH

AS FALL OF 1962 ROLLED AROUND, MY PARENTS AND I WERE GLAD TO put the events of the summer behind us, and with the new school year under way, by all appearances things had returned to normal or whatever our version of that was. Beneath the surface, though, all was not well with us. My father was becoming restless once more. He wasn't speaking about California or philosophy or change, but that didn't stop fate, or something like it, from intervening.

One night before leaving his studio my father must have put out a cigarette in a trash can. The next day we went to his now-charred sanctuary to dig through the rubble and ashes to salvage anything of his work. We found scraps of his illustrations and charred canvases. I found the portrait of me that used to hang in our big beautiful home completely ruined and burned. The only thing I recognized was some of my hair and the wicker chair I had been sitting on when I posed for him.

Only in retrospect did I question whether he might have thrown the cigarette in the can on purpose. He'd been sullen ever since the confrontation with Grandpa, and while he'd continued to paint, he'd been melancholy and lacking in purpose, at least in part because he had been forced to accept that his own father was a miscreant. As I would learn years later, there had been other suspicions about his father's behavior, but people either didn't believe it or looked the other way. It wasn't until years after Grandpa's death that other people spoke up about how he'd isolated Grandma from her own relatives, verbally abused her, and had been caught molesting the daughter of his own brother.

My father may have been angry at his father, but he also never seemed to like it when things were going too well. He was a five-pack-a-day chain-smoker, so he should have known better than to put his cigarette out where it could set things ablaze—unless of course that was what he wanted to do. I've long wondered if my father, the man who traded our house for a trailer, was looking for another way out of a normal family life when he left his studio that night.

Whether the fire was an accident or not, the blaze accentuated how my father was outgrowing his surroundings. Around the same time, he started receiving some backlash for his artwork, which had begun to border on the controversial. We belonged to a Lutheran church that had always welcomed his contributions, at least until he painted a dark-skinned Jesus. This caused a scandal among the staid Christian community who couldn't imagine such a heretical statement. Then they came to our house to try to force a greater tithe, which only upset my father more.

After the fire and the rejection from the church, my father fell into a deep depression. I would overhear the grumblings after my parents thought we were all asleep. He made it clear the drive and desire to go to California had never disappeared. He implied that it was our fault that he had been forced to settle in Minneapolis again after his first try for freedom. His unhappiness was visible on his face and in his body, the tension trapped in his muscles. At first his books and music had fanned the flames of his wanderlust. When they could no longer distract him, he focused on blaming the people of Minnesota for being too small-minded to "get it" or to "get him." My mother, in her reverence for my father and his genius, would agree with him, while encouraging him not to make any more waves.

My father had a complex relationship with the church. A seeker by nature, he was inspired by the teachings of Christ. At one point he had even tried studying for the ministry but had felt stifled by the dogma of Christianity. The people of our church made sure there was no home for him there. My mother had been brought up in a Norwegian family with a conspicuous lack of outward affection. She had a strong faith in God but was looking for a way to define this that was inclusive and loving. She seemed torn between pleasing my father by being avant-garde and fitting in with the church crowd. She liked the artists in our home but also enjoyed the community the church had afforded her.

But my father's depression this time was not just petulance at things not going his way. He was drinking and staying out until all hours. My mother covered for him and told us that he was just working through the loss of his studio and we had to give him time. Then I would hear her cry at night while I listened to the clock ticking the seconds until dawn. I didn't know how to comfort her, so I would bury myself in cleaning and vacuuming the house. We didn't have any relatives to visit, and our eclectic mix of creatives must have sensed the tension—they no longer came around.

We had only one car, and my mother encouraged my father to take it when he needed to get away. He would often stay out late, eventually stumbling home sometime during the early morning hours. I have always been a light sleeper, so I would mark the time in my mind and then listen for any conversation between my parents. There typically wasn't much. My mother would let Clarence into the bed or if he passed out on the couch would cover him with a blanket. She was desperate for him to show some sign of happiness. She made few demands and gave him a very wide berth as she went to her now full-time job as an executive secretary by bus.

I am not sure how long this went on, but finally one night he didn't come home at all. I heard my mother toss and turn, but she didn't get up. The next day we all went to school as usual, and she left for the bus.

That night at dinner there was no sign of Clarence. My mother's red-rimmed eyes betrayed that she had been crying. She still held her composure. "Children, your father has decided to leave us. He is going to California to pursue his art studies."

Danny didn't say anything and Kathy started to cry, mostly because she was confused. She was too young to fully understand what was happening and knew only that Daddy wasn't going to come home. I wanted to tell her that things would be much as they were, but I knew that she wouldn't understand what I meant. I simply held her to me and calmed her enough so I could ask my mother some questions.

"What does this mean for us?" I asked in my most grown-up tone. There had been signs of his unhappiness, so I wasn't completely surprised; I put together that we were living in a house that was given to us by Clarence's art patron and that we would have to leave. I was right, of course. My mother explained that we would have to move, but that when our dad had time to sort out his career and his work after the fire, we could be a family again. That seemed simple enough and Danny and Kathy took it at face value, but all I heard was that he had left us. He was taking time away from us to sort out his life—but we were his life.

My mother got some boxes at the local grocery store and told each of us, in a line that was becoming increasingly familiar, that we could bring only the things that were necessary or really important to us. Once again, we were paring down our belongings and starting over in a new place. I helped Kathy pack her things into a box. If Kathy could stay busy, she might not realize that we were starting over. Perhaps she could be more resilient if I showed her that everything would be fine.

"How is the packing coming?" my mother called from her bedroom. I walked over to her room, where she was putting some photo albums into a box and covering them with a few shirts my father had left behind, holding one of them up to her cheek. I sat on her bed and said nothing.

My mother was the first to break the silence. "Dianne, your father left us for another woman," she said, breaking down in tears. "It's my fault that he is leaving us."

I hadn't seen my mother cry this way before. I was used to her sobbing out of frustration and screaming at us when we were out of control, but I had never seen her in such deep pain. As I'd learn later, the other woman was my mother's best friend, Barbara. My father had been living a double life for quite a while, it turned out. My mother took it as a rejection of her as a woman and a wife, but apparently we were all holding him back from the life he wanted.

As we sat folding sweaters and wrapping paper around the few knickknacks that had survived our many moves, my mother told me how she found out about the affair.

"Remember the morning your father didn't come home," Mom said. I nodded and listened, even though I wanted to put my hands over my ears. That morning did stick in my mind because my mother was very upset and concerned. My first thought was to worry that he was in the hospital, but my mother never mentioned anything like that. She just got dressed for work and caught an early bus.

"There I was on the bus on my way to work and I saw our car in Barbara's driveway."

"There could have been a lot of reasons for him to be there, Mom." I was trying to make her feel better, but I wasn't even sure what the problem was.

"I caught your father and Barbara in bed together," she went on. Now her tears were streaming uncontrollably. I sat there stunned. While I was pleased that I was enough of a comfort that she would confide in me, I would have preferred not knowing all the dirty details. I didn't understand sex beyond what my grandpa had told me, and that was frightening enough. It scared me to know that sex had played a role in why we were now living without my father. I had never thought of my mother and father in bed together, and the thought of him with another woman made me sick. I put my arms around her and held her while she gasped for air. After she calmed down, we both finished putting some of my father's remaining items into a box and taped it shut, the reality sinking in that he'd left my mother, Danny, Kathy, and me alone in Minneapolis with little money and no car. From that moment on he was not my father, he was "Clarence"—and I would never forgive him.

The life we'd been living came to a sudden and abrupt end. We moved into the projects and my mother went to work full-time, but it still was not enough for a single mother to support three children, so we had to go on welfare as well. At age ten, I was now the wife to my mother as husband. I would do the wife and mother things for the family while my mother went out into the world to earn the money to take care of us. While I'd always been a mini momma to my siblings and helped with housework, now I felt a whole new kind of responsibility toward my family. Almost overnight I grew up. I no longer had time for the fantasy world of Barbie and Ken. The normal interests of other children my age were no longer important. It was my job to step into the adult role left vacant by my selfish and unreliable father. I played my part with fervor and felt much older than my ten years.

Of course, I didn't understand the full extent of the toll this would take both on me and on our family. But though I couldn't articulate my feelings, I somehow understood that our family possessed an instability that was different from others. In 1963 parents weren't splitting up every day. There weren't many homes without fathers. We had all held on through the moves, the trailer home, the burned studio, but now we were fragmented. Clearly family was a fragile thing, and preserving that sense of family meant finding it within myself and others—because my father could not be trusted.

STRANGE AS IT MAY SOUND, OUR TIME IN THE PROJECTS AND ON WEL-fare produced some of my best memories of growing up. This was low-income housing, but it was not a bad or unsafe place to live. We didn't have very much, but we had a home that was not living under a gray cloud. We could rely on my mother's moods from one day to the next and this gave us some respite.

My mother was working and making her own decisions, so one of the first things she did once she could afford it was buy us a television. Not only was it a luxury purchase from money she had saved, it was a clear sign she was exerting her independence. Clarence would never have allowed an "idiot box," as he called it, saying it would rot our minds. There weren't many things to watch in 1963, but it was a great distraction that we could all enjoy. It was also a connection to the world. Similarly, my personal prized possession was a white transistor radio. The Beatles had just crossed the pond and were filling the airwaves with excitement beyond anything any of us had heard before. We all sang "I Want to Hold Your Hand" to the radio that became my constant companion.

At school, no one said anything about my family's financial status. My mother made sure we were all clean and nicely dressed every day just like any other student. Instead they focused on what they said were my squinty eyes and Big Bertha butt. I think sometimes children have radar for locating the weakest animal in the herd. They zeroed in on me, the big-butt, squinty-eyed project kid whose father didn't even care enough to stick around.

During that first year without my father, being second-in-command at home gave me the confidence that I couldn't find in school. My mom confided in me and continued giving me extra responsibilities, so that I felt important in our home. Eventually that confidence spilled over to school as well. The 1964–1965 school year began with my blossoming into a great student, with a love for science in particular, working with Bunsen burners and making things out of pipettes. I even had a boyfriend. Because the projects were a diverse place with different kinds of people, I met a young black boy named Michael who was also very studious and lived nearby. We would take walks together after school and talk about everything under the sun. We would listen to Wee-Gee, WDGY on the AM dial, and make lists of our favorite songs.

Meanwhile, my mom was relaxed and focused on us. Even when she dated a few men, it was evident that my sister, brother, and I were her top priority. We had fun together. One night in June of 1965, we all piled into my mother's bed to watch *The Ed Sullivan Show*. Herman's Hermits were making their debut, and I was so excited I was squealing. Then my mother started to giggle. Then she started to laugh. Then she laughed so hard I thought she was going to pee her pants. She was laughing so much she could hardly breathe.

"Mom, why are you laughing?" I started laughing with her, and Kathy and Danny joined in. "Come on, what is so funny?"

"Don't you see them?" she asked.

"What do you mean? That's Herman's Hermits. Aren't they fab?"

"Fab? They're hilarious," she snorted. "Look at those mop tops!" It was so funny seeing my mother in hysterical abandon that I couldn't take offense at what she was saying about my new favorite musical group.

Ultimately, though, all the independence I'd achieved started to change things with my mother. Every night my mother's ritual would be to kiss us good night. She would go room to room. One night she skipped me.

"Mom, you forgot to kiss me good night," I called to her at her apparent oversight.

"No, I didn't," she replied. I lay there for a few minutes contemplating her returning for our nightly ritual so I could go to bed.

"Mom, are you coming?" I shouted again.

"Dianne, you are too old to kiss good night. It is time for you to go to sleep on your own."

I was dumbfounded. I couldn't believe that my mother had decided I didn't need my good-night kiss. This had been our routine since I could remember, and now because of some arbitrary passage of time of which I was completely unaware, this expected sign of love and affection would be withheld from me. At the time, I was deeply wounded, but I swore to myself that I wouldn't show it. I was eleven years old, but I'd felt older than my age ever since my father had left home. Now, as the tears rolled down my cheeks, I decided that if this was what was expected of me, it was time to grow up. Only babies needed good-night kisses from their mothers.

4

CALIFORNIA

IN THE SUMMER OF 1965, TWO YEARS AFTER CLARENCE LEFT, MY MOM received a call from him. She rounded us all up at the dinner table and I knew from her expression that she had news. What I couldn't tell was if it was going to be good news or bad.

"Your dad wants us back," she said, her eyes filled with tears. "He wants us to move to California." My mom turned to me and whispered in my ear so Danny and Kathy couldn't hear her, "He and Barbara broke up a long time ago. Isn't that great?" I nodded. I knew my mother was still missing Clarence and that she'd been just going through the motions with her feeble efforts at dating. No one would ever measure up to him and what she believed was his brilliance. She had mourned him as if he had died.

My eyes puddled up too, but for different reasons. While it pained me that my mother had been heartbroken at his departure, I could see that our family was on a more even keel without him. We had lived without Clarence for two years now, and I was settled into a life that was stable. I was doing fine without him. Our life without Clarence had been good for me. Without his moods and constant dissatisfaction, we had settled into a routine. School was a place where I could excel and I had good friends and my boyfriend. Michael had just found the courage to hold my hand on the swing set. The thought of leaving made my first taste of romance seem star-crossed.

In truth, Clarence's interest in reclaiming his family had been building for some time. Before his call about moving to California, he had been weaseling his way back into our lives, calling on occasion and sending gifts every now and then. He sent a cowboy outfit for Kathy—chaps, a shirt, a hat, a holster, a fake gun, and cowboy boots. She insisted on wearing it so often that we had to sneak it away from her at night to throw it in the washing machine. Surely Kathy wanted to be reunited with the father she could barely remember. Danny seemed indifferent, but since he was generally agreeable and quiet, he was always difficult to read.

"Your father is on the phone, Dianne. He wants to speak to you." Mom handed me the receiver before I could walk out of the room. I had no idea what I wanted to say to him.

"I hear you have been helping hold down the fort," he said. It was good to hear his voice but all I could say was "uh-huh."

"I really think you will like it out here in California. Not only is the weather here great, the people are free thinkers." Another un-huh.

I wasn't really listening. I knew his efforts to convince me wouldn't matter. He liked California and my mother would agree to anything to be with him again.

There were more phone calls, and my mother assured us that our father really wanted to give our family another try. She said he missed us kids and was getting his life together out there. Mom was trying to make it easier for us to make the move, so she kept asking us how we felt about it, feigning that we had any choice in the matter. I resisted as long as I could because I knew that life with Clarence was unpredictable at best, and despite his promises that things would be different, I wasn't buying into it. Somehow his presence always led to upheaval. Living without him may have been hard, but living with him had been harder.

After a while, my resistance started to break down. I was angry at my father, but a part of me missed him too. The prospect of being with him made me feel hopeful about our future as a family. Leaving Minnesota would be hard, but my dad was settled and working in Santa Monica. California could be a new adventure for us.

And so in the summer of 1965, with my seventh-grade year only a couple of months away, we made the move to California. We flew on an airplane for the first time, and when we landed at Los Angeles International Airport, my father was there to greet us.

"Daddy," I said running into his arms. He had a bouquet of flowers for my mother, but I got to him first. Then I remembered how angry I was at him and went into a sulk. He held my mother for a long time and kissed her passionately. He then hugged and kissed Danny and lifted Kathy in his arms. He carried her on his hip as we met up with the porter who had our luggage. We had shipped our boxes ahead, so we had only one suitcase each. Kathy wore her cowboy outfit on the plane to show Dad how much she loved it. It barely fit anymore and was threadbare, but she insisted.

My dad looked tan and handsome and held my mother's hand. He kept telling her he would do better this time. I hadn't realized how much I missed all of us together until we were there at the airport; it felt like when you go into a restaurant not realizing how hungry you are until you see the menu and smell the food. I wanted nothing more than to believe that we could be a real family again, but a part of me couldn't shake the uncomfortable feeling that this would not last. I was becoming superstitious—anything I loved was bound to fall apart.

Still, by the time we arrived at the house, I had lowered my guard. Our house was only nine blocks from the beach. I had never seen the ocean before and immediately fell in love with it.

"Look how close we are to the beach, kids," he said as he gave us a tour of the new neighborhood. He drove around the block and showed me the school I would be attending and then pulled up in front of a Craftsman-style house with a big front porch. We all piled out of the car to check out our new home.

A far cry from our trailer and the projects, the house itself had ample space for us. The Santa Monica house had two huge bedrooms, one that my sister and I would share. My dad and mom would have the biggest room and my brother had a nice spot in the breakfast room off the kitchen. With large living and dining rooms as well, the whole house felt like a place in which we could be a family again.

Right away my parents started thriving. They already had friends that my father had met before we arrived. My mother got a job for the Rand Corporation think tank and took pride in her appearance as she dressed for her job every day. My father had a steady job working for the telephone company designing advertising displays for the different stores. This was a good fit for him because it used his artistic ability but also gave him a structure that he could live with. It also gave him a steady paycheck. My siblings and I each got to pick out new clothes and supplies for school, and I noticed the styles were different in Los Angeles. I got my first bikini that summer, and even though I didn't completely fill it out, I was proud that my child's body was starting to develop into that of a young woman.

I entered the seventh grade with a fresh start and a family that was more normal than at any time in my memory. My father was in a good mood when he left for work, and we had regular dinners together. Our new home environment set my mind at ease about my dad's behavior. While he still possessed the same interest in alternative writers and music, the restlessness that had plagued him seemed to have resolved itself. He was no longer searching for something beyond his grasp; instead it was all there for the taking. Tentatively, I began to embrace the bond between us once more and started to feel, for the first time in years, that he was someone I could rely upon. He and my mother seemed in love again. They were never much for overt demonstrations of affection, but they smiled now and were spending time doing simple things together like cooking out in the backyard, relaxing together in the den, and even playing cards. We also played board games as a family.

But despite the fact that things at home were settling into a groove, the adjustment—school, friends, the neighborhood—was hard for me initially. My saving grace was befriending a pair of twin girls, Jan and Joan, who lived nearby. From the start, Jan and Joan helped me to become just a normal girl, interested in boys, hair, *Seventeen* magazine, and, most important, the Beatles.

We truly were Beatlemaniacs. Once we decided who would have which Beatle, we happily gathered around one another during our recess period after lunch to create scenarios about how each of us would marry the Beatle of our choice. I was in love with George Harrison, and the other girls settled on their mates. We planned our weddings and our houses, all the way to what it would be like to make love and how many children we would have. Our notebook was precious and we each took turns guarding it until our secret club could meet again.

It didn't take long for us to become inseparable. We were young, all with surging hormones, and we'd go to the beach to flirt with the locals or head to the Third Street pedestrian mall in Santa Monica to buy clothes, always eyeing pairs of bell-bottoms or shirts covered in colorful embroidery. Together we'd read *Seventeen* magazine and learn about models like Terry Reno, who was a favorite of mine with her turned-up nose and all-American face. She wore mod clothing that I loved, and since I was making most of my clothing, I tried to copy her fashions.

Even though they were twins, Jan and Joan had very different tastes. When it came to clothes, Jan favored feminine things like I did, while Joan was more practical in her choice of clothing, preferring to wear oxford button-downs. I couldn't wait to be old enough to try out the different styles of makeup, and whenever we got ahold of some, Jan and I would practice putting makeup on in the mirror. Joan had nice long hair with bangs, so she made braids and different hairstyles, but mostly she just humored us—makeup and hair weren't really her things. Joan had the idea to get the chameleon the two shared as a pet. I think if such a decision had been up to Jan, as much as we enjoyed playing with it to see it change color, she could have lived without it.

By the time the first anniversary of our arriving in California approached, I had an experience that would have been impossible in Minnesota: I saw the Beatles in person. The summer of 1966 ended for me with the Beatles concert at Dodger Stadium on August 28. My father drove me, Jan, and Joan and waited in the car for us during the entire concert. There were ten thousand screaming fans at that event, and we were in what was probably the highest row you could be in without being on the roof. But we didn't care that the miniature people onstage who we knew were the Beatles could be seen only if we squinted.

In addition to spending time with Jan and Joan, I began babysitting, and soon my services were in great demand until I made a fateful rookie decision. One day while I was babysitting I invited a boy I'd met in Santa Monica to keep me company. It was innocent enough, but someone saw us making out (a pleasure I had only recently experienced) through open drapes. We kept it light, but the nosy neighbors spread the word and my babysitting jobs dried up. If my parents knew about it, they never said anything to me. I was glad to avoid the "discussion." At the time, we were a conservative family (or so I thought), and I didn't want the heat or the embarrassment.

If this all seems the California version of normal, well, it was. And I loved it. As of the summer of 1966 my life in Southern California was exactly where I wanted it to be. For the first time, I was living an ordinary life in a stable house with plenty of sunshine, good friends, and the Beatles. We weren't in a trailer or the projects, my father wasn't running off with other women, and I was able to enjoy simply being a teenager. Things were, for lack of a better word, ordinary.

What I didn't realize was just how fleeting it all would be.

5

HOW TO BE-IN

OF ALL THE IRONIES OF MY CHILDHOOD, PERHAPS THE GREATEST WAS that it was my mother who introduced my father to drugs. He was forever asking her to loosen up, so one day she did.

It happened in early 1967, while I was in the middle of eighth grade. My mom was friendly with a couple who lived down the street and went over to their house after dinner one night while my father was working late. I was doing homework in my room when I heard my mother come in and go into the kitchen. She sometimes liked to have a bowl of ice cream in the evenings, but from the clanging of pots and pans, it sounded like she was having a party. She kept opening and shutting cabinets and taking stuff out. Then it sounded like she was cooking something, so I went in to investigate.

As I walked into the kitchen, she was cracking eggs into a flour mixture and pouring in sugar and chocolate chips. She wasn't measuring anything and she had a strange look on her face.

"Hi, Mom," I said. I must have startled her, because she knocked an egg off the counter. I was expecting her to become upset, but instead she started laughing so hard she ended up sitting on the floor next to the yellow mess. I sat next to her and started laughing too, even though I had no idea what was so funny.

She handed me the bowl and told me to mix it.

"I'm making cookies," she said between giggles.

"I can see that." I mixed the flour and sugar into the egg mixture and watched her catch her breath. "Mom, are you okay?"

"Yes, I am very okay," she replied, wiping some flour off her cheek. "If you must know the truth, I am just a little bit stoned." She held her thumb and index finger an inch apart to indicate how little she was stoned and then started laughing again.

"Mom! You're stoned? How did that happen?" At the time, I really had no idea how people got stoned.

"Marijuana. I smoked some marijuana with our neighbors," she said, working her way up to a standing position. She didn't look drunk like my grandparents after a few drinks at their bar. She just looked happy and silly. And she was really hungry. This was not like her. She was never a big eater, but tonight she was making cookies without a recipe and snacking on all kinds of things we had in the refrigerator. I turned on the oven for her and we sat at the table.

"I can't wait to tell your father about this," she said. I wasn't sure how he would take it. Sure, he'd been listening to Timothy Leary and Allen Ginsberg talk about LSD and mind expansion, but that sounded serious and profound. This just looked like fun and silliness, though it did make my mother more relaxed. She even left the dishes in the sink to soak instead of immediately washing and drying them before my father came home.

My mother went to sleep, so I made sure to tidy up the kitchen, leaving the strange cookies on a plate for him to see. Then I went to bed and listened for him. He didn't seem to notice the cookies and nothing else was out of place, so he just went right to bed.

The next night I overheard them talking about her experience. She showed him a marijuana cigarette the neighbors had given her and I watched them get stoned. My mother got silly right away, but it didn't affect my father at all. At that point I didn't know that the first time people smoke pot, they don't always experience a high. He seemed very disappointed, so they made plans to go over to the neighbors to try it again. My mom thought maybe it was also the atmosphere that helped her get high. My father seemed all for it.

That weekend they went over to the neighbors and came home arm in arm and laughing.

From then on, the change in my parents was not gradual. After they started smoking pot, their attitudes toward a lot of things changed. I liked that they seemed happy together, but the more nights they went out and came in stoned, the more absorbed they were with getting high instead of what was happening at home. My mom started relying on me more and more to take care of my brother and sister. She seemed very preoccupied with when my father would be coming home so they could indulge in their new hobby together. They would also often disappear into their bedroom before we were asleep and close the door. I knew not to bother them, so I would have the task of getting my sister bathed and ready for bed and seeing that my brother had finished his homework and brushed his teeth. On the one hand, I was so happy that they seemed to be in love with each other again, but on the other hand, it was lonely. I could feel them slipping away from me.

Some nights my parents would sit on the couch smoking a joint together and my mother joined in with my father discussing things like Beat poetry. I don't know how much my mother was really interested or if she understood the poetry, but they seemed to be on the same wavelength. They became much less physically active when they smoked. They would often just sit together not talking or doing anything that I could see.

One weekend, my father was sitting on the couch smoking a joint and I was reading one of my teen magazines. He held in the smoke as he spoke to me, breathing it in between words.

"You want to try some of this?" He held out the hand-rolled joint to me. I always felt my father thought I was a square. I was a good kid and didn't talk back. I liked school, and at the school dances we had at the beginning of the year, I was clearly a wallflower. When he offered me a puff, I took it as a bit of a challenge.

"This is not like a cigarette, Dianne." He showed me how to hold the joint between my fingers. I had already secretly tried smoking cigarettes with my friends after school by stealing some half-smoked butts we found in my backyard. Since my father was still a chain-smoker, that was easy. But I hated smoking cigarettes; in fact, it made me feel sick. I took the joint and hoped that I wouldn't get queasy. Then my father would know for certain how square I was.

"You want to inhale the smoke deeply into your lungs and hold it there if you can. It might burn at first, so try not to cough." I inhaled the marijuana and held it in my lungs as long as I could. Then I let out the smoke with a cough, just like he'd warned.

"Good job for your first time," my father exclaimed. I was surprised by his praise. I didn't feel anything from the pot, so I took another drag. This time I held it in longer. He told me I might not feel anything the first time. I thanked him and walked outside with my magazine and sat on a lawn chair. After a while I opened the magazine and all the words looked like they were in little trains on the page. I closed the magazine and opened it again. No change. The words were still in little trains moving on the page. I then closed my eyes and waited for the pot to wear off.

My mother had been out shopping with my brother and sister. When they got home, my sister ran out to see me. I opened my eyes and she was looking right at me.

"What were you saying?" she asked. I guess I had been mumbling something that I couldn't remember. I know I wasn't sleeping.

By this time, the pot had worn off, but my mouth was dry.

"I thought you might get some cotton mouth," my father said, offering me a cold soda. The soda felt great on my parched throat. I looked at my family sitting in the backyard and was content with everything. My mother stood by him smiling at me. He had obviously told her that I was now turned on to the pot. We grilled hamburgers that night, and I ate two of them. The picture seemed perfect, but I was completely unaware of how quickly my life was going to change. It was only a small marijuana cigarette, but it opened the door to a new way of thinking and a new way of life. When we stepped through, there would be no turning back for us and especially for me.

Our family wasn't the only thing changing in 1967. Almost overnight we embraced the happenings around Los Angeles. The counterculture was in full swing in San Francisco and was moving down the coast to our neighborhood. In 1967 over thirty head shops cropped up to support the growing demand for pot-smoking paraphernalia. The sale of pipes, hookahs, and fancy roach clips became part of the local economy. We were in the center of the hippie movement, with all its lofty goals of love and freedom to believe in whatever you wished. At the first Human Be-In at Griffith Park on January 14, 1967, people were encouraged to bring incense, pictures of their own gurus, flowers, and anything the color of gold as gifts of the magi. Like those wise men presented at the birth of Christ, these gifts were to represent the birth of a movement where people could be brought together in bonds of love.

There was a small crowd at that first gathering, about six hundred people, and my family blended right in. There was no central organizer. People simply created a makeshift bandstand to the north side of the Greek theater in the park and did their own thing. Attendees played acoustic guitars, banged on drums, and plunked out tunes on African thumb pianos. I had never seen anything like this. People were scantily dressed, but there was no full nudity—not that I would have been surprised. Everyone was caught up in the same fever and no one was a stranger.

For this be-in, my father shirked his typical work clothes—slicked back hair and shoes—for a fringed suede vest, blue jeans, and sandals. Freed from the greasy pomade styling of the workweek, his hair stuck up in tufts as if it had been waiting for the right opportunity to express itself. My mother adapted to the dress code of the fashion free by wearing a long, flowing skirt with a cotton peasant blouse. She also wore a beaded headband across her forehead and made one to match for Kathy. I wore plain shorts and sneakers, but when someone handed me some beads I gladly wore them around my neck.

This was a be-in in which everyone was encouraged to just "be" themselves. Most people were older teenagers and people in their twenties. While there were little children running around with their faces painted, they fit into the scene as naturally as the beads and feathers. My parents were probably older than others there, but they looked the part, so no one made them feel unwelcome.

Meanwhile I felt like one of the few awkward young teens barely through puberty, but people were passing around joints and tangerines and no one questioned my age or asked me where my parents were. When I was offered a joint, I looked over to see if my father would approve of me smoking with strangers, but he wasn't even watching what I was doing.

BY EARLY SPRING THAT YEAR, AFTER I TURNED FOURTEEN, IT WAS OBVI-
ous things were changing at home, and it wasn't just because my parents had started smoking pot. The agitation in my father was coming back, first in smaller ways and eventually in bigger ones. One day I walked into the dining room to find my father sawing the legs off our dining room table, one that he had made from a solid core door.

"Dad, what are you doing?" I asked. He was so focused he didn't see me watching him.

"Check it out! The table wanted to be shorter. It told me so. *Shhh*, I have to be careful so I do it right." His eyes were glassy and dilated, staring intently at the table. "There, isn't that better?"

I wasn't sure if he was addressing me or the table. He walked around the table admiring his work. Then he looked at the barrel chairs, which were now towering over what used to be our dinette. One by one he sawed the legs off the chairs until they matched the height of what now resembled a Japanese chabudai. When he took the chair legs off, each chair was tipped back. Somehow this seemed to work with the new design.

When Jan and Joan saw what my dad had done to our table, they thought it was hysterical, but not for the same reasons I did.

"Holy shit, Dianne," Joan said. "Either your father has lost his mind or he was totally tripping."

"What do you mean he was tripping?" I asked.

"LSD, lysergic acid diethylamide," she replied.

"What is that?" I asked. Though I'd heard my father's Timothy Leary records, I really didn't know what LSD was for.

"LSD is a drug that causes hallucinations," Jan explained.

"Some people say it opens your consciousness and makes you smarter," Joan said.

I'm not sure if this remodeled table was a sign that my father was smarter, but the table did become a central gathering place for our little family and my best friends. My parents invited different kinds of people—artists, musicians, actors—over to the house for large potlucks. Before the meal, they would pass around joints. I was used to smoking marijuana by now and often got high with Jan and Joan. We had fun together and were now hanging out at the A Be & See Head Shop near our homes; we were becoming part of a cool group of people who all got high.

After all those at our potlucks were buzzed, we would eat heartily. We were now more vegetarians than meat eaters, but I don't think that was on purpose. People were experimenting with new types of fresh health foods, so the contributions to the table were often dishes with nuts, seeds, sprouts, and tofu. Along with the new foods, there was also a gradual change in the people who were attending the potlucks. Previously there had been a lot of lively conversation bordering on the loud. Now some of my parents' new friends, instead of talking, would spend a lot of time quietly staring off into space.

My dad enjoyed intellectual stimulation, so he would often start a discussion.

"Robert, what do you think a woman's role should be?" Robert was a long-haired man who had been living with his girlfriend for over ten years.

"Why are you asking him?" my mom interjected. "He is not a woman."

"I mean from a man's point of view," my father said, sitting back in his chair as my mother got up to clear the dishes. "See, that is what I mean. Is it the woman's job to clear the dishes?"

Carol, Robert's girlfriend, started to laugh.

"Why are you laughing?" my dad asked. He seemed genuinely curious.

"Why am I laughing, Shirley?" Carol shouted to the kitchen. She had been involved with my father's theoretical discussions about how women's roles were changing and how my mom should spend more time with him expanding her consciousness.

My mom returned from the kitchen with dessert and then got some plates and forks.

"Why do you think I am laughing, Shirley?"

"Because what Clarence is saying is not reality."

"What do you mean? You read the papers. Women want to be liberated from the shackles of domesticity."

"Yeah, right." My mom sighed. "The women who are fighting for liberation don't have three children to feed, clothe, and raise, and they don't have a house to keep clean. And furthermore, when would I have any time to even read the paper, let alone contemplate my navel like that?"

"Don't you want to be equal to men?" my father insisted.

"I am equal. But you say you are going to help me with the household chores. When is the last time you cleaned a dish or cooked a meal? What do you think would happen if I stopped doing all of these things?"

This is how their discussions went. My father would try to "liberate" my mother from domestic drudgery so she could be more passionate about the things he found interesting. Of course he wasn't willing to make any changes to himself. While he talked a great deal about changing the order of things, when it came to his role in the family, it was just talk. Looking back, I can't ignore the fact that they would have conversations like these while my mother was actively doing the housework while he sat and watched. He was never a participant in the household chores. Still, it never seemed to bother her. Much as she always did with him, she just shrugged it off and let him "philosophize," as she termed it.

The fact that my father's attitudes were changing so fast would have been amusing if it didn't portend trouble. My father could never do anything halfway. Instead of being a casual pot smoker, he was smoking all the time, his cigarettes replaced with expertly hand-rolled joints. His eyes were always glassy and he was much more talkative unless he was being pensive. Then he could pontificate on one subject as if no one in the world could understand it with the intensity he could. He was not as excited about his work as he had been and was starting to grow out his hair. He kept it neat with Brylcreem for work, but it was beginning to appear incongruous.

As word spread of the scene happening every weekend at Griffith Park, the sea of happy hippies outgrew its environment. After the first be-in in January, there had been another one in February, a week before my fourteenth birthday, with more than five thousand people in attendance. Exciting as it was, it was like a warm-up to the main attraction. On Easter Sunday that year, March 26, 1967, the be-in moved to Elysian Park in Central Los Angeles. It provided more than six hundred acres for people to picnic, dance, groove, and embrace the counterculture.

The love-in as the "Be In" was now called, started in the very early morning and we got there with the sunrise. There were already what appeared to be thousands of people, including young families with small children and people embracing their muses. My parents set up a place to sit and listen to the music, but I didn't want to stay in one spot. A chain of people passed by and reached out a hand to add me as a link. I turned to my parents expectantly, and they nodded and told me to meet them later back at the car. At least that is what I thought they said, and before they could change their mind, I was off.

There was too much going on for me not to explore on my own. The chain of people ran together along trails through hills, laughing and singing until we ended up somewhere on the far end of the park. We split up and I found myself in the middle of something special. The sweet smell of incense was intoxicating mixed with the pungent aroma of grass. The Doors were playing in the distance, but we were used to seeing them at these events. They weren't famous yet; they had just released their first album in 1967. They were almost like a local band. As I walked through the path between blankets, people handed me joints and shared their bounty.

There was a circle of drummers oblivious to the music coming from other instruments just a few feet away. They were surrounded by a small tribe of men in loincloths who appeared caught up in the rapturous beats. Women were free of any confining clothing. Many were wearing muslin, and some were wrapped in blankets and not much else. There were people of every shape and size dancing together or alone as dogs wove in and out of the crowd. Little children, many golden-haired from the California sun, wore flower crowns. They were busily engaged in finger-painting on paper while their parents were decorating one another.

I was slightly buzzed, and as I wandered through the throng, a guy flashed me a peace sign as his girlfriend handed me a flower and gave me a hug. Next to them was a cute boy who had caught my eye.

"Hey, pretty," he said. He grabbed my hand and invited me to sit with his group. They were definitely older than I was, but without my parents, I am sure I looked older than my age to them.

"Hey, you hungry?" A dark-haired girl in an Indian-print dress handed me a bunch of sunflower seeds. I eagerly accepted them and proffered money for some sodas. The boy who brought me over volunteered to get them for us, and without thinking I gave him what was left of my babysitting money. In a few minutes he returned with sodas, hot pretzels, and candy.

"Thanks, Red," he said and squeezed in next to me.

I felt myself blush. I hadn't realized how lonely I had been. I wasn't seeing anyone anymore, not even the boy who got me fired from my babysitting job. I wanted someone to touch me and think I was pretty. We were now fairly stoned, and instead of getting the munchies and craving food, I fixated on wanting to be kissed. I longed to be wanted, and this boy did not disappoint. He brushed his lips softly on mine and I felt a twinge of desire. He pulled me up and we danced. I wanted to find a place behind a tree so we could explore each other's bodies. I knew the warmth of his body next to mine would make me feel the love that everyone was talking about.

We danced and kissed and I noticed it was getting late. I told him I needed to find my parents, which probably made him aware just how young I was. I hinted that he might walk me back, but he seemed to lose interest, so I just gave him a halfhearted wave and took off.

The sun was low on the horizon. I moved through the late-afternoon shadows, dizzied and energized by the mass of people around me. Stepping over tangles of bodies and around those who were still dancing, I understood, perhaps clearly for the first time, that I was on the periphery of something—not just the spectacle in the park, but something larger than all of this. What had been going on in my house, with my parents and their friends, was happening all over California. It wasn't just my parents, and it wasn't just my father—it was a moment, it was in the air, and everyone in that park seemed to sense it, moving in unison to its rhythm. I didn't understand what it was all about, but I wanted to. No one asked too many questions. They were going with the flow. And even though I was younger than the people around me, I was old enough to see the power of it all and didn't want to be left behind.

My thoughts about the day were interrupted when I returned to where my parents had parked our car and found it wasn't there. I retraced some of my steps to make sure I hadn't miscalculated, but I am always careful to find landmarks in an unfamiliar place. As I realized that I was definitely where the car had been, reality set in: They had left without me. At first, I was angry that they would do that to me—it wasn't even that late and I'd told them I would catch up with them. Quickly, though, my anger turned to fear. I had no idea how I was going to get home.

I held back tears and thought about it logically. I had just turned fourteen and didn't want to look like a baby, but I had never been completely on my own. I had never feared the police, even though people would joke about them and call them the fuzz, so I headed right for the station, confident they could help me get home. As I was walking to the police station in the park, an older-looking boy stopped me. He must have seen that my eyes were tearing up.

"Where are you headed?" he asked. "You look lost."

"My ride left me," I squeaked.

"You mean your parents?" he chided.

He told me that he was in college and that he would be happy to give me a lift. He was so disarming that it didn't occur to me until later that he might have wanted something in return. I was so upset at the fact that my parents had apparently abandoned me that I wasn't even thinking that going with this stranger could be dangerous.

"You better wipe your eyes before you go in," he said as he pulled the car in front of my house. He opened the door for me and handed me a handkerchief. I wiped the salt and dirt off my face, thanked him for the final time, put on my best glare, and walked inside.

When I got in, my mother burst out crying. "Dianne, I was so worried about you."

"I told you she would find her way back home," Clarence interjected before I got a word out.

"We needed to go and couldn't find you," my mother blurted out.

"She's fine, Shirley. I told you she would be. She is resourceful," my father said.

"I was praying that the universe would protect you and bring you home." My mother sobbed.

All I could do was stare at her. I didn't know how my parents' words were supposed to affect me, but they certainly didn't make me feel better. I grabbed a Coke and went to bed.

Their decision to leave me there was not easy to forget. It was obvious from their reactions when I returned that my mother had known leaving me was a bad idea, but she had let my father talk her into it anyway. He'd been right that I would get home safely, but that was beside the point. Like any teenager, I wanted my freedom; however, I also wanted my parents to act like parents. At heart I was conservative and shy. While I liked the colorful clothes and the music at the "happenings" I attended with my family and they were fun, I would have been just as happy staying at home and helping my mom cook and clean the house. It wasn't my idea to become a hippie.

Ever since we'd moved to California, my father's more impulsive instincts had been largely absent from our lives, but after the love-in, I realized they'd been just below the surface all along. I loved my father, but as had so often been the case back in Minnesota, my mother still deferred to him. Only this time it wasn't about our house, our stuff, or a hi-fi. It was about me.

* * *

WITH EACH DAY, MY FAMILY BECAME MORE AND MORE ENMESHED IN hippie culture. Our home was filled with the sounds of Buffalo Springfield, the Doors, and other new bands. In particular, the Doors were becoming more popular, so when I noticed that they would be playing in Santa Barbara, I asked my father if he would take some of my friends and me to the concert. As it turned out, no one could go with me, but my father wanted to go. It was just the two of us at a concert at the Earl Warren Showgrounds on the Saturday of the Memorial Day weekend, 1967. The lineup was the Doors, Country Joe and the Fish, Andrew Staples, Captain Speed.

It was strange being with my father by myself for the drive to the concert. I was typically never alone with him for very long. If I visited him when he was working on something he would talk to me, but we were now stuck in a car for well over an hour and a half of awkward.

I listened intently while he droned on about his new philosophies. Some of his talk seemed circular, but I liked hearing him describe his thoughts even when they confused me.

We were driving along the coast with the windows down. He had his hand with its ever-present cigarette dangling loosely out of the window while I rested my elbow on the armrest. I was humming "Light My Fire" from the new album by the Doors when my father cleared his throat.

"It's okay for people to have sex, you know that, don't you?"

I felt nauseated.

"If you have a boyfriend and want to have sex, it can be a beautiful thing," he said matter-of-factly. I wanted to stop listening. I had no idea why he was telling me this. He probably figured sexual activity was inevitable in light of everything that was happening around me. "Just make sure the boy uses birth control."

I was glad that was the gist of the discussion. This was the second time one of my parents had offered either birth control or advice about birth control. My mother had brought it up out of nowhere when I was in seventh grade. I had been going on some dates with a Jewish boy I met at the beach. I went to his house a few times and he came to mine. We did a lot of closed-mouth kissing and we talked about how much we liked each other, but that was where it ended. It never occurred to me to do anything other than kissing, and he'd never even tried.

My mother must have assumed something more was going on at the time because she asked me if I wanted to go on the pill. I was so embarrassed that I simply said no. I have no idea why my parents thought I was having sex or even wanted to. They never discussed anything with me other than birth control. I figured there must have been more to it than that, but I wasn't about to ask.

It was hard to see it at the time, but the love-ins and rock concerts were just the start of some radical shifts in our family life. As eighth grade wound down, my parents became more enmeshed in psychedelic culture, though I didn't realize just how much things had changed until my father gave me LSD for the first time.

It was in early June, and Jan, Joan, and I were sitting around the shortened table with my parents and a bunch of their friends. We'd just eaten a great home-cooked meal.

My father got a twinkle in his eye. "Dianne," he said dramatically, "it is time for you to know more about who you are." The pronouncement, especially coming from him, was mysterious, but I figured nothing could be worse than our sex discussion.

My father walked around the table passing out tabs of acid to the guests and giving smaller tabs to me, Jan, and Joan.

"Put the tab on your tongue," he said. "I have some surprises for you."

I was already surprised, but since my father was giving us the drugs, I didn't hesitate to accept. He told us he would be right in the next room and that it would be best if we didn't leave the house. He beseeched us to stay inside where he could see us if we needed his help. I had no idea what to expect, but my father's obvious concern made the expectation exhilarating. I felt a buzz even before the drug took effect.

My father put on the new Beatles album, *Sgt. Pepper's Lonely Hearts Club Band*, and at first I didn't feel anything. Then I started to feel the music. I laughed and had to lie down. I couldn't imagine wanting to leave the house. I had a realization of being a me that was more than me. I would never be able to put it into words, but somehow I knew in that moment that everything I would ever need was with me and inside me. When the song "Being for the Benefit of Mr. Kite!" came on, I was enthralled.

"Jan, Joan, do you see the notes?" I asked. They had to see them. They were everywhere. The notes were alive. Then I heard the calliope. It took up the entire room and filled me with ecstasy. I never heard anything so beautiful; it penetrated me from my fingertips down to my toes.

My father came into the room to check on us and handed us *The Psychedelic Experience: A Manual Based on the Tibetan Book of the Dead*. He treated it as if it were an ancient tome. He described it as sacred writings that would give us the key to everything we ever wanted to know and ever would. I focused in on the writing on the cover. It was written by my father's hero Timothy Leary and dedicated to the psychedelic explorer and author Aldous Huxley.

I read the title aloud: "*The Psychedelic Experience: A Manual Based on the Tibetan Book of the Dead*." We each looked at each other and repeated the word *dead* as if it held special meaning. Then we took turns reading passages to one another.

It began:

A psychedelic experience is a journey to new realms of consciousness. The scope and content of the experience is limitless, but its characteristic features are the transcendence of verbal concepts, of space-time dimensions, and of the ego or identity.

In that moment I understood why I would never be able to explain what I was feeling. There were no words.

We decided to walk around the house in our state of altered perception, stopping to look at some of my father's paintings on the walls. His art was now reflecting the change in his interior world, and he had many of what were now being called psychedelic abstractions hanging in our house. They were very colorful and visually symbolic. We paused in front of each of the paintings and stared as the colors blended into a kaleidoscope of pattern.

When we all returned to earth, Jan and Joan went home, leaving me alone to contemplate what I'd experienced. During the acid trip, I'd seen a physical cable connecting my head to the heads of my parents, but at one point, I felt a strong sensation that this cable had been cut. In hindsight, I find it hard to say how much of this was just the acid exposing emotions that most teenagers experience as they try to separate themselves from their parents and understand who they are becoming. But in light of my parents' behavior toward me, the experience was potent, the symbolism impossible for me to ignore. More and more, they were showing a desire for me to grow up, to consider myself an adult, to think and act independently. Whether I felt ready for that seemed irrelevant. What had started with my mother's telling me I was too old for a good-night kiss, and continued with my parents leaving me at the love-in, had progressed to the point that both my parents were assuming I was already having sex. As much as I wanted to stay a child in an uncomplicated world, I now understood that I had to grow up.

After that first trip, my sense of self was unmistakably different. From then on, I was an individual taking a journey that was all my own, not a child lingering in the shadow of my parents. They wanted me to mature, so that's what I would do. Though I didn't fully understand the ramifications of that vision, some part of me was aware that things were shifting in our family and those changes seemed to be speeding up, building toward something. The sense of normality that had defined my life a few short months ago was rapidly coming undone.

6

HIPPIES IN NEWSPRINT

THE TURBULENCE MY FAMILY HAD BEEN EXPERIENCING DURING THE spring of 1967 was magnified when my parents became involved with an underground newspaper called the *Oracle*, run by a group of like-minded hippies.

At the time, the landscape of the counterculture was changing rapidly, and the *Oracle* was at the forefront of these shifts, appealing to people like my father who were already prone to questioning societal norms. Every few months it seemed that new ideas arrived and were quickly adopted by this pioneering fringe, creating a shifting cocktail of philosophy, spirituality, faith, communal ideas about property and love, and drugs that pushed the boundaries further outward. The *Oracle* was instrumental in preaching about much of this, drawing in my parents and others like them, and eventually shaping the beliefs that would alter all our lives.

The Southern California *Oracle* was the offspring of the *San Francisco Oracle* newspaper, which had started as a small underground rag but eventually boasted a major circulation. Here is how they described themselves in their second issue in 1967:

The incredible growth of the *SF Oracle* from 1200 copies to over 60000 in only six issues suggests that it meets a tremendous need for some form of spiritual communication that young people can accept. Nowhere is this need more obvious than right here in Los Angeles. It is with the blessing of the *San Francisco Oracle* that we now exist.

The *Oracle* is a newspaper, but it is more than that. It will shortly be incorporated as a religious association dedicated to sharing the insights gained from the psychedelic experience that others may ennoble their lives and place these in harmony with the forces that animate the universe. The *Oracle* is interested in any style of living that provides greater satisfaction, greater self-awareness, more joy, love and fulfillment. On these pages, we will explore the many roads to life enhancement, the many ways of centering one's consciousness of releasing the joyous spirit within.

The *Oracle* is dedicated to making life a wondrous experience for all. In keeping with that notion, we will originate gatherings, parties, dances and other excuses for the tribes to gather and celebrate.

The paper itself was pieced together like an artistic acid trip. Each page had a different-colored font, and the artwork pushed the parameters of what would have been considered decent by the standards of the "straight world." However, some of the writers were very serious and discussed the topic of chemically induced mystical experiences. In one issue, they did an extensive interview with Alan Watts. They took themselves seriously, and so did my father.

The paper and the people dedicated to its cause were perfect for my parents and their changing sensibilities. I don't know if the *Oracle* newspaper inspired my parents' thinking, or how much my dad had any influence on the content and artwork beyond his credit as an artist in the June 1967 edition, but those dedicated to the paper became our new community, and as a family we began to attend some of the "tribal meetings" mentioned in the paper.

The *Oracle* staff had an office where they put together the paper, but they also lived communally in a house in Laurel Canyon. Laurel Canyon itself was a melting pot of musical talent; hippies and artists were drawn to it as if by a gravitational pull. The house itself was described in many accounts as cavernous and was dubbed the Log Cabin, but only because it was made of wood and nestled in a forest. Any other resemblance to a cabin was greatly understating its grandeur. It was on five different levels, with a bowling alley in the basement painted in Day-Glo colors. The living room where they would hold their meetings must have been at least two thousand square feet, which was bigger than our Santa Monica home. It had fancy chandeliers and a fireplace that took up an entire wall. The thing I remember the most was the glassed-in addition, which looked like a tree house. It was more like an atrium, and during the few times I went there with my parents, there were always musicians jamming in this space. It overlooked water, and staring fixedly into the reflections of trees on the still water below, I could ignore the odd people who used the place as a crash pad.

The Log Cabin would later become the home of Frank Zappa and was legendary in the lore of Laurel Canyon and the music scene in the 1960s, but when we were there, the Oracle commune shared the space with another hippie commune led by Vito Paulekas and Carl Franzoni. They ran a free-form dance troupe and liked to refer to themselves as freaks rather than hippies. Vito was an ex-con who shared many qualities with someone else I was destined to meet, especially his almost hypnotic methods for attracting nubile young women into his sex-fueled lair. Vito was a common sight at Venice Beach, and even though he was already in his early fifties, he was considered one of the inspirations for the fashion and attitudes of the hippie movement, including his reputation for sex orgies.

I went to the Log Cabin with my parents on at least three weekends and witnessed a circus of people all doing their own thing. My parents had no problem with my seeing the goings-on of the movement regardless of whether it was technically appropriate, and now that I had taken LSD, I could tell those who were into their own trip from those who were simply hangers-on. Being older than the children, I was once again stuck in the middle, where young teens are forced to dwell; I found myself attracted to some of the men who were partying at the Log Cabin, but they hardly noticed me because they saw me as a kid.

Our house in Santa Monica also became full of life and creativity. Through these group gatherings, we became friendly with other Oracle families, and several had children close in age to Kathy and Danny. It seemed like every weekend we began hosting meetings, cookouts, and picnics at our house. All of which got more interesting after my father, fresh off of studying the work of R. Buckminster Fuller, figured out how to build a geodesic dome in our backyard. One of my favorite photographs is of my brother, sister, and father and me inside the dome, with my father smoking a joint and grinning from ear to ear. People were always coming and going from our house, but after a while they stopped going. Little by little people started crashing there. I could see why. My father made things interesting and his enthusiasm gave credence and a sense of possibility to all the new ideas the group was considering.

The Oracle group had a big vision for everything from obtaining religious status to the creation of schools and employment opportunities. I know my parents had something to do with the ideas for alternative education that the *Oracle* was espousing. They had been very disappointed with the education I was receiving at the Santa Monica junior high. I never thought of myself as unusually bright, but I guess my education in Minneapolis had been far more advanced than what these schools were teaching us. My parents and the members of their Oracle tribe also believed children should be taught to think differently, something that was never going to happen in the public school system.

Despite their reservations with my public education, to be honest, I didn't have a problem with school. In fact, I liked my school and my friends—both offered a structure that was becoming elusive at home. I might have been a little bored with having to study things I already knew, but it was comfortable to know where I was going and what I would be doing every day. Rules and expectations made me feel secure. Being around my parents and the free-thinking Oracle members had the opposite effect on me.

Increasingly, though, my parents weren't listening to what I had to say about such things.

IN LATE JUNE, I TURNED THE GUILT TRIP AROUND ON MY PARENTS FOR leaving me at the Elysian Park Love-In. If I was old enough for them to leave me there, then I was old enough to go to the Monterey Pop Festival with my uncle, my father's brother, who was the only relative with whom we were still speaking. Like most people, I had no idea that the concert would become a cultural touchstone and a centerpiece to the Summer of Love. I just wanted to see groups and performers like the Who, the Jimi Hendrix Experience, Big Brother and the Holding Company, and Otis Redding. My uncle was younger than my father and a musician, and when I heard he was going to the concert, I promised that I would bring pot brownies if he'd let me come along. He agreed, and I begged my parents to let me go. I expected more of a fight from at least my mother, but they both said it would be okay—my mother even helped me bake the brownies.

When we got to the concert, we didn't have tickets to get into the venue, but it didn't matter. Right outside the fence was a festival of counterculture revelers that made the Elysian Park Love-In look like a family picnic. My uncle was sick with either the flu or food poisoning, so he stayed close to the truck to wait it out. He didn't want to ruin my good time, so he pretty much told me to go on without him.

The feeling around the festival was electric and I was completely free to explore. It's difficult to recognize history when it's happening all around you, but I knew this was something special.

I wandered around and met people, enjoying the generosity of freely shared food and marijuana and getting the freedom I'd craved to meet people who wouldn't simply dismiss me as Clarence and Shirley's little kid. I shared my brownies, which I hoped was not the cause of my uncle's malady, and got myself very stoned. The festival was set for about seven thousand attendees in the arena, but there had to be over fifty thousand people on the grounds. At night, I fell asleep for a few hours in a horse barn. The horse wasn't there, but there was a soft blanket of straw for me to crash on. There were long-hairs and hippie girls sitting on the barn roof to watch the concert, which is probably how I wound up inside.

When I woke up, some people invited me to a party where I met Tiny Tim, who was tall and very funny. Or maybe everyone was funny. We were passing around joints and feeling the electricity of the music and the times. There was so much to see with the soundtrack of the music in the background—every now and then you'd perk up your ears and hear the Byrds, Jefferson Airplane, or the Grateful Dead. People were sitting together weaving yarn "eyes of God," and others were selling handmade colorful jewelry and wind chimes. It was tactile and sensual, and wherever you looked, there was something beautiful.

Sunday was raining, but it was perfect for listening to Ravi Shankar. The strange and haunting sounds he produced on the sitar were transporting. He created a sacred atmosphere by requiring that everyone put out cigarettes if they wanted to hear him play. People complied. He encouraged them to light incense, what he referred to as joy sticks, and the sweet smell was everywhere. At the end of the performance, people threw flowers on the stage. That night brought the festival to a close with performances by the Mamas and the Pa-

pas and the Who. As I peered through the fence, I watched as Peter Townshend smashed his sunburst, maple-neck Fender Stratocaster. The crowd went wild.

I had been away for only a weekend, but when I returned my good mood quickly deflated. My home was now filled with more Oracle members who had evidently lost their lease or decided that sharing their environment with the Paulekas freak commune was no longer serving their goals. Somehow it became our responsibility to take care of these now-homeless hippies, another one of my father's great ideas that he came up with unilaterally. As I walked through the door, I saw that our spacious living and dining rooms were both filled with transients on mattresses or in sleeping bags. Confused, I went looking for my parents.

"The Oracle had to move out of their house," my father explained when I found him. "We told them they could crash here."

While my mother seemed to agree with my father, I knew she wasn't completely comfortable with the idea. I knew objecting to this would have been futile, but as was always the case, they never asked us how we would feel about our home being taken over. Adding insult to injury—there was another surprise waiting for me: My father and his friend Bob, another member of the Oracle group, had purchased bread trucks from the nearby Pioneer bakery with plans to turn them into mobile homes.

"This way if we ever want to go anywhere, we have our home with us," my dad said.

Maybe I was missing something, but I had vivid memories of how this same scenario worked out the last time we tried living in a mobile home. When we finally did land somewhere, we were cramped and miserable. My father had the "this time will be different" look on his face so I kept my mouth shut.

The two men quickly got to work on their trucks. At first it was a matter of taking things out. Then it was a matter of putting things in. My father figured out a way to insulate the truck with soundproofing Styrofoam that I think he got from work at the telephone company. Admittedly, we all thought it was clever how he figured out how to use what was essentially trash to make a home out of a cast-off vehicle.

He worked on that truck every day for the entire summer, building a foldout table that converted into a bed as well as bunk beds that doubled as storage. My mother and I helped sew a curtain that would go completely around the truck to create privacy for anyone who might be inside. My father created a pop-up awning that extended the truck out the back to provide shade from the sun. My brother worked alongside of him soaping up screws so they could go into the metal without being stripped. Even Kathy helped sweep up the shavings from any woodwork that he did in the garage.

Despite all the work he was putting into the truck, I didn't see the big picture at the time. Given how often he seemed to latch on to new ideas, I didn't realize how serious this plan of his actually was. He had pretty much shut down his painting studio and had quit his job. Every bit of energy and focus was put into this truck and the apparent freedom it was going to give our family. It didn't occur to me or anyone else that this was my father's pattern rearing its head again.

With so much focus on the truck, it was easy to forget that our actual house didn't seem to belong to us anymore. During that summer of 1967 the entire Oracle commune lived with us, ate with us, and slept under our roof. In general, I grew to like most of the people staying at the house—after all, it could be fun always having people around. One night a bunch of us decided to try making the legendary "mellow yellow." Someone had been advertising it in the *Oracle*, and it was supposed to be made from the insides of the banana peel. They espoused it as a cheap legal high. We were typically not out of pot, but on this night, we scraped the insides of the bananas and smoked them. I didn't feel anything, but we all laughed anyway because of how silly we felt to have fallen for the rumor.

"It's Donovan's fault." I laughed when I told Jan and Joan about our experiment. We'd played Donovan's song "Mellow Yellow" constantly, as it had been on the top of the charts in 1966 and was still going strong.

Still, some aspects of the arrangement were uncomfortable. There were people in every room, and many of them slept in the nude. From what I understood, these people weren't used to holding back on anything they wanted to do when they wanted to do it. They were at ease with their bodies and showed no modesty at all. I felt awkward about it but didn't say anything. Kathy walked in on a couple in the middle of having sex and started to ask a lot of questions. I doubt my parents answered them, but it did lead them to tell the couple to "cool it." Whatever freedoms the *Oracle* staff enjoyed at the Log Cabin would have to be limited at least in the presence of the children.

Understandably, Jan and Joan were also apprehensive with the setup when they came over. They told me how some of the men from the Oracle kept talking to them about loosening up and asking them to come sit with them. The girls said no and laughed it off as if they had no idea what the guys had in mind. They knew what these guys wanted from them probably more than I did. Jan and Joan lived with a single mother who had taught them how to protect themselves. I wasn't even told that I needed to protect myself or from what.

When my friends did come over, we avoided the Oracle guys and headed straight to my room. We'd talk about sex and share what we knew. Jan and Joan didn't have much more awareness about sex than I did at this time, but we were all feeling our raging hormones and were curious. Though we wanted to experiment with boys beyond kissing, the leering eyes and suggestive comments of the Oracle members were intimidating. There really wasn't anything romantic or sexy about the way the men from the Oracle were trying to persuade us to get close to them. It made all of us uneasy, so we started spending more time at Jan and Joan's apartment or at the beach to dodge any situations we didn't feel ready to handle.

Not every awkward situation could be avoided though. People would come and go from our house, which meant there were a lot of strangers around. And all of them acted friendly with one another, even if they'd just met, which made it hard to know who was trustworthy. One of the couples that moved in with us had been part of the adult film industry. Initially I didn't think much about it, and it didn't seem to bother anyone else. In this atmosphere of sexual freedom, no one was into making judgments.

One day this couple told me about their friend who was a photographer, saying how I would make a great subject, that with my beautiful skin and hair I should consider becoming a magazine model. The suggestion was more than flattering—in my mind I was still the girl with the squinty eyes and the fat rear end. I was vulnerable in a way ripe for exploitation, particularly since my parents' lack of attention lowered my self-confidence.

A few days later, the photographer, an overweight guy in his mid-thirties, came to pick me up. He was wearing a button-down shirt with a suit vest that didn't close in the front. It didn't have any pockets, so it didn't serve much of a purpose except to mask the sweat stains forming under his arms. He helped me select a few outfits, including the new orange bikini that I'd bought for the summer. I was finally getting breasts, so that was a positive change. I still felt fat but was hoping the rest of me would reshape itself like the women I saw in the magazines.

We drove into the woods, and he had me pose in my bathing suit on a log. He told me to imagine that I was a fairy in the forest. I thought about all the beautiful hippie girls I had seen floating through the love-ins, with flowers in their hair like wood nymphs. That is how I imagined myself, completely free and completely beautiful. Then I imagined the forest was alive and welcoming me as its fairy queen, with each leaf and plant in awe of my flowing red hair. I was no longer a freckle-faced little girl, awkward in her body. Instead I was the goddess of the forest who with one wave of my hand could bring all the flowers to life.

The reality was, we were in a remote wooded area somewhere close to my house. The photographer asked me to pose in a hundred different ways all the while clicking his shutter with each shot. I imagined myself as a redheaded not skinny Twiggy, one of the world's most photographed models of the time. As I was lost in my imagination, he asked me to take off my top. As soon as I hesitated, he said the first words he had uttered the entire time we were there:

"There is no one here but us, and only you will see these," he insisted. It is funny how it seemed like there was no one else in the world while he was taking my picture. He made it so I was very unaware that he was even behind the camera. I don't know why, but I took off my top for him.

"That's it, there is my girl," he said as he snapped the shutter. "Now take off your bottoms. Only you will see how beautiful you are."

At that point, I know I was caught up in the moment and the excitement of thinking that someone, even an overweight sweaty photographer, saw me as beautiful. The hippie women were not shy about their bodies, so I decided to do what he asked. I took off my bottoms and let him photograph me. I felt beautiful. I imagined myself to be the most desirable girl in the world, thinking that all the boys at the beach would want me. This would be my secret that they could see only if I let them. When we finished, I dressed and we got back into the car. When we began to drive, I realized I had no idea where we were going.

"I thought my house was back there," I pointed. It felt like we were going in the wrong direction.

"Don't worry, we are going to my studio. It isn't very far from here. I have a few more photo ideas I would like to shoot."

We got to this little cabin, which was far away from any other houses. He had a key, so I figured it must be okay. It smelled musty when we entered it, like it had not been used for a while, but it was clearly a place where he had been before. He told me to lie on the bed and give him a smile. He shot some photographs.

Then he went into the bathroom and started the bathwater. "I would like to get some shots of you in the bathtub with some bubbles," he shouted from the other room.

I sat there for a moment, looking at the fading light in the cabin. All at once I came to the realization that none of this was okay. I was alone in a cabin in a place I would never recognize again, and no one had any idea I was there. My stomach tensed up.

"That's all right," I said hesitantly. "I have to go home now."

I heard him turn off the faucet. He came back into the bedroom, where I was now sitting up straight.

"You don't have to do a shot in the bath if you don't want to." He started to stroke my hair, and I felt my heart race. He noticed me tense up and began rubbing my shoulders. I became aware that part of the musky smell permeating the air when we entered the cabin was coming from him.

"I really need to go home now," I said, standing up.

"What is your hurry?"

I started to cry. I wasn't a wood nymph or a hippie girl. I was a dumb girl who was alone in the woods with someone I didn't know who was trying to get me to have sex with him. That much I figured out. I only hoped it wasn't too late.

He sat with me for a minute and said, "I thought you wanted to do this."

My chest began to heave. I couldn't speak.

"Get dressed," he said. "I will give you all the photographs and we will forget this ever happened." We got back into the car and he drove me back to the house. He said he would call when the pictures were ready and would give them all to me if I promised not to tell anyone about it. I nodded and wiped my eyes on my sleeve.

Surprisingly true to his word, he showed up a few weeks later with over two hundred and fifty photos of me, mostly in the nude. I really liked one in which I was smiling and in my orange bikini. I took that one out and put the rest of them back in the brown envelope they came in and hid them under the bed.

Young as I was, I still understood how lucky I'd been to return home safely, and that there was something very wrong with what had happened. The photographer was disturbing, of course, but the fact that I'd met him because of people living in my house was equally troubling. Though I hadn't considered it before, the people my parents were involved with were relative strangers to us, and we took most of them at their word about their pasts. These were people my parents had invited into our home, a place that was supposed to be safe, but now it turned out I couldn't trust them.

Beyond these uncomfortable questions of the modeling shoot, there was also a larger, more problematic reality for me. No longer a child, like Danny and Kathy, but not an adult either, I was in a precarious position, and no one—not my parents and not me—seemed willing to acknowledge it or to recognize just how vulnerable I was. My father was plunging our family headfirst into the ethos of the moment, opening us up to a communal existence without fully understanding the risks that this posed for me specifically. Or perhaps as I would like to believe, he too was simply naive about some of the very real dangers hidden in the idealism of the moment. Acting as hastily and impulsively as he always had, he didn't stop to consider that as a parent of a teenage girl he had different responsibilities. It was a miscalculation that would prove dangerous.

*   *   *

LOS ANGELES DURING THAT SUMMER OF 1967 WAS A CRAZY SCENE.
There were happenings every weekend, and it was easy to get caught
up in the wave of change. This was a revolution led by the young,
and more of them were arriving every day, flooding into Los Angeles and into San Francisco to find the tribes of hippies they'd heard
about. California was at the epicenter of the counterculture, and
eventually it just came to blend in with the sunshine and the palm
trees.

While it was becoming increasingly clear that this way of life was
taking over, I still had my own reservations. I had enough maturity
to know that school and a stable living environment had been good
for me. I had ambitions and goals for myself. But it also became
more difficult to resist the forces around me, especially since my parents' blind enthusiasm clouded their judgment. They were thinking
and acting like the teenagers streaming into L.A., as though they
didn't have responsibilities or kids of their own; after all, it's a lot
easier to live in the moment when you don't have three mouths to
feed. They were adults, but apparently they were rejecting that role.
And though I had plenty of misgivings about their approach, at a
certain point that summer I decided to simply give up the fight—if
living in the now was my future, so be it.

In mid-July, my parents let me go to the Fantasy Faire &
Magic Music Festival at Devonshire Downs with Jan and Joan. It
was a two-day festival in Northridge, which wasn't too far from
us. The radio ads described it as a "magic meadow where people
would partake of a spectacular gathering, an adventure in light
and sound with twenty groups including the Doors, the Iron Butterfly, Jefferson Airplane, Canned Heat, in forests and meadows
filled with a thousand wonders." There was no way we were going
to miss it.

The bands were as spectacular as advertised, but there was something else that caught my eye as we wandered throughout the sea of hippies. The promoter of the event was a tall, handsome, curly-headed man in his late twenties named Kim Fowley. My eyes followed him as he walked the grounds greeting people he knew. Jan and Joan teased me because it was obvious that I was hot for the guy. He was just my type and he was in charge—that was very appealing. Eventually, he started to notice me, and toward the end of the day, he approached me and asked how I liked the show.

I don't know why, but I felt like a different person as I flirted with Kim. It was like I was intoxicated, but not on drugs, on him. I didn't want to come across as a dumb little kid, so I acted as poised as I could. While we spoke, I made up my mind: If he made any kind of move, I wouldn't turn him down. There was sex everywhere, but more than that, the *expectation* of sex was everywhere; if I was expected to do it, I at least wanted it to be with someone I found exciting and sexy. Not some leering perv with sweat stains or a longhair who happened to be living under my parents' roof.

Kim got the message, asking my name and giving me little things to do as he made sure the show ended without any difficulties. Jan and Joan decided to leave, and when they came up to tell me they wanted to go, Kim offered to give me a lift home. With the cleanup under way, he talked and I listened, and a few times he took me by the hand. My body was reacting to every touch and I decided that this night would be the night for me to go for it.

I didn't say anything to him as we got into his car, but he came up with the idea to take me to his apartment first, since it was near to where I lived. When we got into his apartment, I saw that it was surprisingly modest for someone as important as he apparently was. He offered me a drink and I asked for an Orange Crush, realizing too late any ambiguity about my age was now gone. He smiled and offered me a 7UP instead. Then he took out a joint that we shared while sitting on his couch.

As we became buzzed, he grabbed my hand and led me toward his bedroom. He undressed me slowly and I knew I wanted him. With each piece of clothing removed he told me how beautiful I looked and that I was like a goddess. Then he surprised me.

"Come here," he said as he sat on the bed. "I just want to look at you." He leaned back on his pillow and asked me to stand on the bed over him. At this point I was completely naked and ready to try sex. I stood over him and that was all he did. He looked at me and admired my body. He never laid a hand on me, even though I gave him every signal that I would be happy to have sex with him.

Then he told me he should take me home and that was that. He had me dress and he kissed me on my forehead. I was totally confused about what had happened but I figured "different strokes for different folks," as the expression went. Even though it was a rejection, it didn't feel that way at all. Rather, it was just confusing. Sex was all around me, but some people considered me too young for it, and others seemed to think I was already doing it. Once again, I was in that awkward teenage space—the sexual liberation of the sixties apparently wasn't sure what to do with a teenage girl.

IT WASN'T UNTIL MY FATHER PUT CARPET ON THE FLOOR OF THE CONverted bread truck—the final touch—that I fully understood the scope of his plan.

With the truck complete, my parents called us together and told us their news.

"We've decided to drop out," my father explained.

I questioned the "we" part but bit my tongue, instead asking, "What does that mean?" I had never heard that expression before and didn't know what my parents were talking about.

"Just as it sounds," my mother continued, as if hearing it from her would soften the blow. "We've decided that we are going to drop out of society and live on our own. Other families will be coming along with us. That is why your dad has been working so hard on the bread truck. We are going to live in it." I knew that was what my father had been planning for us to be able to live in the bread truck, but I didn't think he meant permanently. In my mind, it would have been for vacations or trips.

The idea, as it became clear, was for several Oracle families to "drop out" with us. This was a way to live out their philosophies, not just talk about them. For us, though, it was more about a return to form for my father as he attempted to get out from under responsibility and societal expectations. The difference this time was that he had other people who would encourage and support his views without giving him a reality check. They were all gung ho about the idea that people could successfully drop out and that this action in itself would make a difference in society.

"What about school?" I asked.

"We should be ready to go by the end of August, so you won't be going back to that idiot school," my father replied.

This news landed hard. Even as our life had been turned upside down, school had been a constant for me. I was getting good grades and got the only A in my sewing class. I was making all my own clothing and having fun with my friends. While it was true that Jan and Joan had also stopped going regularly to school, this felt like a more definitive break. I wasn't so sure about this plan, not to mention the fact that, once again, we were going to have to pare down our belongings to fit into a truck. Anything that didn't fit would have to be sold or left behind.

I was upset, not just because they had decided all this without discussing it with me, but because it demonstrated just how little we spoke, period. This was especially pronounced with my mother. Our relationship was so much different than it had been a year ago—we hardly talked. Most of the time her conversation was with my father, and either they were arguing about the roles of women and men or she was nodding her head in agreement with his ideas.

With my father, the times he and I did speak tended to involve his ruminating on one thing or another, with him doing most of the talking about his philosophical concepts and periodically asking me for my opinion. Still, we never talked about the things that mattered to me, and we certainly hadn't talked about uprooting our lives all over again.

As I was struggling with the news, my brother had the opposite reaction, elated that he didn't have to go to junior high in the fall. He would have hit the road that day if our things had been packed.

Kathy was similarly excited. "Whee!" she exclaimed. "Can I sleep on the top bunk?"

That afternoon I went to see Jan and Joan to tell them what was happening. The minute I got to their house, I started to cry. They both hugged me and sat me down on their couch.

"It is a good thing," Jan said. "You should get out of here." Jan and Joan hated school and thought my new life sounded like a great adventure. Even though they lived only with their mother, they didn't understand how just living in the same place for more than a year would have been a luxury for me. As alternative as they thought their lives to be, they at least knew where they would be sleeping every night and who would be under their roof.

Joan stroked my hair as I cried into her sweater. "I know, let's go to A Be & See and grab some guys to go to the beach," she suggested. I wasn't feeling very attractive or motivated to try out my inept efforts at flirtation, but they talked me into it.

A Be & See was a seedy little head shop where we were now regulars. It was owned by a gay couple named Del and Monty who had decorated the front with stained glass. I had status with Del and Monty because my father was doing silk screening for the *Oracle*. His artwork was becoming collectible by the local heads, who would remove the free black light posters found in the middle of the newspaper and tape them to their walls. Del and Monty let the local kids hang around and get high in the back room of their shop. The other regulars, some cute local boys from the Catholic school, got a kick out of it when I brought Kathy with me because she would bogart the joint until one of them ran around chasing her to get it back. We also showed them how she could give me a shotgun, which is when you hold the joint between your teeth and blow the smoke into someone else's mouth.

When we got to A Be & See, some boys were there who had been hanging around with Jan and Joan. I wouldn't say they were exactly dating, but they would get high together and hold hands on the beach. They grabbed the guys to go to the beach with us and asked them if they had a friend for me. I wasn't in the mood but tried to be nice to the shy redhead they invited along. He seemed okay and I had nothing better to do. We walked to the beach to do one of our favorite things: get high and watch the surfers wipe out. There was an ongoing rivalry between the surfers and the heads. The surfers never touched marijuana because they said it wasn't good for surfing and looked down on us for even sharing the beach. We thought they were total establishment and that they would be better off with a little bit of altered consciousness.

After a few hits, I was feeling better about the bombshell my parents had dropped. The pot was kicking in and I was feeling more relaxed. Jan, Joan, and their guys were sitting on the sand making out when the not-so-shy-after-all redhead took me by the hand and led me to the pier. It was late afternoon; the space underneath the pier was quiet, peaceful, and secluded. You could see, smell, and hear the ocean from that vantage point, but no one could see you. My body felt fuzzy with the pot and tingled when he touched me. I didn't feel turned on, as I had with Kim. This was a boy close to my own age and acted it. I wanted the attention but was nervous. We kissed and his tongue softly probed my lips. I didn't know what to do. The other times I made out, the boys didn't open their mouths. The boy started to breathe heavy and pushed his tongue all the way into my mouth to the point I thought I might choke. It felt strange, but after a while we got into a rhythm that felt good and exciting.

He was moving on top of me and I tried to push him off, but his rocking back and forth as he opened my legs felt natural. Even though my mind was scared, my body was responding to his. He slipped his hand under my shirt, and I thought about stopping him. I put my hand on his, but he kept massaging my breast until it felt like my breast was moving against his hand. He kissed my nipple and I felt him slide his hand into the drawstring pants that I had sewn myself. It wasn't difficult for him to slip his finger into me.

"Relax," he whispered. "I am going to make you feel good."

Again, I thought I should move his hand, but it did feel good. I wanted him to probe deeper. I knew I should stop him, but I was feeling things I hadn't felt before, and as I told him I thought we should stop, he kept reassuring me it would be okay. Though I liked feeling his finger inside me, what I didn't expect was how quickly his finger became his erect penis. It was inside me before I could push him off and tell him to stop. It just happened. He penetrated me, and in a minute was finished. I am not sure if he pulled out. I was too embarrassed to check. I was too embarrassed to say anything. *Did he think I had ever done this before?*

We got dressed and walked silently back to the others. When we were walking home, the girls asked me if I liked him. They could probably read my expression. I must have looked different, but they didn't ask and I didn't say anything. I did see the boy at the A Be & See Head Shop after that, but we never had sex again.

I wanted to tell my mother about what had happened, but I couldn't bring myself to do it. The last time she talked to me about birth control, it was humiliating, and this seemed even worse. I didn't know how to talk to her about it—it would be too awkward. The truth was, the idea of sex scared me, even though my body told me otherwise, especially when I was high. And now that I'd had it, it was clear to me I still wasn't ready. What I'd really craved that day was for someone to kiss and hold me, but instead I felt used and ashamed. I was also worried I was pregnant. I'd heard you couldn't get pregnant the first time, but I was too scared to ask anybody, so I worried in silence until I got my period. I was so relieved I swore I wouldn't have sex again until it was with someone special and we were in love.

My resolve didn't last very long. Later that summer I changed my mind, only this time I knew what was happening. That other person inside of me emerged, the one that had followed Kim Fowley around until he had no choice but to notice me, and that person knew there had to be more to sex than what I'd done under the pier.

It started when I noticed a guy named Kenneth around Venice Beach. Venice was a place where ideas flourished. Hippies flocked there every day to sell their wares, show off their music, or try to influence the masses. Kenneth had set up an event from late July until early August for people to come together to pick up trash on the beach. The idea was to promote environmentalism and ecology. Of course I went to the event and met Kenneth at the table he set up to hand out pamphlets about stopping pollution. He was at least ten years older than I was, which made him even more appealing. He was handsome and he stood for something. He told anyone who would listen how wrong it was to destroy the earth and how we need to teach children when they are at a very impressionable and important time in their lives. We could use their creativity to raise consciousness about ecology. He was an activist who was doing something good with his time, something practical and not simply self-indulgent. I listened to his pitch about not using plastic and other throwaways and positioned myself so eventually he would notice me. He didn't notice me at first, but I wasn't deterred. I started hanging out by his table every day, and eventually he started paying attention.

He started the conversation, but I was actively trying to draw him in. He invited me to walk along the beach and I listened to everything he had to say. I don't remember if he ever asked me anything. I didn't really care. I wanted him to kiss me, and he finally did on one of the benches behind a palm tree. He took things slowly, and it was obvious he was experienced. When he French-kissed me, I didn't feel like I was drowning in tongue. He touched me in places that I didn't realize were sensitive and spent time doing nothing but kissing me on my neck. He invited me to his house and we eagerly made love.

Smart and sexy, Kenneth made me feel like a woman. There was only one problem: He had a girlfriend, a fact he neglected to tell me until after we had sex. The awful thing was, I didn't really care. When he invited me to his house when his girlfriend wasn't there, I didn't hesitate to say yes. He never asked my age or where I lived; for the first time, it felt like I'd been able to shake my age and just be myself. I just showed up at the beach, and if the coast was clear, we would go to his place and make love. When I was with him, he paid attention to me and made sure the sex was satisfying and affectionate. He didn't jump out of bed when we were finished to signal it was time for me to leave. We held each other and sometimes even took showers together. It was everything my first experience was not.

Kenneth opened my eyes up to what sex could be like—and the fact that an older man had educated me was not lost on me. Now that I'd been with a man, a part of me knew I was going to find it hard to be satisfied with boys my own age. Whether my assessment was accurate or not, I felt that I was now officially a part of the sexual revolution I'd been witnessing around me for the last several months. I might not have had a place in my parents' counterculture, but at least I knew how to have sex.

He and I saw each other every so often for the next few weeks, but it was probably because I was following him around like a puppy.

I am not sure he would have pursued me if I had not made myself so available to him. Not surprisingly, things between us ended without much fanfare. The time for my family's departure was coming closer, and though I kept hinting to him about it, he never said anything. Then I stopped seeing him at his usual place. I looked around for him but was careful not to ask anyone, since I didn't want him to be mad at me if his girlfriend found out.

When my parents told me to pack for the move, I finally gave up looking for him.

7

THE NOTE

AS OUR FAMILY PREPARED TO HIT THE ROAD, I DECIDED TO MAKE THE best of what was left of the summer and my remaining time with my friends. We went to the beach, shopped, and hung out on the strip whenever we could. The strip was a place where things were happening musically, but we couldn't get into most of the clubs, so we just wandered around watching the boys watching the girls, who were watching them back.

It was all fun, but little could distract me from the reality that I was leaving this life behind. I worried incessantly about the bread truck becoming our movable house. No more bedroom, no more neighborhood, no more buying Twinkies at the liquor store or visiting the corner A&W with my friends. Any way I looked at it, there was something that didn't feel right about this decision to leave our lives behind. My uneasiness only grew when my father showed me where all my stuff was supposed to fit in the bread truck.

"That's all the room you get, so use it wisely," he said.

Much like our failed attempt to drive to California in the trailer, he told us to select only our most important belongings to take with us—the rest would go to a huge yard sale. Most everything we had went into the sale, including my sewing machine, which would never fit in my storage space. One by one I put my books, most of my clothing, old magazines, and even records on the folding tables and tarps my parents set out on the front lawn. I stuffed some clothes and my favorite orange bikini into my knapsack along with some underwear and a skirt.

When we had almost emptied the room, I grabbed the brown envelope of my photographs from under the mattress and hid them at the bottom of a box of fabric and embroidery thread I was taking with me. Then my mother gave me another box to sort out. It had my Barbie and Ken dolls with the bed my father made for them.

"We won't have room for all that," my father said as he passed by my room. Only the essentials. I reluctantly handed these remnants of my childhood to my mother and never saw them again.

Once everything was packed, we stocked the converted bread truck with food items and extra blankets. The last things to go in were our new sleeping bags and camping gear. That purchase was to be a consolation for the loss of everything else. The next morning when we were about to say goodbye to our home, Danny caught some hippie running down the street with his new sleeping bag. Even when we'd had the entire Oracle commune living in our house, no one had ever tried to steal anything from us. It seemed an auspicious start to our adventure.

As we stared at all of our stuff packed into the back of a bread truck, the real meaning of the phrase *dropping out* hit home. It is easy through a contemporary lens to assume that the people who dropped out back then were thrill seekers. In spite of their questionable decisions, my parents didn't do things just to do them. They were too serious for that. For its part, the *Oracle* went to great lengths to explain the spiritual rationalizations for dropping out and becoming more connected with other people, returning to some sort of a more natural state. These may sound like excuses for quitting work, but to my parents, they were much more than that. As misguided as this seems today, they believed in what they were doing, giving up their own security to pursue what they hoped would be a better life for us and for the world.

Still, my mom had her reservations. She had a crying fit the night before we left; the reality of taking us out of school and her once again stepping into the unknown was too much for her and she came close to backing out. Apparently, she wasn't the only Oracle member with hesitations. Of the original nine families, only one other family from the Oracle did the dropout thing with us. Everyone else moved on and either got jobs or moved in with other people.

As a fourteen-year-old, I was too focused on my own experience to think about how my mother was coping. I didn't consider that her hysteria the night before, which had led my father to give her a smack across the face, meant that she too had doubts. I didn't consider the pressure she was under to try to hold her family together, please her husband, and still make a life for herself and her children. We were going to be living off the savings that my mother had carefully squirreled away when my father was employed. With only one other Oracle family willing to embark on this "statement of independence," it meant they were essentially on their own. They had no real experience with this kind of living. The "turn on, tune in, drop out" lectures of Timothy Leary and his peers didn't provide a blueprint for how you were to go on taking care of a family while living off the land.

It was early in the morning when we prepared to leave. Jan, Joan, and our friend Sarah surprised me and came to my house to say goodbye. They gave me some flowers they had picked along the road, probably from somebody's garden. Before I got into the truck, they each hugged me and we all cried together. My mother reassured them that we would still be in the area for a while and could keep in touch, but I knew that was unlikely. We wouldn't know where we were from one day to the next because my father was in charge. For all I knew, he would be licking his finger, holding it up to the wind to determine our next direction—his restlessness finally in the literal driver's seat. Even though we would likely be mere miles away from

Jan and Joan, something told me that the space between us would feel much larger.

My father called for me to get into the truck. I held on to my friends' hands as I walked away until eventually it was only our fingertips touching. They each waved as we pulled out of the driveway and continued until they were completely out of my sight.

IT DIDN'T TAKE LONG FOR THE REALITY OF THE "TURN ON, TUNE IN, drop out" existence to sink in—and much as I suspected, it was not nearly as idyllic as Timothy Leary had made it sound.

That first day we got as far as the Will Rogers State Beach in Pacific Palisades on the Santa Monica Bay, not far from where we'd started. It was our first stop as "free people," and initially my parents seemed to think we could just park there and stay as long as we liked. It turned out to be an aborted effort when, after two days, the police told us to move on. My father ranted about the establishment's trying to own and regulate everything. He thought we should be able to land and stay anywhere we wanted in this "free country." My mother didn't want to fight the law, so we packed up and moved on to Zuma Beach in Malibu, which was prettier anyway. We were allowed to stay there, so we set up the camper awning and planned to relax for a little while on our own; we'd already managed to lose the other Oracle family somewhere along the coast.

But relaxing wasn't really possible in the bread truck. We were in a cramped space, always getting in one another's way, and my mother struggled with maintaining control. Since we'd left, my mother had been on my back about everything and kept getting on my nerves. Less than a week in, and already it was difficult to keep a converted bread truck camper clean and tidy when parking it at the beach. And with less space to move, she couldn't distract herself with other tasks and household duties.

Shortly after we got to Zuma Beach, her frustrations boiled over, and so did mine. We got into a fight over, of all things, pancakes, and angry and frustrated with the entire situation, I stormed off to get away from the whole scene. *They* were the ones who'd forced us to do this. What did *they* think was going to happen with the five of us living in a bread truck? What did *they* expect? I wasn't going to hang around if they didn't appreciate me or were going to treat me like a little kid.

I went out to the beach where I came across a cute little curly-headed boy, about three years old, trying to swing on a swing set in a nearby playground. His parents were lying on a blanket and his mother had a sun hat covering her eyes.

"Swing me, swing me," he said when he saw me looking over at him. I related to how ignored he must have felt, so I pushed him on the swing.

"I Stevie." He giggled. "Swing me higher!"

I don't know how much time had passed until his parents saw me playing with him. They invited me to sit with them and offered me a sandwich.

I found out that the father's name was Ronald and the mother was Linda and they were living in his mother's house while she was on her honeymoon. Ronald was a writer and Linda was a silk screen artist and they had been living in a commune before moving into his mother's home. I gathered the mother was well-to-do and was not going to be home for a while.

I told them a bit about who I was and why I was there. Reluctant as I was about our journey, I had started to parrot my father's philosophy because he kept the radio tuned to the Timothy Leary lectures all day. I might have been frustrated with the situation, but it was difficult to avoid the mind-set and the language of what it was all about—even if I didn't fully understand it myself. Convincing people, and perhaps even myself a bit, that what our family was doing made sense. As it turned out, Ronald and Linda already shared our communal mind-set, so they were intrigued, and after a while, the couple and little Stevie followed me back to where my family had set up camp.

"There you are," my mom said. She didn't seem too concerned, just making a statement of fact. I didn't feel all that welcome.

"This is our home," I told Ronald and Linda.

"It's cool, but it doesn't seem to be very big for a family of five," Linda commented.

"Oh, we're managing fine," my father interjected, always proud of his work to rid us of the trappings of the establishment. Ronald told them about where they had been living before moving to Malibu and I could see my father become more interested in what he had to say.

We spent some time with Ronald and Linda, and they started to visit us when they came to the beach. I got the feeling they were relieved to have me play with Stevie so they could enjoy some adult conversation with my parents. They had some friends living with them named Scott and Tracy, and the four adults and Stevie joined us on several nights to cook out on the beach and smoke grass.

"You guys should take advantage of the space I have at my old lady's house," Ronald said one night, exhaling puffs of smoke between words.

"Yeah," Linda added as Scott and Tracy nodded their heads in agreement. Wearing a pair of loose-fitting drawstring pants, Scott was sitting on the sand while Tracy leaned with her head in his lap. We were all listening to the waves come in, and I fixated on the shadows from the campfire we'd built. The flames fascinated me and drew me in—I had to fight the urge to get too close. I was always struggling with the allure of things that could hurt me.

It didn't take much convincing for my parents to accept Ronald and Linda's invitation. Even though we were dropping out, there didn't seem to be any conflict in temporarily living in a beautiful home as long as it belonged to someone else. Ronald's mother's house at Zuma Beach was ultramodern and spacious, located in the middle of a citrus grove overlooking the ocean.

We all settled into a rhythm at Ronald's mom's house. We ate what we wanted during the day and tried to be together for a communally cooked dinner. It reminded me of how things had been with the Oracle members living at our house in Santa Monica, only now we had so much more space and not as many people. It almost felt normal again. We could spread out and I even stayed in my own room.

One afternoon Stevie saw me looking at my envelope of photos and squealed, "Dat Dianne!" He looked at each one and didn't see the secret I was holding. He didn't notice I was nude in most of the shots. I don't know why, but I gave him the envelope of photos. I never wanted to see them again. I had the one photo of me in the orange bikini that I kept in my backpack with a few other keepsakes—I never knew what became of the rest of the photographs.

Although they were on a type of vacation while housesitting, Ronald managed an alternative bookstore and Linda was gaining a reputation with printed fabrics. She took us to a place that carried her work. It was also a club with light shows and music that were meant to create a trippy environment, the feeling of being on LSD. Tracy and Linda were both former heroin addicts, and while they took every opportunity to lecture about the evils of heroin and how it could steal a person's soul, no one felt that way about acid, which we discussed regularly.

Ronald and Linda set up a special acid trip for all of us that started in the middle of the day. We had been smoking pot frequently and discussing the benefits of acid but had not tripped together. We were becoming more comfortable with one another, and there was no question that I would be included. They set up mood music, candles, and a bowl of fresh oranges in the center of the room. I took my tab and watched as they put the tabs on my sister's and brother's tongues. This was the first time for them, and my father reassured me that he would keep a watchful eye.

When the drug kicked in, Kathy and I lay on the grass and she became mesmerized by an anthill. As I was now more experienced at tripping, I was fascinated by how natural it was for Kathy. She didn't seem affected in any visible way; she was just more of Kathy. I have no idea how long we were staring at the ants at work. Time disappears on an acid trip. I remember the taste of the oranges exploding on our tongues. We tried to describe it to each other, but there were no adequate words even from her.

Eventually Kathy got bored with the oranges and skipped off to find something else to examine, which left me alone sitting under a tree. As I was contemplating the orange grove, thinking how miraculous it was that these pulpy round oranges grew from flowers on a tree, I distinctly heard what I believed was the voice of God.

Dianne, it is time for you to leave home.

I didn't answer the voice. I knew it wasn't my own inner voice and I couldn't tell from which direction it had emanated. But I knew it was God. And it was the voice of authority. "Dianne, it is time for you to leave home."

Even as I struggled to understand just what *home* meant, these new words held power, especially when combined with the vision I'd had on my first acid trip. You don't forget a huge cable being severed from the heads of your parents, leaving you floating on your own. This had to be the second part of the message.

This must be the next step, I thought.

We were all doing our own thing during this acid trip, and I began drifting into different rooms in search of a change of scenery or maybe a record player. I opened a door, and there was Ronald lying across a bed. He put out his hand for me and I joined him. It was like he was expecting me. I know that I was tripping, but I was aware of what was happening and it seemed right. As I lay next to him, the room felt like it was vibrating. There were colors swirling in patterns on the wall and I squeezed his hand tighter. He leaned up on his arm and looked at me. He took some of my hair and twirled it around his fingers.

"You are so beautiful," he said. He kissed me on my forehead and around my eyes. Then he kissed my nose.

"Your skin is so smooth," he said as he rubbed my young stomach and barely there breasts. I knew that Ronald was married with a pregnant wife and a little boy, and that my entire family was in the house, but my reality in that moment was only that room, only that bed. There was nothing outside that door—no parents, no siblings, no former heroin addicts, no Stevie, and no Linda. Ronald filled me up with the same sense of desire and being desired that I'd felt with Kenneth. Sophisticated and worldly, he was younger than my father and Kenneth, but he was at least eight years older than I was, so he was undoubtedly a man.

For the first time, I came to see that my sexuality was empowering—something I had that older men seemed to want. In part because no one was talking to me about sex, I didn't realize how dangerous a situation this could be. In my mind, sex with older men meant I was a woman, despite the fact that nothing could have been further from the truth. But with each older man I was attracted to, the age difference between us became less and less consequential.

Following that acid trip, we began to meet secretly to make love. At least that's what I thought was happening. I don't know how secretive we were being or if my parents figured it out; we weren't exactly being careful to hide our infatuation. Furtive stares, pats on my ass, stolen kisses didn't seem to raise anyone's eyebrows. I suppose people see what they want to see. Ronald seemed to always want sex, assuring me that Linda didn't know and that she would likely be okay with it anyway. That surprised me, but weirdly made it even more exciting.

We had been living with Ronald and Linda and the others in this arrangement for several weeks when we got the news that Ronald's mother was coming home. The first step was to return the home to its formerly pristine shape, and the next was to find a new place to live. It was October when we started looking for our next move. Scott and Tracy decided to move on. They were planning to travel and then return to the commune where they'd originally met Ronald and Linda. My parents, meanwhile, had other plans. They had been trying to sell a car they had stored in Santa Monica, a '57 two-tone four-door Chevrolet, to raise funds for a trip to the Grand Canyon. Under other circumstances, I would have jumped at the idea of a real road trip—even if it meant being crammed into the bread truck. But I was taking the messages from my acid trips to heart and I wasn't ready to leave the setup I had with Ronald. While my feelings weren't as intense as those I'd had for Kenneth, Ronald made me feel like an equal. If I went with my parents in the truck, we would likely revert back to arguing, as they treated me more like a kid sister than their daughter. They behaved as though their parental guidance had reached its limits; they wanted me to be a free person able to make my own decisions, and I just wanted them to notice me.

I knew that my mother believed in divine messages, so I told her what I had heard during the acid trip, appealing to her sense of the fates.

"That must have been heavy," she replied and took my hand. If she wasn't angry or upset, my mother was always good at trying to see all sides of something.

The two families discussed the option of me staying with Ronald and Linda to be their live-in babysitter and everyone agreed. My parents may have even believed in the innocence of the situation. After all, Ronald and Linda were a couple with a young child and a baby on the way; a live-in mother's helper was not so out of the ordinary.

I don't know who came up with the idea, but to make things official, my parents wrote out a note indicating that I was permitted to be living on my own in case they could not be reached and Ronald and Linda needed something for me. It was not a legal or enforceable document, but it was intended to be the equivalent of emancipation at age fourteen.

Elated, I took care of the note and kept it in a safe place. More than letting me stay behind while my parents embarked on a road trip, the letter represented something far greater in my mind: freedom. Freedom from my parents, from the bread truck, and most of all, from my father's unpredictability. I didn't know where I would be going with Ronald and Linda, but it had to be better than being with my parents.

LINDA KNEW OF A HOUSE ON TOPANGA LANE, IN A LITTLE VALLEY JUST below the Pacific Coast Highway and north of Topanga Boulevard, called the Spiral Staircase House. The name came from the fact that the wooden house had a spiral staircase on the outside, which was the only way to access its upper floor. There was no first floor to speak of because years of neglect had left it filled with sand. It was nestled into an area people dubbed the snake pit, probably because it was in a floodplain and had a lot of perfect hiding places for snakes. Up the road a bit was the Rancho Hotel, which had small bungalows where people would stay to have easy access to the beach. All you had to do was walk across the PCH and there you were. An infamous crash pad, the Spiral Staircase House appealed to drifters, drug users, musicians, and devil worshippers, and in one of its previous incarnations it had been a heroin den. That was almost certainly how Linda knew about it in the first place.

Ronald and Linda worked out a deal with the house's owner, a woman named Ginger, that we would clean it up in exchange for living there for a while. Ginger knew she was getting a better deal than from the other tenants, and she didn't seem to care about the place or if she collected any rent. Because my parents couldn't leave for the Grand Canyon until they sold the car, they worked with us to clean up the house, sleeping in the bread truck at night and sharing the space with us during the day.

We all rolled up our sleeves to clean up the Spiral Staircase House before any of us would be comfortable using the kitchen or bathroom. It was a wreck, but if my parents questioned letting their daughter stay in such a place, they didn't say anything to me about it. Linda, however, was quite vocal about how awful the addicts were to leave such a mess. To her, pot and LSD were sacraments. She now saw hard drugs as signs of inferior moral and mental decay. The syringes and drug paraphernalia strewn about confirmed my resolve that I would never shoot anything in my veins. The cleanup became a mission because we needed gloves, bleach, and buckets of hot water to remove the grime and filth left by the spaced-out heroin addicts and speed freaks chasing their next fix. The house might have been disgusting, but at least it had hot water, which was more than I could say for the bread truck.

Once the house was clean, I could see why people liked it there. The staircase entrance led right into one of two living rooms. The bathroom and small galley kitchen were just the right size. Surprisingly, all the plumbing worked and the fixtures were brought to a shine. The view from the kitchen window reminded me of a jungle, the trees and vines so overgrown that they created a natural barrier to the rest of the world. Even though the Pacific Coast Highway was a short walk away, this house was far back enough from the road to feel isolated.

My parents hung around for about a week until my father came home with the good news that he'd sold the car and now they could leave. As they loaded up the bread truck, I hugged my sister and brother goodbye and gave each parent a perfunctory squeeze. Before they left, my parents made sure I had my note tucked safely in my pocket and they were off. They said they would swing by on their way back from their trip, but I wasn't too worried. I was ready to be on my own without them, so wherever they landed next was not my concern. As confident as I felt in my choice to remain with Ronald and Linda, I had no idea that this decision to stay on my own would be the first in a series of questionable decisions that I was ill equipped to make as a fourteen-year-old.

With my parents gone, the next night at dinner the energy had changed. I ate quietly and tried to figure out what was happening around me.

"She knows," Ronald said, nodding his head toward Linda. Linda smiled coyly, which was not the expression I was expecting. She took my hand and held it between both of hers.

"It's okay, really, sweetie," Linda said, nuzzling my hand with her cheek. I looked to Ronald for a reaction, but he simply nodded.

"We threw the *I Ching* before we decided to ask you to live with us," she added, "and it said we would have a young love maiden in our lives. That young maiden is you. We didn't want to say anything when your parents were here because we didn't know if they would be cool with it." It seemed a bit hypocritical for everyone to be okay with an arrangement yet so secretive about it. Suddenly I wasn't sure what I'd signed up for.

"We want you to be our love maiden," Linda explained, her dark eyes suddenly alert. It took me a while to understand what they were saying, which should have given me a clue that I was not as worldly as I thought.

"We share everything," Ronald explained. "I didn't think it was cool to keep it to myself what we have been sharing together. Linda is my old lady and she thinks you are as beautiful as I do."

I hadn't thought about being in a relationship with two people and wouldn't know the first thing about being with a woman. I was hoping that wasn't what they were asking.

"We are both going to share Ronald," Linda explained. "We can all sleep together and it will be groovy. I don't mind sharing my man with you because you make him happy and so that makes me happy. It is all love."

I felt relieved because, even though I was curious about women and liked to see their bodies, it was usually to compare theirs to my own. The idea of sex with a woman was not something I was interested in. Still, the *I Ching*, a Chinese oracle, had apparently given cosmic permission to our somewhat awkward ménage à trois. We decided that Ronald would sleep in the middle of the two of us, so he could have whichever one of us he chose when the mood struck. Or we would watch each other please him. It was all new to me, but with Linda's belly growing, I was getting more attention from Ronald than she was, which in turn made me feel desired.

We were together like this for about a month. Ronald had gone back to work and was gone much of the time, working on a novel and buying books for the store. Linda was nesting in the house by painting the rooms in different colors. Sometimes I joined in, but she would become very focused on her work and her own vision for how it should look. Linda wasn't like a mother figure and didn't really have time to be a friend like Jan and Joan. Nor was she exactly sisterly.

Eventually it became clear that, although we shared a bed, I was basically an appendage to their creative life. I was in charge of Stevie, which was the ostensible arrangement, but when put into practice, it became less interesting and fun by the day. I grew bored, unhappy, and even a bit resentful of my parents and my current situation. I thought about how close I had been with my mother when my father had left us. She said time and time again that I had been her rock, that she didn't know how she could have gotten along without me. That was the mother I thought about when I missed her; the one who talked to me, noticed me, and cared about me. I didn't have a place in my own family, but it felt less and less like I had a place in this one either.

Some time toward the end of October my parents returned from their trip to the Grand Canyon and stopped at the Spiral Staircase House to visit me. Kathy and Danny acted like nothing had happened; to them I simply missed a great trip, I hadn't pulled away from the family to be on my own. Maybe my parents were getting used to the dropout life and were getting along better. They were not planning to stay at the Spiral Staircase House for more than a day, but even so I moved surreptitiously into the bedroom with Stevie. They might have been cool with the arrangements I had with Linda and Ronald, but I wasn't sure I was anymore.

"We are heading to Big Sur," my mother announced over a dinner of brown rice, tofu, and fresh vegetables. Kathy and Danny ate at least two plates full, which made it obvious that the food supplies were waning in the bread truck. "We heard that Esalen is a groovy place to go. A lot of hippies are there, and we met some people on the road who said it is far out."

In 1967, the Esalen Institute was a place to probe the boundaries of human potential. It was a natural place for my parents to explore. It brought in leaders from different fields and speakers that would have appealed to my father's intellectual curiosity and my mother's need to have a life that made more sense. The workshops at Esalen were supposed to be experimental to help people transcend the limits of the rational mind so they could learn to communicate more intimately in a feeling and nonverbal way. It was exactly the kind of place to draw in people like my parents.

My father was smoking a joint and passing it around. He looked at me for an answer but didn't seem to care one way or another. My mother seemed excited for me to join them, so I pretended like I would go because that's what she wanted. I didn't know what Big Sur or Esalen would bring, but it was perhaps our last best shot at being a family.

WHEN WE GOT TO ESALEN, IT WAS OBVIOUS IT REFLECTED THE ESSENCE of the times. The Esalen philosophy was for people to experience the present, to get in touch with their feelings, and to communicate intimately with others. To say nothing of these beliefs and the drugs, the grounds themselves were likely the reason so many people, especially hippies, flocked to the place for retreat and refocus. There were redwood buildings on bluffs above the Pacific Ocean, gardens blanketed with colorful flowers, and bathtubs built into the sides of the mountains filled with water from a natural hot sulfur spring. Artists set up easels to capture the impressionistic blending of texture and light, but none could fully capture how I experienced it.

That is, until I saw Jerry. Jerry interested me more than the scenery. He was youngish, about twenty-six to what was still my fourteen, quite good-looking, and he drove a sports car. It was clear he had money and he knew a lot of the people in Big Sur. We met during some outdoor talk that I immediately forgot, and I eagerly accepted his invitation to take a walk together.

He was very into the whole existential thing, but coming from him it made sense. He said things like "Man, if I could be nothing, I would be everything." I nodded and watched his lips, which were part of a perfectly symmetrical face. "The establishment is more interested in the news than what is happening within themselves," again a profound statement of wisdom coming from a man emanating pheromones. Or maybe it was me.

While we were sitting in the grass, Jerry asked me to walk on his back. "This is the way Asian women give back massages."

It didn't seem like such a strange request, so I grabbed onto a tree branch and wiggled across his back making sure to dig my toes into the crevices of his spine. He responded to my touch, so we got into some kissing and exploring. We hung around together for the next few days, and when it looked like my parents were finally getting ready to pull up stakes for a new destination, I told Jerry in the hope that he would ask me to stay. He did something better. He sang the words to the popular song "San Francisco (Be Sure to Wear Flowers in Your Hair)." That was where he was headed next and he invited me to go with him.

I never gave my parents a chance to say anything about my leaving with Jerry. I remembered the note in my pocket that didn't have a specific location on it or expiration date, so I simply announced my plans.

"Mom, this is Jerry, I am going with him to San Francisco."

"Uh, uh, when are you leaving?" she asked.

I didn't give her any details other than I was leaving right away and headed for the Haight. It never occurred to me that my mother might be concerned because at this point I assumed it was easier for my parents without my tagging along.

Off I went with Jerry as we headed for his grandmother's house to shack up on Nob Hill. It wasn't quite Hippie Hill, but it was better than a bread truck. When we got to San Francisco we bypassed the hippie hangouts and went right to the house. Pale yellow, it was two stories and had a huge bay window in the front. There wasn't much furniture, but there was a wing chair sitting right where the sun came in. We brought in some meager groceries like goat cheese and bread and got ready to hole up together for a while.

After a few nights of energetic sex, Jerry left me at the house to wait while he went off to score some drugs or something. I didn't mind waiting for him. I relaxed and stayed in bed until the food ran out. It took me a while to figure out I was alone in the Haight. Jerry was so casual with his instructions that I had no idea when he was coming back or where he had gone. I just assumed that because we were having sex and I was staying at his grandmother's house that he felt some sort of minimal obligation to me. People weren't suspicious back then. Sometimes the pot made you feel that you were all old friends without taking the time to find out the basics.

One night, after about a week, I decided to look around. I was wearing the same makeshift dress I'd made out of a skirt that I had to rinse out at night and a pair of sandals I had made with some twine and old pieces of leather held to my feet by wrapping the twine around my big toe. The dress was still damp but I didn't have the patience to wait for it to dry. I needed a change of scenery. When I walked a few blocks, I found there were people all over the streets with long hair and beads and outfits like one would expect. They looked like they could have been a tourist attraction. Sometimes I had to step over people lying on the sidewalk who were high on drugs, simply strung out, or grooving to some music pouring into the streets.

After walking in circles for about an hour, I heard music coming from an apartment on the second floor of a building. I went upstairs and the door was open. No one cared when I walked right in, and in fact the first thing they did was hand me a joint. I took a drag and looked around for a friendly face. All the faces were friendly but vacant. The trick would be to find someone with whom to make eye contact that would elicit a response. A guy with curly hair and an open muslin shirt was sitting on the floor strumming a guitar. There was a girl sitting next to him with her head on his shoulder, and he motioned for me to join them.

It was good to sit down with other people. I took a drag of the weed and handed it to the girl, whose eyes were half shut. She took a toke and handed it down the line. They offered me some food, and after a bit, I figured I might as well go back to the nice bed on Nob Hill rather than crash with everyone in the apartment. It was dark out at this point, and I walked back to Jerry's grandmother's house and waited.

The next morning Jerry showed up with some food and his father, acting like nothing had happened and I hadn't been waiting for over a week with no food or money. For all he knew I was exactly where he left me, sitting in a wing chair looking out the bay window watching the world go by.

Attracted to him as I was, I got over my anger the minute I saw him. He signaled for me to come into the bedroom, and as I followed him, my stomach jumped with excitement. That was until I saw his father in the bed without any clothes.

"Why don't you give my dad a good blow job, Red?" That was the name he had been calling me, and my excitement instantly turned to nausea. I had been feeling lousy anyway since walking all night in the cold air of San Francisco in nothing but a damp mini-dress and almost bare feet.

"I don't feel well," I coughed. Then I really started to cough. And I kept coughing for days until I had developed a fever and could hardly breathe. I was too sick to care about the humiliation of his expecting me to service his father or the fact that he didn't seem to care at all about me.

"I think we need to get you some help," Jerry said softly after feeling my head. I would not make any eye contact with his father, who was still there leering at me from behind his newspaper. Later that day Jerry took me to see some of his friends in Big Sur. My chest felt heavy and I could hardly breathe. I should have been grateful to the couple who wound up taking care of me. They met us at the door dressed in white cotton and said they practiced some form of Zen macrobiotics.

The couple's house was very clean but rustic. They had open shelving with all kinds of jars filled with beans, grains, and what looked like dried seaweed. They also had herbs and something they called lotus root. They created a poultice and put it on my chest. They fed me miso soup and a twig tea and said it would take time but I would feel better. I was full of fever that first night. I don't recall if Jerry ever said goodbye. I didn't see him after that, not that I expected I would. I was becoming wiser and less vulnerable. At least that is what I thought. I wasn't allowing myself to feel the deep hurt of once again being tossed aside like nothing after I shared my body with a man. But that was what sexual freedom was about. If they didn't care, then I wouldn't either.

The Zen couple was very kind, and in a few days, I felt well enough to leave. They hinted I should stay, which made me leery. I left through a window at four in the morning and climbed a fence to freedom. I wound up hitchhiking back to Hollywood to find my parents. I had no idea where they were and was on the road with my thumb out when it hit me that I had no place to go. It was a good thing I was picked up hitchhiking by a carful of New Zealanders on their way to Hollywood. They were in a white Cadillac and seemed like angels rescuing me, essentially barefooted with my thumb out and no money in my pocket. One of the girls in the back had a typewriter and said she was a writer. They all said they were on their way to Hollywood to meet Dean Martin. The girls were happy to drop me off someplace specific, except I had no idea where to go. The only place I could think of was Ronald's bookstore so I could figure out where to find my parents. They could have been anywhere, and in my rush to escape to San Francisco, it didn't occur to me to find out if they had any plans.

When I got to the bookstore, Ronald wasn't there, but his partner was. He knew that my parents had returned to the Spiral Staircase House, where they'd rejoined Ronald and Linda, and all of them had been pointed in the direction of the nearby Hog Farm commune. So that's where I headed next.

8

WELCOME TO THE HOG FARM

RONALD'S BUSINESS PARTNER DID HIS BEST TO AVOID THE DEEP RUTS in the dirt road leading up to the Hog Farm commune. As we kicked up the dust, I had no idea that I was heading toward what would become known as one of the focal points of the 1960s counterculture experience—I just wanted to find my parents.

The Hog Farm was founded by a man named Hugh Romney (later known as Wavy Gravy) and his wife, Bonnie Jean. Hugh had been an entertainer admired for his comedy and poetry. He had already had some success in New York and California, performing at various bohemian locales. Bonnie Jean, then Beecher, had been an actress who guest-starred in such TV shows as *The Twilight Zone* and *Star Trek*. They'd married in 1965 and began a journey together that came to represent much of what the 1960s were about. Hugh had been along with Ken Kesey and his Merry Pranksters for some of the famous Kool-Aid Acid Tests when the Merry Pranksters, traveling in a painted bus they named Further, set up Acid Tests, turning people on with LSD to have an uncontrolled psychedelic experience. The Merry Pranksters were not welcome in many communities, so they wound up staying with Hugh Romney and his wife Bonnie Jean in their one-room cabin in Sunland, California. And after they arrived, more and more people kept showing up at Hugh and Bonnie Jean's house, including some not-yet-famous musicians like Jerry Garcia and the members of the Grateful Dead. This arrangement was fine with Hugh and Bonnie

Jean but not with their landlord. They had no place to go until a local hog farmer named Doty had a stroke and needed someone to run his farm for him. That was how a hog farm with its forty or so hogs became the Hog Farm commune.

Hugh formed this community with him at the center and Bonnie Jean at his side in 1966. He wanted it to be a fun place where people could live in freedom and peace. As he described the experience in an interview for *The Realist* in 1969, the early days were about creating "an expanded family, a mobile hallucination, a sociological experiment, an army of clowns. We were living on a pig farm for about two years, feeding forty real pigs breakfast and dinner for free rent."

Of course I knew none of this as the car sputtered its way up the road, nor did I know how my parents had ended up there. In October, while I'd been in the Haight, my parents and siblings had reconnected with Ronald, Linda, Stevie, and their new baby, and together all of them went on a visit to the Hog Farm. Ronald, Linda, Scott, and Tracy had lived there before house sitting so for them it was a return. My parents and siblings went back several times before getting the official invitation to stay shortly before Thanksgiving, not long before I found my way to them.

The closer we got to the Hog Farm, the more unsettled I became about how I'd be received. While I wanted my parents to greet me like the returning prodigal daughter, it was difficult to admit to them or myself how much I had missed them. Being in the Haight had opened my eyes to what it really felt like to be alone and gave me a small taste of the dangers inherent in the life we were living. My decision to go with Jerry had been impulsive and reckless, and from the fact that I barely knew him to the flimsy barefoot sandals I was wearing, I wasn't equipped for the consequences of my choices. Though I didn't feel like I belonged with my parents, now I understood that being by myself posed risks that were greater than I'd imagined.

As we pulled into the Hog Farm, I spotted the bread truck right away and felt a pang of familiarity. It was parked near other vans and scattered about were tepees, makeshift shanties, and a partially constructed geodesic dome. I didn't realize until that moment how much I'd been expecting to feel relief at the mere sight of that truck, but instead I was struck with a different visceral reaction: *I don't fit in here.*

I got out of the car and scanned the scene for familiar faces. There were couples with young children and people doing their own thing. I noticed my father, with Danny at his side, adding piping to the dome. I couldn't be sure if it was the same dome we had at our house in Santa Monica or if it was a new one, but Clarence and Danny didn't look up from their work. Then I saw my mother sitting with Kathy admiring flowers. She barely shifted her gaze when I walked up to her. I probably should have assumed she was high, but my first impression was that she didn't care. Kathy was the first to greet me with excitement. She hugged me and grabbed my hand to show me around. My mother gave me a quick squeeze and said she was happy I was there.

As I surveyed the grounds, I could see that the Hog Farm appealed to my parents for the same reasons I resisted it. In the time since we'd dropped out, my parents had been searching for like-minded people who shared their values and goals for the counterculture. At the Hog Farm, it seemed they'd found that. Suddenly my parents were surrounded by people who actually had a plan and were in a place where they could be "dropped out" but not alone. The communal life—everyone taking care of everyone else—had always appealed to my father, yet even better was how this place would allow him to avoid the burden and responsibility of feeding his family without a job. His skills at building things and creating art made him valuable to the commune and gave him a sense of importance. It was also helpful that they no longer had to eat into their savings, since they didn't have any real plans for how to survive when the money ran out.

My mom and Kathy walked me around the farm. The first place we stopped was the hog pen. There really were hogs and they were big and smelly. The pen was falling apart, and every place you looked was muddy. Some of the hogs were painted with bright colors; one even had an American flag painted on its sizable rump. Kathy pulled me over to where my father and Danny were working. Danny stopped what he was doing and gave me a hug. He was about eleven now and was starting to look like a young man. I hadn't been gone from the family for more than a few weeks, but everything seemed to have changed. Danny seemed different and happy.

"What are those glad rags you are wearing?" my father sniffed while looking me up and down. He flicked the ashes off his cigarette. I thought I looked good and I suddenly felt dirty and self-conscious. When Ronald's partner had been driving me to the Hog Farm, a place I had never heard of, he'd explained it was a happening place where hippies were now gathering around a cool dude named Hugh. I had "borrowed" a bit of money from Jerry's Zen friends, and I'd asked Ronald's partner to stop at a thrift store so I could fix myself up with some cleaner clothes. The shirt I'd picked out was full and embroidered and I was wearing drawstring pants that might have looked a little big on me. I even bought new sandals so I could get rid of the ones I made myself. I looked around the commune and saw other people dressed even more oddly than me. Maybe they were artists and knew something I didn't about appropriate hippie attire. Either way, I was stung by his instant dismissal.

I didn't have time to dwell on his insult—Kathy grabbed my hand and skipped off with me toward the other parts of the commune. On the way to the Haight, Jerry had taken me to a couple of communes to visit his friends. Neither looked anything like this place. One was built into the side of a mountain at Big Sur and was focused on holistic health; those living in this commune grew their own food and raised goats. The atmosphere at the Hog Farm was more circus than farm. Everyone seemed to be doing something expressive, with no real rhyme or reason. Hog Farm residents were interacting and working together, but it was more of a gathering of people with different agendas who all liked to smoke pot and make fun of things.

As I would learn, there was a structure to the commune even though from the outside it looked like everyone was doing whatever they wanted. Hugh was a quiet leader but made it clear that everyone would pull his or her weight and that conflict would be resolved before it would be allowed to fester. Kathy, who had made an impression on everyone with her joint-rolling skills, told me the immediate rule that there would be no smoking inside the house. People were taught to hide their stash in case the cops wanted to cause a hassle. The Hog Farmers were also allowed to smoke on what was fondly dubbed High Hill. You could see people climb up the hill first thing in the morning for a breakfast toke and late in the evening to wind down for the night. In between everyone smoked wherever they wanted as long as they were careful.

I slept in the bread truck that night with my parents and Kathy. My mother was legitimately interested in my stories about the Haight. My father smoked a joint and remained silent as I told her how awful it was.

"I am glad you are back with us, sweetie," my mom said, her hand on my arm. It felt good to have her look at me with sympathy and concern. "That guy was a jerk to do that to you." I hadn't even told her about the father and what Jerry wanted me to do with him. I was too embarrassed to tell anyone. That night, for the first time in weeks, I slept soundly, with Kathy snuggled up to me.

In the morning, my mother took me around to meet everyone. She brought me over to meet Hugh Romney after morning meditation. From the moment we locked eyes, I think there was a mutual distrust. I am not sure if he was counting on another member of the Lake family, especially one that was a budding adolescent with attitude to match. He asked me a lot of questions like "Where are you coming from?" "What you been doing?" "What are you into?" and of course "How old are you?"

I didn't have a good feeling after I told him I was fourteen—something changed. As I'd been walking around after my arrival, I'd noticed that I seemed to be the only person my age. That morning I'd watched him interacting with the small children. He was jovial and playful. He'd been the same way with the couples who were members of the commune. With me, he was cold and unwelcoming, and upon hearing my age, he seemed to grow skeptical, almost suspicious, as though I represented a danger that neither one of us could see.

As I shifted my body awkwardly, I tried not to read too much into the look on his face, but his displeasure was impossible to ignore.

IN THOSE FIRST FEW DAYS, I MET A LOT OF PEOPLE, INCLUDING A WOMAN everyone called Big Cathy. She filled me in on the other rules, which were in place to keep things running. Otherwise there were no rules about personal expression. Hugh and Bonnie Jean, whom I had not yet met, set up a system of dance mistresses and dance masters. Everyone took turns with jobs while the dance mistress ran the inside like the kitchen to keep everyone fed and the dance master ran the outside to see that things were working and the hogs were cared for properly.

Big Cathy explained that people tended to fall into steady jobs because of what they liked to do and what they were good at, but everything seemed to get done the way it was supposed to. Big Cathy showed me her mattress in the hallway of the main house in case I needed anything. There were mattresses or sleeping bags everywhere, including a makeshift bed occupied by my brother behind the sink of an unfinished bathroom. It made our Santa Monica home with the Oracle members look spacious.

Even though it was a commune, couples seemed to be pretty straight and together with each other. Though I saw Ronald and Linda around, none of us acknowledged our shared past or our shared bed, which was probably just as well. There weren't many single people, with the exception perhaps of Big Cathy and a few more. Not all the couples were married, but if they were together, they pretty much stayed with each other.

Admittedly, aspects of the Hog Farm were interesting at first. Hugh set up Sunday happenings at the Hog Farm, often following the suggestions people would leave in the fantasy box. These fantasy events included a Tiny Tim Day, on which Tiny Tim came and performed; a Dress Like Children Day; a Build and Fly a Kite Day; and a Hog Farm State Fair Day, when they had bake-offs and picnics.

More important, despite my initial skepticism, being back with my mother and sister felt as refreshing as I'd hoped it would. Together with them, I experienced shades of our previous life, but to say we were reconnecting as a family would be to stretch the truth. In reality, I hardly saw my father. He was going through his own shifts and had now changed his name to Chance, which he also wrote on a bandanna that he wore. It wasn't until later that he explained to me how he saw his life at the Hog Farm as a second chance. It was also an opportunity for him to create distance from us. Hog Farmers were taking temporary oaths of silence so they could get in touch with their inner selves, a step that my father took as well. Naturally the silence only pushed us further apart.

Our family of five became part of the communal family, but we had very little to do with one another. The younger children like Kathy seemed to be raising themselves under the semi-watchful eye of all the adults, but they were largely given the freedom to do what they wished. Meanwhile Danny spent time with the men, who were repairing, building, and caring for the hogs, so he seemed to be learning some good values.

My mother kept me occupied by inviting me to help in the kitchen, a place where she seemed to be most comfortable. It gave her a reliable way to express her domestic needs for certainty and a clear role to play in the communal hierarchy. The time I spent with my mother in the kitchen helped me see how she was changing. She seemed more relaxed and now wore flowing clothing and no makeup. I thought she looked more beautiful than ever. She kept busy, but we hardly spoke about the tangled thoughts that were going through my mind. We'd been through so much in such a short period of time. All of the changes had left me untethered and confused, unsure of myself and my place in her life. I wanted to speak with her about all that I was experiencing, but she was always preoccupied and seemed unavailable. She seemed to put me in the category of all the other women at the commune, as if I were now her friend or her sister, not her daughter.

I tried to do my own thing, but I didn't know what that was. Each day I observed people simply being themselves or playacting. I could never tell which. During the day people walked around in top hats and roller-skated. They painted things and had fun in between chores and people from the town would come up to the Hog Farm to play music and enjoy the atmosphere. In the evening, we would sit under the dome and listen to people playing music. We chanted "Ommm, Om, Om." The sound of *Om* is supposed to be the vibration of the universe. You chant the sound, and if you do it right, it eventually becomes like no sound at all. When you do it in a group, it becomes pure vibration. Sometimes Hugh would tell jokes and people would share stories. Hugh spoke a circular philosophy while pot-saturated acolytes nodded in agreement. I didn't always follow what he was saying and didn't see him as a guru as other people did. He was too aloof toward me.

When I shared how I didn't fit in with my mother or mentioned that I was lonely, she told me to make the best of the situation, so finally I decided to follow that advice.

While my parents and everyone else were off doing their thing, I did my thing with the boys who came up the hill from town. One day I met a cute musician who was close to my age. I decided to have him stay over with me on a mattress in the large living room where everyone slept. I knew my dad was somewhere in the room, but the boy and I were both high, and honestly, since my father wasn't speaking to anyone, it seemed unlikely he would say anything if he had a problem with me. Besides, pot always made me focus on what was in front of me, and what was in front of me was the boy.

We tried to be quiet, but we weren't that successful. While the other people in the room were either stoned or tripping, someone almost certainly heard us having sex. Even if no one caught us in the act, they probably put two and two together when they saw us sleeping naked barely covered by a blanket the next morning.

Honestly, though, I didn't think anyone would really care. Everyone was talking about sex, and everyone who wasn't talking about it was doing it. They were talking about love, free love, living free, and no one was saying that these things didn't apply to me. In one way or another, I'd been absorbing these lessons ever since our family had joined the Oracle. Now I was just acting on impulse and living in the now, following what I thought was the spirit of the whole commune. I had no idea how wrong I was.

MY ACTUAL TIME AT THE HOG FARM WAS SHORT, LESS THAN A MONTH. Hugh Romney and Bonnie Jean made sure of that.

Hugh and Bonnie Jean called me into the kitchen one afternoon. Hugh didn't have any teeth in the front and often wore a clown's nose. This day he wasn't smiling. His tone became uncharacteristically serious, at least in contrast to the persona he showed most of the commune members and his audiences. Bonnie Jean nodded in agreement as he laid out my fate. He sat back in his chair and put his fingers together so they formed a little box. I looked all over the room to try to avoid their gaze, but no one else was around. That was unusual. There was never no one around. No matter where you looked, someone would be there doing something. And the kitchen was at the heart of everything.

"Dianne, we have been talking with people and we don't think it is a good idea for you to be living with us here." Bonnie Jean nodded and tried to look sympathetic. The more her eyes puddled with tears, the more I wanted to throw something at her.

"What do my parents think about that?" I asked.

"They have left it up to us to decide."

"We know you don't really have a place to go, so the best we can do is let you stay in the attic of the main house, but you have to follow certain rules."

Nobody seemed to be following any rules, so I was feeling a bit put out. "We want you to be able to stay here, but we have to be careful," Bonnie Jean added.

"To put it plainly," Hugh explained, "you are jailbait. Do you know what that means?"

I really didn't, but I knew it must have something to do with sex—everything always had something to do with sex.

"You are under the age to have sex, particularly with people who are older than you." He spoke to me slowly as if I were stupid.

As he said the words, I wasn't surprised. Everyone else was doing it, but they wanted me to follow a different set of rules. They'd built an entire movement around relinquishing responsibility about sex that they now expected a teenager to bear. The hypocrisy would have been laughable if it hadn't been so aggravating.

"We are already getting heat from down the hill," he said referring to other run-ins they'd had with members of the neighboring community and the police. "If anyone figures that you are having sex with anyone here, we can get into big trouble."

I looked at him blankly. I was a potential thorn in their side who could hurt their reputation or put an end to their fun. Until that point, it had never seemed to me that anyone at the Hog Farm had any particular rules to follow. We had assigned chores to do every day, but everyone was pretty much free to be who they wanted. Apparently, it was a free society within the commune only if you followed the dictates of Hugh and Bonnie Jean. I looked out the door at the painted hogs and the mud and the squalor and the people going about their day. They weren't being asked to live in the attic.

I wanted to talk to my parents, but Hugh and Bonnie Jean seemed to speak as though my parents knew about this ultimatum I was being given. Based on how the conversation unfolded, my assumption was that my parents asked Hugh and Bonnie Jean to take care of this conversation for them. I didn't know if I was more upset by the statements of these relative strangers or by my parents' apparent choice of this place over their own daughter.

What I didn't know until years later was that my mother had no idea this conversation with Hugh and Bonnie Jean ever took place. Maybe my father did know, but my mother certainly did not. It's difficult to imagine what she would have done had she known—perhaps she would have intervened, but that would have risked our family's presence. Membership in the Hog Farm commune meant acquiescence to the rules, and the rules were not created by consensus but rather by Hugh and Bonnie Jean, who also decided who could stay and who could not stay. I came to them by default because they liked my parents, but prior to my arrival, they had been able to avoid people in my age group by careful selection because it raised too many uncomfortable issues. Apparently not even the sexual revolution knew what to do with a teenage girl.

Regardless of whether my parents knew about Hugh and Bonnie Jean's decision, the legacy of this rejection undoubtedly shaped my path. In my mind, my parents had abdicated their role to communal parenting. I was no longer their personal daughter. I belonged to the Hog Farm, which made Hugh Romney a sort of father. And it was clear that he and his wife didn't want me around.

In the end, all I could mutter was "Uh-huh, I understand," as I got up to leave.

I would have to think of something more, but for now all I could do was kick the door on the way out. I grabbed an apple even though it wasn't mealtime and ran off. There weren't many places to hide from everyone, so I found a large rock and leaned up against it. I was scraping my feet in the dirt when this guy and his girlfriend came up to me.

Richard was tall and slender, maybe in his early thirties, with long dark hair balding on top and a mustache. He didn't live at the Hog Farm, but I had seen him and his girlfriend Allegra several times at our circle time or playing music. Allegra was thin but was the kind of thin that surprisingly still showed ample breasts. She was also tall, something I was certain would never happen to me. There was still some hope that my breasts would get bigger, since I was only fourteen, but my height had probably reached its limit.

"What's up, Chicken Little?" Richard asked. I looked up at them both as they stood over me. "Is the sky falling?" I realized that I was sulking and was happy that at least someone noticed.

"I guess you could say that."

"Why so glum, chum?" This got me giggling. It was so corny, and he and Allegra were smiling at me. They sat down next to the rock and I offered them a bite of my apple. They each took a delicate bite of my offering and handed it back to me.

"Here you go, princess. Thank you for sharing your bounty."

When I told them of my plight and rejection from the Hog Farm, they moved away from me, whispering and gesticulating. Then they came back arm in arm.

"Chicken Little, we would love for you to come live with us. This place is not everyone's scene and it sounds like you are getting the shaft."

"We dig that," Allegra added. "Our folks didn't get what we were all about either, so we moved on a long time ago."

I took Richard and Allegra over to my parents to ask their permission. They were both busy and I couldn't get their attention. Since I already had the note they had given me to live on my own, I decided just to leave, telling Hugh and Bonnie Jean of my plan to go with Richard and Allegra. I was pretty sure my parents wouldn't even notice I was gone.

I didn't know that my leaving hurt my mother terribly and led to my parents ultimately splitting up. I found out later that when I chose to leave, my mother cried and spoke to her friends about the loss. My father became angered that my mother was "airing her dirty laundry" to the commune. When she protested, he kicked her out of the van. That was the beginning of the end for them.

If we had been able to talk about it, she would have known that I didn't want to be on my own and I would have known that she actually wanted me with her. But my immaturity made that conversation difficult; I was stubborn and headstrong and would never have let on that I wanted to be a kid with parents. I would never have told them how much I needed to belong to them, to be their child, to feel I was important to them. As a fourteen-year-old, I couldn't articulate any of that. All I could do was seethe. So I took off with Allegra and Richard, fully believing that my parents didn't want me with them.

I didn't know Richard and Allegra, and while this move was nearly as impulsive as the decision to run off with Jerry, somehow it felt safer. They were familiar; there was some connection, however tenuous, to my parents and their life. What I didn't know, what I couldn't have known, was that Richard and Allegra, well-meaning as they were, would lead me straight into the arms of Charles Manson.

9

SOMEONE GROOVY

I DIDN'T WIND UP WITH CHARLES MANSON THE WAY MOST PEOPLE COM-monly assume. Over the years, different accounts have written that my parents handed me over to him with a note that specifically said I had permission to join his family. While my parents made many mistakes that contributed to my joining Charlie, deliberately hand-ing me over to him was not one of them. Instead, my direct path to him began not with my parents, but with a handful of seemingly innocent words from Richard: "Hey, Chicken Little, we want you to meet someone groovy."

I'd been with Richard and Allegra for a couple of weeks, going back and forth between Richard's house and the Hog Farm, when Richard and Allegra invited me out with them to a party. It was going to be a nice change for me, as Richard and Allegra were speed freaks and many of their speed-freak friends used their house as a crash pad. At least pot smokers liked to eat. The speed freaks seemed to live on air and whatever they popped into their veins. I was dying for a hamburger and a soda.

"That sounds far out," I said. Anything that was a change of pace was going to be fine with me.

"We are going to a party in Topanga at this place called the Spi-ral Staircase House." I didn't bother telling them that I was already quite familiar with the place. After all the work we did cleaning it up, I hoped it had not been reclaimed by addicts, who like weeds would try to overpower the flowers.

And with that, we were off.

When we arrived, we climbed the stairs that led into the living room, and a red-haired girl got up to greet us. She stared at me for a minute and ran back to her friends yelling, "Dianne is here! Dianne is here!"

I was incredibly confused. As far as I knew we weren't planning to go to the party until the last minute, so I couldn't imagine they were expecting me.

The girl returned with three other girls, who all took turns hugging me. The red-haired girl who called herself Lynette said, "You are even prettier than your picture. Charlie is going to be so happy to meet you."

She took my hand and led me to where a bunch of people were sitting in a circle, and in the middle of the floor sat a small man playing the guitar. There were girls surrounding him, singing along to his soulful music of songs I'd never heard before. The girls sat me down and Lynette kept her arms around my shoulder. As soon as the music stopped, she jumped up and pulled me by the hand.

"Charlie, we found Dianne. She's here!" They weren't just excited, they were overjoyed. It had been ages since I felt truly wanted, and all the attention made me feel like royalty. They were beaming with love and I felt it. Without hesitation, they sat me in their circle as if I belonged, and strange as it may seem, I felt like I belonged there too.

Lynette must have sensed my confusion, because she began to explain how they recognized me. While I'd been off in the Haight, they'd met my mother at the Hog Farm. Apparently, my mother had given them my photo and told them to keep an eye out for me if they made it to San Francisco.

What I didn't understand then and only learned much later was that my parents and siblings had done more than just run into the Family at the Hog Farm and given them my photo. They'd actually taken a trip into the desert with them, traveling in the black school bus that Charlie drove around in and outfitted for his followers.

Many people during this period were painting buses, bread trucks, and VW vans with psychedelic Day-Glo colors. Charlie and the girls chose to make a different statement with their monochrome home on wheels, tricking out a surplus school bus by painting it all black, including the windows, which made him easy to spot. To the residents of Tujunga and the Hog Farm, Charlie was known as Black Bus Charlie.

As it turned out, all my family members had a story about an encounter with Charlie before I'd even met him. Back then, the alternative community in Southern California was still relatively small, but it fascinates me how Charlie and the girls had been circling my orbit long before our paths intersected. Riding on the bus with the crew, my mother had thought Charlie was interesting and that his girls were nice—she'd even dropped acid with him. As I'd later find out, a couple of Charlie's girls even introduced my then-eleven-year-old brother to French-kissing.

While my mother and Danny had more positive experiences with the Family, my father's run-in, which I learned of only years afterward, proved eerily foreshadowing. One afternoon my father was sitting in the bread truck with a friend drinking scotch. Even though the drug of choice at the Hog Farm was marijuana, my father always appreciated a belt or two of the hard stuff. Chance and his friend were engaged in one of my father's favorite topics of discussion that would become more animated with the amount of alcohol he consumed.

"Owning stuff is a trap. That is why we gave it all up and hit the road." It is likely he went on and on with the same clichés he repeated when we lived in Santa Monica about the establishment and the benefits of not owning anything. Incongruously, at that point he was playing a record on a battery-operated phonograph that was his pride and joy.

While Chance and his friend were indulging in their fantasy of nonconformity, Charlie climbed up the stairs to the bread truck and said to Chance, "Hey, man, if you really believe that stuff, you will give me that phonograph."

"Don't listen to that asshole," my father's friend interjected.

My father's integrity was being challenged and his ego was on the line. After a brief pause Chance said, "Go ahead and take it." Before he could change his mind, Charlie wrapped the phonograph up in a bag and disappeared with it—a con man and a thief from the very first.

Ominous as signs like this were, back at the Spiral Staircase House, I knew nothing about them, and even if I had, I doubt it would have changed anything. I was far too enthralled by these people who wanted me with them. Lynette was adamant that I'd finally found my way home—to them—and quickly I came to agree.

"We went to San Francisco looking for you," she said as she pulled me closer to Charlie. I couldn't believe that they went to all that trouble for me. It never occurred to me to consider how strange a statement that was. To me it was magical and beautiful. It was the answer to what my heart had been missing.

Charlie stood up and looked into my eyes so deeply and intimately that I almost turned away on instinct. Instead I held his gaze and felt like he was looking into me.

"So, this is our Dianne," he said and pulled me to his chest in a hug so close I could feel his heartbeat. He held on for several seconds and I felt my resistance fade. I was used to the hippie hugs at the Hog Farm, but this felt warm and real. Tears welled up into my eyes as I took in his embrace. Charlie held me at arm's length, looked at me and said "oh, you're beautiful. I want to talk to you. I've been looking for you."

I sat next to him and listened as he sang and told funny stories. My first impression of him was that he was charming, witty, and most of all intriguing.

"Have some root beer, little darling. I give you the last sip in honor of your arrival."

Lynette and a girl named Patty stroked my hair and passed me a joint while Charlie strummed out more tunes on the guitar. At first I thought Patty was homely. She had a prominent bulbous nose and thin lips. But when she smiled, her face became beautiful to me. She exuded a motherly warmth and was obviously completely smitten with Charlie. His presence was disarming. He continued to sing and seemed to make up the words as he went along.

"Dianne is home," he sang out and the girls joined in with the chorus: "Home is where you are happy."

Everything felt like a dream. I had been around groups of people grooving on music, but they were often into their own trip. These girls seemed to love one another. They were affectionate like best friends or sisters, but it didn't seem fake. They weren't trying to outdo each other in their outrageousness, as was true of those at the Hog Farm, where everything seemed like one big joke. There was something different about this group of girls and about Charlie, and while I wasn't sure what it was, I immediately knew I wanted to be a part of it. Like a raindrop joining a puddle, I blended in easily, my loneliness disappearing. For the first time in my life, I felt like I was in the right place at the right time.

There was a lot of unspoken communication between Charlie and the girls. His expression changed slightly, and as if the scene had been rehearsed, Patty took his guitar from him. He stood, took my hand, and led me outside. We walked hand in hand to the black bus. He went in first and motioned for me to follow. It reminded me of a raja's palace, with mattresses on the floor and Indian-print bedspreads and carpets hanging from the walls. Pillows were strewn about and colorful swirls were painted on any surface not already covered with fabric. This explosion of color was the last thing I'd expected from the blackness of the exterior.

We sat facing each other and the anticipation swelled up inside me. I expected a kiss, but instead Charlie had me put my hands up against his. He moved his hands in different directions until I caught on that I was to follow his every move. It was a game and I was more than eager to play. It was like he was syncing up our energy. He sped up until I could no longer follow and he started to laugh. Then he guided me onto the mattress and again looked into my eyes so that I felt there was no one else but the two of us in the entire world.

"You are so beautiful, my little one." His voice was barely above a whisper, but I heard it reverberate through my consciousness. We had only smoked pot, but I felt as if I were on a trip, his trip, and he was guiding my every move. Charlie was older than the other men I had slept with, but his body seemed younger. He had tattoos on his arms and a small tuft of hair on his chest. There was something magnetic about him, even though I wasn't sure I even found him attractive. He was small and nice looking but not as classically handsome as some of the men I had pursued. The attraction was more chemical and inevitable without any thought about whether I would or wouldn't.

He took his time to explore my body. He avoided the places that made me purr until I could barely stand it. After a few minutes, he put himself inside me while staring into my eyes. He was tender as he held me up to meet his deep thrusts. When he finished, he sighed; I exhaled and realized I was hooked.

I watched as Charlie put on his jeans. He was clearly a man but also seemed like a boy. He was playful, and that made me feel even more comfortable with him. Sometimes after I would sleep with a man, I would be left feeling empty. My experience with Charlie was the beginning of something. I felt appreciated by him, not just like some pretty young thing. Charlie was offering me more than sex. He told me I should forget my parents and give up my inhibitions. He made it clear he wanted me to be a part of the group; his group. It felt as if there was no turning back. When I'd been with other older men, I'd been playing the role of a woman—Charlie made me feel like I'd actually become one. He said everything I needed to hear.

That night I went home with Richard and Allegra, but I knew I would return. The decision seemed so natural; a date with destiny. Charlie and the girls were now living at the Spiral Staircase House. It was only a matter of time before I joined them.

THINGS WITH RICHARD AND ALLEGRA CONTINUED MUCH AS THEY HAD been, with them taking me back and forth to the Hog Farm. Whatever threads bound me to that place were finally severed as it became clear there was nothing left for me there. I was an outsider, and my parents and brother and sister were having a life without me. Each time I took a trip there, my presence seemed to make less and less sense.

When I eventually made it back to visit Charlie and the girls at the Spiral Staircase House, Lynette and Patty told me I should stay with them. Creating a sense of urgency, they told me they were planning to take a trip soon, and I had to make up my mind. I wasn't sure yet about leaving my parents for good; in living with Richard and Allegra, I still had a connection to the Hog Farm as well as the possibility that my parents would tell me they wanted me to stay. It was a childish fantasy, but it helped ground me. As long as I was near them, I wasn't truly alone. Still, I was concerned that I would lose my new friends if I hesitated for too long.

When I got back from the Spiral Staircase House I told Richard and Allegra about the possibility of going with Charlie and the girls.

"I don't know about that, Chicken Little," Richard said. For some reason, he had changed his mind about Charlie. "It may not be such a cool scene. Maybe you should stick around here for a little while."

That was the one warning I got about Charles Manson. It was not from my parents or from people at the Hog Farm. It was from my speed-addict friend who somehow understood something that the rest of us did not. Richard never gave me any specifics about why he felt the way he did, so I don't know where his hesitation came from, and thus there was nothing to dampen my growing crush on Charlie and his girls. But honestly, I'm not sure anyone could have kept me away. The pull of belonging had become too great.

I thought about the note my parents had given me. Even though it was for a specific purpose, it had given me my freedom to be on my own. I didn't see any reason not to use it as my passport to Charlie's world. I visited the Hog Farm one last time, stuffing what few belongings I had in the bread truck into my knapsack and saying goodbyes to my father, mother, brother, and sister. As we parted, I was surprised how little I felt toward them. The rift that had been growing for months was finally complete.

When Richard and Allegra took me to the Spiral Staircase House, all the girls ran out to greet me. It turned out they were packing the bus for a drive and told me I was just in time. Charlie reached out his hand to me.

And I took it.

Remembering his face in the December light, I find it hard to reconcile the man I followed onto that bus with the monster the world now knows him to be. Over the years, I've wished that I could go back and show my younger self what he was to become, changing the story from the start. Clearly that's not something anyone can do, so I'm left trying to defend the indefensible: Why did I get on that bus?

In the decades since I first met him, I've turned the question over in my mind countless times. The obvious answer was that I felt an attraction to him, and as a fourteen-year-old girl, I reacted to that hormonally. But that's not really the answer, or at least the full answer. More than just attraction, I felt a deep connection. It seemed as if he understood me completely and wouldn't let me down or betray me as all the other important people in my life had. Ever since we'd "dropped out," I'd been an afterthought, at various points a mouth to feed, jailbait, and a reminder of a previous life in the straight world.

With Charlie and the Family, from the beginning, there was none of that baggage. I had a place with them from that first night. I belonged in a way that I hadn't anywhere in months. Charlie and the girls also made it okay for me to want and have sex. It seems so simple, yet this freed me from some of the deepest confusion and shame I'd been experiencing since I was nine.

There is no doubt that Charlie took advantage of me. This small man oozed self-confidence and sex appeal, and as he would demonstrate time and time again in the months and years ahead, he knew exactly what he was doing. He was a master manipulator, while I was fourteen and essentially on my own. I was a naive, lonely, love-starved little girl looking for a parental figure to tell me "No, don't do that." As I discovered that first day in his magic bus, when he focused his attention on you, he made you believe there was no one else in the world. He also had the uncanny sensibility bestowed upon mystics, yet misused by sociopaths and con men, to know exactly what you needed. Charlie knew what you were afraid of, and could paint a scenario that would use all those insights to his advantage—traits that I would see in equal parts over time. Of course, in this moment, as I walked up the bus steps I saw none of these things. Instead, all I saw was acceptance.

But perhaps the most impressive trick of all was how he made this seem as if it was my idea. Ever since my father first left home, I'd cultivated a sense of independence. I'd taken care of my siblings, I'd cooked, I'd become a free thinker, I'd taken drugs. I might have been fourteen, but I thought I understood who I was and what was missing from my life.

What I needed was a family. And now it seemed I'd found one.

PART II

TUNE IN

10

THE BLACK BUS

THE BUS LURCHED FORWARD AND I STUMBLED TO THE FLOOR AS WE took off. This was not the grand entrance I had envisioned, but everyone simply laughed as I crawled to an open space on the floor. The bus was fitted with a wall behind the driver's seat, a place against which Charlie could lean and play his guitar while facing outward toward all of us. Charlie rarely drove, but rather relied upon the few men who traveled with us. Today it was Larry, the boyfriend of Ella Jo Bailey. As I scanned around the bus I became aware of how much care had gone into its decorations. There was a platform with a mattress in the back, which I had hardly noticed the first time Charlie had taken me into the bus with him.

The front and side windows were clear, but all the other windows were painted black in sharp contrast to the vibrant psychedelic images painted on the inside of the bus. All the seats had been removed, and in the center, suspended from the ceiling, was a table. The rest of the bus was cozy with overstuffed pillows and beanbags and more Indian-print bedspreads, giving it the feel of a motorized scene from the Arabian Nights. Charlie strummed his guitar as the girls sang along to his original music.

We passed around a joint, and as I listened to Charlie's songs, I took in the faces of everyone around me. Their voices bounced off the metal of the bus's walls and filled the space around us. I looked from girl to girl, soaking in the whole scene. It had been only three weeks since we first met, but I felt I was becoming one of them. I scanned the circle of young women, their smiles wide and their voices in harmony as Charlie led us to whatever destination he had in mind.

I knew little else about these women except how they made me feel about myself. In time I would come to learn their stories, and how, like me, each had found her place in Charlie's family. Sitting toward the front of the bus was Mary Brunner, who'd given me the impression she was the matriarch by default. She had been the first girl to join up with Charlie. Not classically beautiful, she had light hair and solid features, but also possessed a mischievous smile. She'd apparently been quite straitlaced when Charlie first met her on the Berkeley campus, where he would go to check out the scene and play his guitar.

She and Charlie became friends, and she let him stay at her apartment. All he brought was a single box with his belongings and a guitar. Still, she made it clear they would not be having sex together. And that was just fine with Charlie, because it was all part of his plan. Of course I took everything at face value when I first joined the group. It wouldn't have occurred to me to question the actions of others or assume their choices were calculated. This was a period in which a person's past, particularly if it was on the wrong side of the law, was not considered a deterrent. The counterculture especially trained its adherents to never trust the man, which included all those in the justice system.

Charlie had been open with everyone about his criminal past, and even when I heard about it in passing, I didn't think much about it. But Charlie was different from run-of-the-mill dope dealers or petty thieves. Charlie had been a criminal since he learned to speak, but his plan, such as it grew in the time I knew him, was completely under the radar, at least to me. He told us just enough to make us feel sorry for the awful deprivation he had endured during his early life. He never alluded to his firsthand education at the feet of felons, and I knew nothing of his real past until many years after my time with him, when I learned through various accounts a history that has put things in perspective for me.

Before he met Mary Brunner, Charlie had been in prison a few times, and during each stint he grew more and more interested in the pimps there. Evidently there was a hierarchy in prison, with the con men and the pimps at the highest level of respect. When he got out of jail in the late 1950s he tried to become a pimp like the cons he most admired. He had one major problem: he couldn't hold on to the girls. They weren't loyal, and the minute he was sent back to jail, the few he had in his stable found other situations.

Charlie promised himself that when he got out again, he wouldn't make the same mistakes. He certainly didn't plan on going straight; it was just that this time he was determined to become a successful pimp. Charlie had six years to figure out how to succeed, but his best opportunity came when he was transferred to Terminal Island to serve out the last few months of his stint. This is where he found the mentors who taught him the pimp trade. He wanted to know how to keep the girls loyal. Thus far in his life no woman had ever remained loyal to him, starting with his own mother and subsequently a woman he married who left him for another man.

A wise old pimp gave him the three secrets to keeping women loyal and malleable. Charlie used these as the foundation of everything he did following his release from Terminal Island in March of 1967. The first was to use fear and intimidation, but that didn't always work. The next was becoming the greatest lover in the girl's life—satisfying her like no one else can. The final and most important was making the girl feel fully loved.

And so, when he was released in 1967, Charlie decided to put his education to use. The only problem was that the free-love idealism of that moment, LSD, and current attitudes toward sex—the same forces that had moved my parents to drop out—also meant that the sex trade, at least in the Bay Area, was changing as well.

No matter. Charlie was resilient and creative. It didn't take him long to scope out the world into which he was now released. The new scene of lowered inhibitions, pseudo-philosophy, communal behavior, and young people in search of guidance from new kinds of authorities provided ample opportunity to take advantage of people. It just so happened that Mary Brunner was the first one to take the bait.

Charlie hadn't been out of jail for very long when he met Mary. From what I understand, Charlie didn't have to use fear and intimidation with her, at least at first. He liked her personality, and even though they were from two entirely different worlds, he felt they could communicate. He won her over by being a gentleman, waiting until it was her idea that they become lovers and working on improving his own sexual abilities. He made it a point to focus on pleasing the woman first so she would have more reason to stay. He would make her feel as if she were the only woman in the world and through patience would find out exactly what pleased her the most.

When Charlie and Mary eventually became lovers, they quickly formed a special bond. He made her feel things she had never felt before. A Midwestern girl from Wisconsin, Mary was down to earth and didn't put on any airs, and she was not used to being the center of a man's attention or having him care so much about her sexual needs. Fun and quick-witted, Mary was compatible with Charlie, but more than that, she became devoted to him and had stayed with him ever since. And because she was older than most of us (a good ten years older than I was), she eventually became something of a mother figure to the group, modeling her dedication to him for all the other girls to emulate.

Next to her was Lynette, who like me also had red hair. (Given the fact that Charlie's mother, in his telling, had apparently been a slight young woman with red hair barely out of her teens when she abandoned him, it doesn't take much of a psychologist to realize that he was surrounding himself with a group of maternal stand-ins—young, petite, fair-skinned redheads—that he would make certain never left him for another man.) When I'd first met Lynette at the Spiral Staircase House, I was immediately taken in by her smile and inner glow. She had a childlike quality that immediately made me feel at home, and though she was about five years older than I was, you would never have known it by looking at her.

Charlie had rescued Lynette from a curb in Venice Beach after she had a huge fight with her father. Her father was an aeronautical engineer who ran his home with the same structure and discipline as he must have run his laboratory, and from what Lynette said, he threw her out. She thumbed a ride to Venice, known as a hippie hangout, and she'd been sitting on the curb reading a dictionary when Charlie pulled up in his van.

Charlie parked, got out, and said, "You look like you need a friend."

After taking in her appearance as a little lost girl, Charlie could have chosen any number of things to say, and his words would have appeared brimming with insight. He could size people up within seconds and create the right mirror for them to see in him what they wanted to see for themselves. Of course because Lynette was sitting by herself on a curb in Venice, it wouldn't have taken much prescience to assume she was feeling alone, but Charlie exuded omniscience in his delivery.

At first, after looking at this stranger and his van, Lynette hesitated. But something in his invitation to come away with him aboard his magic VW bus convinced her this was what she had been seeking all along. Of all of us, Lynette became the most dedicated to Charlie and every thread that he spun into a tapestry of illusion.

On the bus was another redhead, Patricia Krenwinkel, or Patty as I'd been introduced to her, who, the story goes, had first met Charlie in Manhattan Beach. She happened to meet Charlie at a party and was swept off her feet by this charismatic little man. Another rootless auburn-haired girl, Patty had always been self-conscious about her looks, seeing herself as plain while struggling with her weight and a hormonal condition that gave her too much body hair. Charlie quickly became her knight in shining armor, making her feel both lovable and loved.

What Patty didn't realize when she first met Charlie was that he came with a small but growing harem. Patty got a huge surprise when Charlie picked up Lynette and Mary. Though I imagine Patty wasn't pleased when she figured out she would be sharing him with others, she didn't likely know where else to go and truly might not have cared after coming under his spell. And of course Charlie, who was becoming a more impressive manipulator seemingly by the day, could talk her into staying with the double-talk that he would deploy so skillfully in the years ahead, explaining that "love was love" and "his love was for each of us," and leading each to believe that she was his number one girl.

Seated next to Lynette was Susan Atkins, the next one to join Charlie. From the moment I joined the family, Susan was always a bit of an intimidating figure, with dark hair and big brown eyes that always telegraphed her state of mind. Though she was only five years older than I was, she had certainly lived a lot more than I had, even when you factored in her tendency to exaggerate. Long before she met Charlie she was attracted to life on the lam. I remember her as a wild woman. She'd run away from her family early and had a collection of sordid tales to prove it. She'd been a stripper and a topless dancer. She'd lived with drug dealers. She had even bragged that she had done a show with the notorious Satanist Anton LaVey, in which she played a vampire during a witches' sabbath. According to her, they did the authentic ceremony and it wasn't an act; she told us she took LSD before she came out of a coffin. The entire thing sounded terrifying to me, but it only added to her allure and mystique.

Eventually she'd found her way to the Haight and joined a commune. This commune turned out to be more of a drug-dealing family of men paired off with women, so Susan joined a man who didn't have a girl of his own. She fit in nicely, and the group gave her a place to belong and a man to take care of her. Another woman, Ella Jo Bailey, was also living with this group, and when the men got busted, the women were available to find another family. And as luck would have it, that's when Susan met Charlie.

The building where Susan and Ella Jo were living also housed other transient crash pads. According to Susan's later testimony, somehow Charlie wound up in one of them and was playing his guitar to an audience gathered for the drugs and the entertainment. The dance of seduction between Charlie and Susan sounds like the introduction he gave to each of his initiates. From her perspective, they vibed from across the room and joined in a shared need for music, passion, and abandonment of inhibition.

I am not sure if Charlie seduced Susan Atkins in the way that he had the rest of us, or if she'd been the one doing the seduction. I'd later come to realize the power struggle between them made their relationship more volatile than the relationships he had with the rest of us, and probably had its roots in their earliest interactions. Because, unlike the rest of us, she seemed worldly and experienced, she was comfortable using her sexuality to get what she wanted. While I was hardly a virgin, I was still trying to understand my own body—pleasing or enticing a man was a mystery. Meanwhile Susan made it obvious that she knew where it was at and what it was for.

As I got to know her, Susan treated me like a little pet, ruffling my hair as if I were a cute little dog. This produced mixed feelings in me. On the one hand, it was about as endearing and affectionate as she got, but on the other hand, I didn't want to be treated like a little girl by anyone in the family, especially in front of Charlie.

I liked looking at Ella Jo Bailey, who sat next to Susan. She often faded into the background, but we shared a love of nature and quiet and often took walks together around the "snake pit." Ella Jo Bailey appeared shy, but it was probably because she was overshadowed by Susan's big personality. She was a curly-haired blonde with a gentle smile and had just a bit of sarcasm in her expression. Her blue eyes twinkled as she amused herself with observations she was too shy to share with the group. Although she stayed on the periphery of things, I enjoyed her playfulness and her open heart.

During this first real trip on the bus I had only my initial impressions of these women who would become my closest friends. I knew few facts about them. I would piece together the stories of these women gradually as I became more familiar with each of them. It wasn't until years later, when I finally compared all the accounts of how each of us met Charlie, that I realized how similar all our stories were, perhaps with the exception of Susan. We'd all been isolated from our families and struggled to find out where we belonged as a result. And it was at that precise time that we'd had our run-ins with Charlie—when we were seemingly at our most vulnerable. Each story highlighted Charlie's ability to make a girl feel as if he only had eyes for her—just as he had with me that first night at the Spiral Staircase House. But even as I learned these stories over time and heard the parallels between them, I wasn't able to connect that Charlie's manipulation was the common thread uniting us—only how lucky we all were that he'd brought us together.

With the bus kicking up dirt and dust behind us, I took in the high female voices as they sang the choruses of his songs, beginning to learn the words, lyrics, and melodies that would become the soundtrack to my time with the family and would serve as the gateway to my indoctrination. I looked around the bus at each of these girls whom I barely knew, yet already I felt connected to them. And I joined in.

AS FATE WOULD HAVE IT, MY INITIAL SEPARATION FROM MY PARENTS was short-lived. We had been driving for only about half an hour when we got stopped on the Pacific Coast Highway in Malibu. The cops hated hippies, and we certainly had the look, especially with the bus. Charlie warned us to be cool with the cops because he had been in the joint, but this was my first experience with any trouble. We all got out of the bus, and the cop walked down the line looking each of us up and down. He stopped in front of me.

"How old are you?"

Before Charlie or anyone could stop me, I blurted out, "Fourteen." I should have at least said I was almost fifteen, since my birthday was coming up in February and it was December, but I didn't think quickly enough. The cop's eyes widened.

"Come with me, young lady." He put handcuffs on my wrists and put me in the back of the squad car.

Another cop showed up with a van and took everyone else with him. I don't know what he thought we were doing. We had been smoking some grass, but we'd finished it, and as far as I knew we were just driving around on our way to a party.

"Where are your parents?" he asked.

"I don't know," I said.

"Don't be smart with me," he said. "You are in a lot of trouble."

"For what?" I asked, but he didn't give me a reply. He seemed really angry so I shut up.

The cop brought me to the Malibu police substation, a small one-story brick building on the mountain side of the Pacific Coast Highway. I was shaking as they put me into a holding cell, where I stayed overnight. There was no one around except the sheriffs, who were more used to drunks than young hippies.

The next morning, I was transported by van to the juvenile hall in Sylmar, and from there, everything happened fast.

"Name?" a matron asked me. The place was clean but looked dirty. Everyone seemed angry and upset.

"Dianne Lake."

"Age?"

"Fourteen."

"Where are your parents?"

"I don't know." This time I gave them their names and explained that I really didn't know where they were. I assumed they were at the Hog Farm, but the last thing I wanted to do was send the cops there in search of my parents.

They took my fingerprints and a photo of me and gave me a change of clothes. Then they led me into a shower room and told me to take everything off. They put my things in a bag, marked the bag with a number, and sprayed me with some awful-smelling insecticide. After they rinsed the insecticide off me, they gave me some rough soap. When I dried off, they gave me the ill-fitting uniform made of a heavy canvas material that was scratchy against my skin, which was now inflamed by the bug spray.

After I was dressed, they took me to a holding cell with other girls. Since it was juvenile hall I assumed we were all around the same age. I figured they were runaways or in there for pot smoking or bad language or disobeying their parents.

"What are you in for?" a heavyset girl asked me. Her uniform pulled against her forming breasts and was tight around her thighs. I didn't want to stare, so I turned away.

"I'm talking to you," she continued.

"I'm not sure. I told them I was fourteen and they brought me here."

"What are you in for?" I figured I would continue the conversation.

"I killed my parents." I wasn't sure if she was kidding me or not. But she seemed distressed when she said it. Then she toughened up.

None of the other girls said anything to me. The matrons took us to our dormitory rooms, which had metal bunk beds with thin mattresses, a sink, and a toilet.

"Why you tell them how old you are?" one of my dormmates asked me as we waited in line. She hit me on the shoulder, but I think she was trying to be friendly.

"I don't know. I didn't know I could get in trouble for that. I had permission to be out."

"They don't give a shit about none of that in juve. Here being young is a crime."

She was right. I was there for only a few nights over a weekend until I could be seen by a family court judge. That was enough for me to see that this was a tough place to be a kid of any age for any reason.

Much to my surprise, my parents showed up for my arraignment. I had no idea how anyone found them; all I could think was that one of the girls must have tracked them down. My parents stood there looking uncharacteristically parental and giving the court the address of a friend as their place of residence. They didn't tell anyone that they were living at the Hog Farm commune, which helped show the court I would have a straight place to go if I was let out of juvenile hall. My parents laid it on thick about how we had just moved to California, devising a decent explanation for why I was with Charlie and the others in the bus in the first place. It was all a charade, but it worked. After the judge warned them to keep a better eye on me, I was released from custody.

Although it had been only a few days, I was happy to be released to the Southern California air. As I soaked in the sunlight, I was surprised how relieved I felt to be with my mother and father. Just having them nearby had been a comfort, something I hadn't felt from them in a long while. More than their presence, though, the words they'd said in the courtroom, the picture they'd painted of what our family had been like not that long ago—dinners together, beds with clean sheets, my siblings with me in a home where we all belonged together—left me overcome with homesickness. What had gone unsaid was the fact that this version of our family had disappeared almost a year earlier, when my father cut the legs off the dinner table and everything had changed.

The mere memory of that time was enough to give me pause. I missed everything about my old life—school, kids my own age, and Danny and Kathy. Seeing my parents there, I knew I wanted to go home with them, but I also hated that I would be banished to the attic if I returned with them, so I tried to engage them to see if they'd changed their minds about being separated from me as well.

"How are Danny and Kathy?" I asked, trying to start any conversation that would prop open a door.

"They are just fine," my mother answered, while my father remained silent. Annoyed, he seemed put out about the whole juvenile court thing. I was assuming how they felt because neither of my parents gave me much to work with.

"Are there any new people at the Hog Farm? Any new hogs?" I asked, grasping for anything that might show a renewed interest in me.

I was met with mumbles and stares. I would have preferred a reprimand, anything rather than these confusing mixed messages.

I was running out of things to ask about, and it became increasingly clear that their indifference had not changed. They'd shown up today not because they wanted me back in their lives, but because it would have been trouble for them if they hadn't. I was an inconvenience.

When we walked outside out of the judge's view, I noticed Charlie and the girls leaning on the black bus waiting for me nearby.

"Mom?" I started to break down, but stopped myself. I wanted them to embrace me and tell me enough was enough—they wanted me back home where I belonged. I wanted to spend time with my mother in the kitchen cooking mushy oatmeal and flat lemon meringue pie since the Hog Farm had no electrical appliances. I was even willing to tolerate Hugh and Bonnie Jean's disapproval if there was a glimmer that they wanted me to go with them.

I looked over at my father, whose expression had not changed. My mother's words caught in her throat. Across the street stood Charlie, smiling at me, while Lynette jumped up and down, saying, "There's Dianne." The contrast couldn't have been clearer: My actual family didn't seem to care one way or the other about what happened to me so long as I wasn't causing problems for them. My new family, however, clearly felt I was supposed to be with them.

I gave my father a quick hug and felt him tense up at my grasp. Then I hugged my mother and held her for a few seconds.

"Mom . . ." I said. She looked like she wanted to answer me, but said nothing. For a brief moment, I thought I saw tears, as she looked away to my father. I felt a wave of nausea, but I held my composure, so that my father wouldn't think I was a baby.

I turned around and waved to Charlie and Lynette, who were motioning for me to join them.

"Goodbye, Mom." I kissed her cheek. I looked at my father, who turned away and started to walk toward the parking lot, with my mother trailing behind him.

Charlie put his arm around my shoulders and led me into the bus. When I got on, Mary hugged me and Lynette, Patty, Ella, Susan, and Mary all clapped. Then they pulled me into the circle and told me how happy they were to see me.

"We love you, Dianne," Lynette exclaimed. "Tell us all about your adventure."

"Oh, it was awful." I told them all about the pesticide bath and they listened to every word I said.

"Well, you are back with us now," Patty reassured me.

"The little one lost her cherry," Charlie quipped. Going to jail for the first time was apparently a rite of passage, but I hoped I wouldn't have to face it again.

Now that I was surrounded by the girls, the sadness I felt about my parents' apathy toward me faded, along with my memories of us all gathered around the dinner table. My parents were leading different lives now, and I was too. I could no longer rely on them to take care of me, even at a distance; they were too immersed in themselves.

It wasn't that I would never see them again—of that I was pretty sure. The scene in L.A. was getting bigger, but it was still relatively small. I was bound to run into them or people that knew them, and I could go visit them at the Hog Farm from time to time. But such run-ins wouldn't mean that they were parenting me, caring for me, or looking out for me. Our relationship would be more like friends who'd grown apart than parents and a child. From here on out, they wouldn't be responsible for me—my new family would.

I didn't look back to see which direction their car went. After all, you can't see anything out of a window that's covered in black paint.

11

WE ARE ALL ONE

THE SPIRAL STAIRCASE HOUSE REMAINED OUR BASE OF OPERATIONS for at least several more weeks after I returned from my stint in the junior joint. This strange place with its history of being a crash pad, a drug den, and a place for all kinds of bizarre rituals felt like the closest thing I had to a home.

It wasn't long before it would outlast its usefulness. It was a good party house and a central location to receive visitors. The small kitchen was convenient, but we spent many of our nights sleeping in the bus, which we had now outfitted with wall-to-wall mattresses. We wanted to be together, especially at night, because we were bonding in a way that I instinctively knew went far beyond a typical commune. I knew what those were like.

I'd been with the Family full-time for at least a couple of weeks now, hanging out with the girls, smoking pot, and periodically having sex with Charlie, but it still wasn't entirely clear to me what the point of our little group was and what we were all about. This group was different, not only in its intimacy but in its core. Like my parents, the Oracle followers, and people at the Hog Farm, Charlie spouted beliefs about communal life and giving up the possessions and inhibitions of the straight world, but what made life with him different was that everything revolved around him. He was beyond our guru. He was our entire reason for being there, the center of our universe. If communal life was at least partially about subverting the self for the benefit of the group, life with Charlie it seemed, was about subverting the self for the benefit of him.

It was on the black bus that I had my first LSD trip with Charlie and the Family. We all sat in a circle and I watched as Charlie placed a tab of acid on each of our tongues. I studied him as he went from person to person—the way he held his small but muscular body, the way he moved, the sensuality of his hands as he administered the sacrament. At his behest each of us put our hands up against another person's hands as he guided us through our psychedelic journey of altered consciousness.

"Feel that energy," Charlie said. "That is the real you. We are all one."

The LSD took effect and I could see the light between our hands. Colors—blues, purples, reds, and yellows—burst from our fingertips. He told us to lay back and close our eyes. Then he spoke softly to us, seeming very far away. I opened my eyes to confirm where he was and to make sure I was still in the room with everyone else. I saw Patty's hand next to mine and wanted to reach for her, but I couldn't move. My hand didn't want me to move it. So instead I saw color going over to her hand and touching her palm. Then I visualized colored light going from my hand over to Charlie's palm. I knew that we were all there and we were together.

I closed my eyes again and heard Charlie talk about his name. "We are all together for a reason," he said in a melodic voice. "Think about my name and you will understand your purpose. I am Manson, man son, man's son."

I pictured the Jesus of my childhood church with a crown of thorns, Jesus comforting children, Jesus with his kind, loving face all knowing and all compassionate. In my mind, we became disciples aware of a truth others could see but not accept. I thought of the misunderstood Jesus on the cross being crucified. I began to feel hot tears falling down my cheeks. Then I opened my eyes and there was Charlie standing in front of us and it looked as though he was hanging on the cross, with a stigmata of color pulsating through his hands and on his ankles.

At some point, I must have fallen asleep, because when I awoke, everyone was sitting in a circle singing with Charlie as he played his guitar. They were some of the same songs I'd heard on the bus, designed to make us feel a part of the whole he was creating. There were no marks on his hands or ankles, but he looked at me as I joined the circle, and I knew that he'd shared my vision. Most likely they all had.

I didn't know what it all meant—I don't believe any of us did in that moment. But scenes like these played out frequently in these early weeks, setting the tone for what our group life would be and establishing powerful rituals that made me feel as if I'd joined something larger than myself. In the weeks and months ahead, I'd hear it during group trips like this, as well as in how Charlie spoke to us.

"We are all one," he'd say over and over to us.

He put these same messages in his songs, repeating the ideas incessantly, until there was little doubt in my mind that I belonged to these people and they to me.

IT WAS ABOUT TWO OR THREE WEEKS AFTER OUR ABORTED MALIBU TRIP when we all knew it was time to travel from the Spiral Staircase House for parts unknown. This was the trip they had been planning, if you could call it planning. Time did not exist in our lives, so if we wanted to live in the now, we would never plan too far ahead. Instead, Charlie would "postulate" for things. He would think about something we needed or wanted and it would appear just at the right time. Things always seemed to be showing up—food, funds, clothing, and other items were a thought away. We were outgrowing the Spiral Staircase House, so Charlie postulated for us to find what we needed by taking a road trip. We would follow the signs to wherever they led us. When we got back, *if* we got back, we would figure out our next move. This was complete freedom without limitation. Everything was possible.

There was no question I would take the trip with everyone. We left California some time between Christmas and New Year's Eve, ringing in 1968 together on the road. We passed the time smoking joints and singing Charlie's songs. I was now learning all the words and harmonizing with everyone, and often Charlie would play his guitar and make up words on the spot to suit the situation. Out of a strange coincidence or design on his part, somehow Charlie had gathered women who could all carry a tune. We all tried to outdo each other with our voices, but after a while we would blend in, despite our subtle competition.

After a couple of weeks on the road and a quick trip through Texas, we ended up in New Mexico, where the terrain changed from lush trees and wildflowers to mountains rising above calm clean waters. We passed through forgotten towns and parked near a lake in a park that seemed to be a well-kept secret. The air felt crisp and dry, and though it was cold, it wasn't the rip-through-your-skin cold of Minnesota winters. We'd stop along the way and stretch our legs, but never ventured too far from the bus. Charlie would go into little mom-and-pop grocery stores or roadhouses to get us sandwiches and candy. He had an instinct when we needed a break and made sure none of us got too restless.

Charlie knew people everywhere who were willing to open their homes to us as if we were their relatives. And if there wasn't someone around that Charlie knew, he would use his charm to convince strangers to open their homes to us. Though his appearance could be menacing, especially to people who were unfamiliar with hippies, he was a difficult person to say no to, given his ability to size people up quickly and find common ground with them. He could change his voice, intonation, and accent depending upon who was on the receiving end. He used every opportunity to show us how to do this as well, and in time, we learned to reflect to people the version of ourselves that they wanted to see. It enabled Charlie to appear harmless and unsophisticated to people. If he wanted to ingratiate himself with someone, he would. It was that simple.

One night we helped cook a meal with one of Charlie's friends, and after dinner we sat around in the living room in what was a comfortable but modest ranch-style house. It had a woodstove for heat, so everyone smelled smoky. I always loved the smell of smoke, whether it was from a woodstove, a fireplace, or leaves burning in someone's backyard—for some reason, it always reminded me of Little Red Riding Hood happily skipping to Grandma's house, even though I never thought about what would happen when she arrived. That night, as I settled into bed, I wrapped myself in the cozy smell of the woodsmoke, overcome by how fortunate I was to be with Charlie and with people who loved me.

The next day I woke up to a different reality. We were in the kitchen preparing some food when Charlie walked in. I thought he just came in to check on when the food was going to be done, but he was clearly distressed. He took some ice out of an ice tray in the Frigidaire, put it in a dish towel, and held it to his mouth. His eyes looked different. I tried to get his attention because he didn't seem in a very good mood. I hated seeing him unhappy, and my instinct was to distract him from whatever was bothering him.

"Charlie, where are we going from here?" I asked.

"Don't ask questions," he snapped.

"Can I help you with anything?" I asked. "Do you want some food?"

Before I knew what was happening, he dropped the ice pack into the sink and whacked me across the face. I slipped back and landed on the floor.

"Do I look like I want any food?" he spat. He gathered up the ice pack and put it back on his mouth before storming out of the kitchen.

I sat on the floor, stunned. No one had ever hit me like that, even my parents. It hurt, but the shock of the moment temporarily absorbed the pain of the blow. I must have looked confused, because Patty came over and helped me get up.

"Charlie has a toothache," Patty explained as if that would take the sting out of my jaw. Her voice made it sound like the slap was a rather routine thing, that it was okay for Charlie to hit me. When she didn't say anything further, I tried to rationalize it. What had I done wrong? Why did that happen to me and not someone else? Now he would be mad at me for not being aware of how he was feeling. I didn't know what I felt worse about: the fact that Charlie had hit me or the fact that he was in pain.

That night there was no singing and I stayed to myself, still trying to understand what had happened. Everyone was quiet around Charlie, so I followed their cue. He had his own bedroom and invited Mary to stay with him. I saw her ministering to his sore mouth, but no one was ministering to mine. I got into the top bunk and lay there silently as warm tears dripped onto my pillow. There was no turning back from this. It was obvious I would have to try harder to be like the other girls, who seemed to know Charlie's needs before he had to teach them the hard way. The more I thought about it, the clearer my conclusion became: When it came to Charlie, the other girls were smarter than I was, so I must have deserved the slap.

When I saw him the next day, Charlie confirmed my thinking.

"You needed me to do that, little one. You have never had any man teach you when to speak or when to be quiet. The man is the head of the household and you have never had a man or a father. You will learn to be a woman."

He kissed me on my forehead. Upset as I was, I was grateful that at least he was no longer angry with me.

In the years since, I've often gone back to moments like this, trying to understand why I didn't see them for the warning signs that they were. As someone who had never been hit by either of my parents growing up, I was disturbed by his slap, but what's equally troubling to acknowledge was how quickly I was able to dismiss it. Despite the clear hypocrisy of his actions—displaying such obvious violent tendencies while incessantly insisting we "love" each other—I was incapable of seeing the act for what it was: physical abuse. Of course, these were contradictions that would play out on a much more horrifying scale later on, but at this point, I was blind to them. Even at this early stage, I was in deep enough that I couldn't see his double standards for what they were.

The most confusing thing was that I wasn't raised to keep my mouth shut and stay quiet. This behavior that Charlie was demanding of me was not something I came by naturally. Both my parents had encouraged my opinions. Sure, they'd argued about the role of men and women as far as their duties in the home, but what I had learned from them was that a woman should share her intelligence and think for herself. This would not be acceptable to Charlie. If I wanted to stay with the Family and remain in Charlie's good graces, I would have to lose the "I do it myself" attitude that had long been central to who I was.

I have no idea how Charlie got rid of his toothache, but he seemed in a better mood for the rest of our stay in New Mexico. After being struck by Charlie, I followed what the other girls were doing, and like them, I began to monitor Charlie's moods more closely. Once I started paying more attention, I realized that his moods dictated everything about our group dynamic, setting the tone for most of our lives. Sometimes he would be happily engaged with us, and we would all reflect that attitude with one another; other times he was very far away and withdrawn, brooding in a way that dampened all our spirits. (Lost on me at the time was the similarity of Charlie's behavior to my father's emotional swings back in Minnesota and how my mother had trained all of us to walk on eggshells for him.)

After about a week in New Mexico, we piled into the bus and headed back toward California. Charlie seemed in good spirits, in one of his more playful moods. As the bus moved through the open vistas of New Mexico, I made myself comfortable, snuggling into a fake fur from our communal clothing pile and feeling better about everything. I looked over at Charlie and he made a face at me, raising his eyebrows so they looked like a separated rainbow and sticking out his tongue. I laughed at how impish he looked.

He quickly changed his expression and stuck out his tongue again, challenging me to play with him. I realized this was a game and began to imitate him. I kept this up for a little while as Charlie used the shape of his eyebrows and the muscles in his face to become different people. He must have practiced a lot in prison, because he could isolate parts of his face that I didn't realize could move separately from the whole, dropping his brows in unison and then raising up only one. Then he made a V with his brows that made him look like the devil. With every movement of his face, his eyes changed as well, like a shapeshifter creating the illusion of different people and personalities.

Eventually I stopped trying to keep up and simply enjoyed the show. Somehow Charlie could even dilate his pupils at will, and the same placement of his eyebrows could telegraph extreme joy or extreme anger depending on the energy he was trying to convey. It was fun, but there was also something unsettling about the display. These were different masks he could wear, seemingly at will. Most people have just a handful of faces and emotions they can wear believably; Charlie's range felt infinite. Despite being relatively new to the group, I believed I was capable of knowing him better than the other girls—all I needed was time—but as this game laid bare, it was hard to discern where the act ended and the man began.

*   *   *

THE WEATHER WAS TURNING TO SNOW AND THE COLD WAS CREEPING IN
when the bus broke down in Winslow, Arizona. The engine refused to turn over, instead making a pathetic grinding sound. As he
rushed out of the bus to see what the problem was, Charlie's mood
turned on a dime, and he exploded with rage. He stomped around,
cursing at the bus and even kicking it under the window we were all
peering out of.

Patty bravely got out of the bus, and I heard her telling Charlie that her father's credit card could be used for repairs. Charlie
thought for a minute.

"Then you take care of it. I'm out of here," he said.

He lit a smoke and lifted the collar of his jacket to block the
wind from his face. Patty gave him a scarf and some gloves from the
communal clothing box, and he walked off, sticking his thumb out
for a ride.

I grew anxious about being alone with just the girls. With Charlie around, I felt safe—we all did. Without him there to make decisions who knew what would happen? I couldn't believe that Charlie
was going to just leave us in the middle of nowhere. Lynette must
have sensed my unease because she reassured me that Charlie just
wanted us to be independent. Susan was sitting next to a guy who
had come on the trip with whom she'd been sleeping with while we
were in New Mexico, and when they both stood up, I was hopeful
they would take charge. Instead, Susan started cursing and stomping much as Charlie had done.

She said, "We're getting out of here and hitching just like Charlie. You girls can figure out this mess on your own."

I couldn't believe she just up and left, but I shouldn't have been
surprised. By this point, it was clear that Susan not only desired to
dominate Charlie's attention she longed to be like him and wanted
us to view her much as we did him. And so with that, she was off,
and we were on our own.

"We'll postulate for help like Charlie does," Lynette said in her typically cheerful voice.

Even though Lynette was from California, at times her accent reminded me of the hills of West Virginia, an affect I think she picked up from Charlie. Much as Charlie modulated his voice to fit a situation, Lynette had grown more adept at manipulating people, often making herself appear childlike, her saccharine pseudo-southern drawl morphing her into a helpless innocent girl that people wanted to help.

Postulating was a way that Charlie demonstrated his magic. I could never figure out how he did it, but it seemed to work out just as he said it would. He taught us that if you imagine what you want and ask for it, it will come to you. I guess it was his version of "ask and it shall be given; seek and ye shall find," which I had heard about in church. He set it up as a test of our faith in him and in our own ability to make things happen. Today people in the new thought or new age movements call it manifesting. While I came to believe completely in Charlie's ability to "postulate," it's clear to me now that what he was manifesting was just his ability to manipulate people into giving us the things we needed.

With Lynette's suggestion in mind, Patty led the way for our group to find help for the broken-down bus. We backed up our efforts at postulating with sex appeal and the fact that Patty had the credit card. She was the senior member of the group, second to Mary Brunner, which also helped me feel confident.

It turned out we weren't far from a gas station, and as we had postulated, there was a mechanic on duty.

"Could you help us out?" Lynette drawled, touching the young mechanic on his arm.

I instinctively pulled my fake fur coat around me to make myself look even more cold and pathetic. Patty explained our situation, while Mary and Ella smiled at him and acted girlie. The mechanic

was young and didn't seem too bright. He blushed when he told us
he would take a look.

We all crowded into the mechanic's office, where he had a
space heater running. Everything smelled like oil, but he had some
candy bars and a Coke machine. He opened it up for us and told
us to help ourselves, and he gave each of us our choice of candy.
I grabbed a Milky Way bar and ate it hungrily, the taste taking
me back to my trips to the candy store with Jan and Joan. I ate it
slowly, savoring both the sugar on my tongue and the memories,
which were really from only a year ago yet felt like they were from
another life.

Patty went with the mechanic to show him the bus. When they
returned, he told us: "You are going to need a new part for your
home." The boy seemed flushed, so I wondered if Patty had shown
him the inside of the bus to sweeten the deal. "I will order it and see
if I can get it in yet today. I might be able to pick it up myself in the
next town." He offered to drive us to a diner to get sandwiches, and
he had the bus towed to his shop for repairs.

As promised, he went to pick up the part while we ate and relaxed in the local diner. No one said anything to us about how we
looked or asked what we were doing there. There were a few locals
eating eggs and waffles, and the waitress was very kind. She asked us
how we were holding up in the snow.

"We got stuck here and our bus broke down," Lynette exclaimed.

"Then you girls need a piece of our homemade pie." They didn't
have lemon meringue, so I asked for apple.

"These are on the house," she said kindly.

We stayed at the diner for several hours and played cards as the
young mechanic made the repair. When it was time to leave, our
waitress said, "You girls take it easy driving home." My mind lin-
gered on the word *home*.

The mechanic made sure we had sandwiches and soda pop for the return trip. Patty gave him a big hug and we each kissed him on his cheek. Patty and Mary took turns driving the bus for the eight or so hours due west it would take us to get back to Topanga and the Spiral Staircase House. I would have helped, but I didn't know how to drive. We all kept each other entertained with singing and warm by sitting close.

As we pulled up past the beach shacks and parked the bus in front of the house, Charlie came out to greet us. If he was surprised to see us, he didn't show it, climbing on board with us and lighting up a joint. He didn't say much. Patty told me later on that Charlie was really ticked off at Susan for taking off and leaving us behind. It occurred to me that maybe Charlie had left us for our own good to see who was going to be loyal and listen to his instructions.

Exhausted from the drive, we fell asleep in the bus. Lying there listening to the sounds of everyone as they drifted off, I felt relieved to be home, or at least what felt like home. By making it back to L.A., we'd all passed a test. Not only had we followed Charlie's orders, but we had worked together. And now, at least for a time, he would be pleased with us.

"DIANNE!"

We had been back in Topanga for a little while when I heard Lynette calling my name. I'd been exploring the hillside around Spiral Staircase and contemplating the places snakes could hide in the daytime. The air smelled of brine and the sounds of seagulls and waves were audible in the distance.

"Dianne, Charlie wants to take us on a road trip," Lynette said, coming over to get my attention. "He has to check in with his parole officer." When Charlie had been released from Terminal Island in March 1967, he had requested to have his parole officer in San

Francisco when he'd thought he would settle in the Haight. Now that he was living in L.A., he still had to keep in contact to stay out of trouble.

"Is everyone going?" I asked.

"No, just us. He also wants to take us to meet the zuzu man."

"The zuzu man?" It sounded like an African ritual that my father's old Ethiopian artist friend might have described.

"Zuzus! That is what Charlie calls candy. We are going to visit the candy man."

Charlie had asked specifically for me. I would be the only one to go with him and Lynette on a special trip. Even though we were all supposed to be equal in Charlie's eyes and in his love, this was a clear sign of favor. This had been all I had wanted since that first day in the bus when he made me feel as if I was the only woman in the world for him. I wanted more of that feeling, and here was my chance. Having Lynette along was as good as being alone with Charlie. Lynette was as close to him as any of the girls. So to be allowed into their tight little circle was as good as any privilege. I was beaming as we climbed into the bus. I wanted both Charlie and Lynette to love me. I would be on my best behavior to make this the best trip ever.

Some people may believe that the zuzu man was a drug connection. I was naive, so maybe it was. But from my vantage point, the zuzu man was really the candy man, with real candy, just as Lynette had said. Charlie wanted us to be childlike and to enjoy the freedoms that were often used by controlling parents to manipulate their children into doing their bidding. These childhood pleasures should be free for the taking, so he made up the name *zuzus* to represent all kinds of treats, and he especially liked hard candies.

We waited in the bus, looking at magazines while Charlie went to see his parole officer. We also thumbed through a copy of the

Kama Sutra—and as I looked at the drawings of the happy men and women in varying poses of intercourse, I began to see just how much I had to learn about sexual positions.

"Charlie says we should all be free to experience love at the highest levels of sexual freedom," Lynette said.

It sounded like she was repeating her explanation verbatim from Charlie, but looking at the book, I didn't really understand what she meant. I wanted to be a better lover, but the people in the illustrations looked like they were twisted into positions that were not humanly possible. I pointed to one picture and said, "Can you do that?"

Lynette took up my challenge and tried to put her legs behind her ears, then fell over laughing. Lynette grabbed the book and showed me a drawing of an Indian man and woman positioned facing each other so that each person's mouth is near the other's genitals.

"This is called sixty-nine," she explained. "It is one of Charlie's favorites."

I thought back to my first experience with him and realized that's what he'd been trying to do with me; I hadn't understood and had no idea how to please him. Hopefully, he didn't think I was a bad lover.

When Charlie returned, he had a big bag of hard candy just like he promised.

"Zuzus!" Lynette squealed.

I was learning to temper my enthusiasm at seeing him. My insides felt like a puppy when his owner comes home, but I had been observing the other girls since our New Mexico trip and saw how they waited for a sign of approval before acting on their impulses. Whenever there were "teachable moments," either Charlie would glare at me to indicate I was doing something wrong or one of the other girls would show me how to behave. I suppose I was somewhat feral. Charlie wanted us to be free but not uncontrollable. I was catching on to Charlie's desire for me to be more subservient, but it wasn't easy.

In these early days, when he was in the mood, Charlie liked to talk to me about things. Sometimes he would discuss his philosophy and beliefs and I would respond approvingly, but not too much. It was similar to how I'd learned to speak with my father, a man who'd also liked the validation of my agreeing with him, even if I didn't always understand what he was talking about. Through Charlie's ramblings, I could be aware of any subtle changes in his demeanor. Then I could gauge my level of response.

I didn't have to ask how the meeting with the parole officer went; it was clear when Charlie got to the bus that he was happy. He had not gotten into any trouble for the arrest when I'd gone to juvie. I could imagine him charming his parole officer into taking his side against the mean officers who were against him for no reason. As we hungrily ate the zuzus, he suggested we take a ride into the park away from all the people. I started to feel excited and Lynette was grinning at me as if she knew something cool was going to happen.

It was daylight, but when you were in the bus, it was completely private, as if there was no one else in the world. The sun shone through the window and Charlie reached out to pull me to sit next to him and Lynette. He looked from me to Lynette and then broke into a wide grin.

"Have you ever been with another chick?" he asked.

While I'd had sex with Ronald and Linda, we had always been having sex with him. I had always been curious about girls, but there was a definite taboo back then. I'd had little crushes on my female teachers in school, but I'd never thought about sex with them. I became nervous because I had no idea what to do or what to expect.

Charlie took the role of instructor. I watched eagerly and nervously as Charlie told Lynette to lie back against the mattress, gently putting a pillow under her hips to raise her up so I could clearly see her vagina. He used his fingers to show me the parts that could be erogenous zones for a woman. I had no idea that my own body could have feelings in so many places. I hadn't really experienced an orgasm, so I hadn't thought about how to give pleasure to a woman.

"This is the clitoris," he pointed out. "Now use your tongue to feel it respond."

I moved slowly toward her and closed my eyes. Her body felt spongy, but I could feel her respond beneath my tongue. She let out a gasp of pleasure, so I knew that I was doing it correctly. I felt her grip my shoulders, and I became excited that I was making her feel good. After a while, her hips rose and she sighed. Then she tenderly returned the love until I too had reached a soft climax. I was too shy to look at her, but she stroked my face and smiled warmly. I didn't feel embarrassed or ashamed.

I believed that Charlie gave me this lesson in lovemaking to make me happier as part of the group. To me, this was about sexual expression and freedom, as described in the *Kama Sutra*. Charlie was always stressing how important it was for us to lose our inhibitions to be free of the shackles of society. I hadn't had much time to be shackled, but I was competitive by nature. I didn't want my age and inexperience to reflect poorly on me, so I embraced whatever he had to teach me.

What I didn't see was that being with another girl also made me more marketable. The more skilled and experienced I was sexually, the more valuable I was as a currency of exchange. For Charlie, sex was always about the pleasing of a man, and because men found two women having sex together to be a sexual thrill, there was value in our ability to perform. And I think that is why Charlie wanted to make sure we knew how to do it properly. In reality, I don't think Charlie wanted us girls to think about each other sexually, except as a way to break down barriers and express his control over us. I don't remember him being particularly kind about homosexuality except as it related to what he called sex of convenience. I don't think he would have approved if two of us had fallen in love with each other or had had a lesbian affair. We might have been loving each other, but really, we were loving him.

As we finished, Charlie reached his hands to each of us and pulled us up to a seated position. We all now faced each other. Charlie had taken off his clothes too.

"You guys did that real good. Now I am going to teach you one of the most important things you can know about a man. You felt how good the softness of a tongue was on your pussy? That is how good it feels for a man to have his dick in a warm, soft mouth."

I always thought men liked to be inside a woman; it never occurred to me that they might even prefer a blow job. It made sense now that I thought about it. They could sit back and enjoy it without any work or fear of getting a girl pregnant; they could be treated like a king, which was what Charlie explained. If you treated a man like a king, you would have power over him. Of course, it never occurred to me that this education would be for anyone's benefit other than Charlie's. In reality, this would become yet another tool that heightened our value to him: It gave Charlie power over other men who wanted in on the sex, leading Charlie to show off my prowess to the men he wanted to impress or manipulate.

Charlie gave me an education in the art of the blow job that left me frightened and nauseated, but pleased that Charlie seemed satisfied with my performance.

"You'll get used to it, little love," Charlie said when he saw that I was upset. "Just don't think about it. When that happens, you have the man completely under your spell. You have no idea how that feels to a man, who really thinks only with his dick."

He gave me a handful of zuzus. I didn't think I would ever get used to any of it no matter how good it felt for the man, but Charlie made sure that I would have plenty of practice.

The whole experience left me shaken and conflicted. In a matter of months, my entire outlook on life, sex, and God had changed. Pleasing a man felt powerful but dirty at the same time. Charlie was telling us to overcome our inhibitions, but it would take a while for me to feel okay about having a man's penis in my mouth. Over time I would separate who I was as a girl from who I became when I gave head to a man. Still, my confusion would deepen as I came to realize that the better I became at it, and the more Charlie was pleased with me, the better I felt about myself.

As we drove back toward L.A., Charlie seemed to notice my melancholy because he decided that we would stop off at Esalen, that magical place overlooking the ocean, where I had gone with my parents. The healing hot springs were just what I needed. There the three of us dropped acid and sat in the tubs built into the mountainside. The hot springs cleansed away my thoughts, making me feel wonderful and alive. The springs combined with the LSD gave me a clear vision of heaven. I may even have believed I *was* in heaven, as I began to rethink men, women, and the whole idea of shame that had been plaguing me. I thought back to what Charlie had said about his name—"Man son." Just like Jesus, Charlie was teaching us that we needed to live like we were intended to live, free of hang-ups, shame, ego, and societal rules about money and possessions. While I was tripping hard on acid, all this made sense to me. Perhaps it was up to me to get over the shame of sex and to fill my heart with what belonged there: love for Charlie.

As we rolled back into town, the giddy elation that had accompanied the start of our trip had been replaced by a misguided sense of maturity. Looking out at the beach through the bus's windshield, I felt older and wiser, not just about sex but about Charlie. I felt as if I possessed a clearer sense of who he was; the personal time with him had helped me understand his message of shedding my inhibitions. To follow him would mean I'd have to fight against my own instincts—to avoid getting hung up on what felt wrong, and instead listen to whatever Charlie said was right.

It was probably by design on Charlie's part that our first group sex session took place not long after my trip to the zuzu man, just as the others were learning, as I did, to lose their inhibitions. It was shortly after we'd returned to the Spiral Staircase House that Charlie called all of us into the bus. As we sat around waiting, Lynette told me why we were together: We were going to take an acid trip and become bonded as one. I knew what she meant. This was beyond the touching of our hands.

The anxiety grew inside me immediately. Sure, I'd had the practice session with Charlie and Lynette, but I wasn't even sure how this would work. Who would do what to whom? Charlie administered the acid tabs to each of us, which took effect in twenty minutes or so. In the meantime, the excitement rose as we sat in a circle next to one another. Along with Charlie there was another man, but the rest of us were Charlie's women.

"We are all going to join with one another," Charlie said as he lifted his hand and held it up to the first person in the circle. It could have been any one of us but was likely Mary. She was and would always be the number one girl, even when Lynette became Charlie's loyal confidante later on. As the acid took effect, I could see the color and the energy pooled at the place where their hands met. Then Mary would raise her hand to the person next to her until their energy blended in color, passing it down the line that way until the circle was complete back to Charlie.

Charlie then told someone to take someone else's shirt off and pass that down the line in the circle. It was ritualistic and methodical—it wasn't a ripping off of everyone's clothes and jumping into a pile. Everything was done slowly and sensually until we were all naked and exposed to one another. By this time, we were all high on the acid, which affected everyone differently. Charlie would try to manage the trip by keeping us focused on each other. Eventually everyone would be touching someone else or two people or everyone at the same time. We became like a stream of water moving in rhythmic motion.

Whatever chaos and conflict I may have been feeling without the drugs, I now felt only love and belonging with them. I think we all believed that we were joined equally to Charlie and that Charlie was something good and godlike, and to be a part of the group in this moment connected us in a way that nothing else had. It strengthened me to feel I belonged to something bigger than myself—even though I had no idea what that thing actually was.

12

PANHANDLING AND POSTULATING

IN THE MONTHS AFTER I JOINED THE FAMILY, NEW PEOPLE WERE ALWAYS coming and going from our group. Some would move on quickly, while others would hang out for a bit before drifting away, but the ones who stayed were often committed to the vision of life that Charlie laid out, a vision that he was using to indoctrinate the group. Such was the case when a girl named Nancy Pitman started hanging around with us shortly after we left the Spiral Staircase House.

As we all knew even before we returned from New Mexico, we were outgrowing the Spiral Staircase House. The longer we stayed the worse it got. There were too many visitors and not enough space, but more likely Charlie and the other girls were simply getting restless. This house was known to the locals, so they wouldn't always respect Charlie's need to control the traffic. He didn't want it to become a hippie crash pad unless he could benefit from the visitors. Though I liked being across the road from the beach, I didn't care much one way or another, so when Charlie found out about a seemingly abandoned house nearby on Fernwood Street, we made that our next destination. The house on Fernwood Street was still in Topanga, about ten to twelve minutes from the Spiral Staircase House, but it was on the opposite side, closer to the mountains. We rode through winding roads and made a hairpin turn back toward the ocean to reach the small two-story house that would become our next home. The first thing I noticed were the eucalyptus trees on the steep property, and then I saw that behind the house was a built-in pool filled not with water, but with trash.

It was easy for us to make the move to Fernwood Street because we were a mobile troupe whose home was really in the black bus; these places were crash pads for us to spread out, but our real home was being together. We shared everything. We were unencumbered by materialism, as Charlie reiterated at every opportunity. I wanted to be fully free and I tried not to get attached to anything, but sometimes I would have my favorite clothes. I wasn't trying to be vain, but certain clothing made me feel better about myself. I imagine some of the other girls felt the same because despite the communal clothing pile, we each let the other choose the clothes we liked the best. That was the closest we got to personal belongings. We didn't wear makeup, so that wasn't a problem, and we didn't read anything, so no one had any books other than what Charlie gave us to read. Sometimes we had blankets or backpacks, but those were if we needed to go somewhere quickly.

So that is how we could quickly pack up our meager belongings, along with a few things that probably didn't belong to us, to move into our new house. Perched at the top of Fernwood Street, the house was built on the side of a hill, so that when you entered off the street, you were on the top floor of the house, with the kitchen in front of you and the living room down a set of stairs. The house itself was completely empty and unfurnished. The garbage pool had become a dumping ground for vagrants, so we would have to make it clear to people that we now occupied this place. That would not be a problem, because people always knew about Charlie and his whereabouts; the black bus was a huge tip-off. The bus was really our home, so the Fernwood house presented a slight inconvenience. The bus had to be parked down the street away from us, something I think made Charlie uncomfortable. As nice as this house was, I knew better by now than to become completely comfortable anyplace.

We hadn't been at the Fernwood house for long when some of

the girls met Nancy at the beach. Nancy, whose father was an aeronautical engineer, was from a wealthy family and must have been looking for adventure, because when the girls told her about Charlie, she asked to be introduced. When she first walked in, I imagined her as the perfect embodiment of a California surfer girl. With a glowing perfect tan, taut strong legs, and a flat stomach, she seemed like she'd stepped right out of a Beach Boys song. She didn't have breasts to speak of, but she didn't need any—they would have ruined her look.

Right away, Charlie liked her—and the fact that she had her own credit card paid for by her father certainly didn't hurt. Some of us just brought ourselves, but when someone brought an asset like a credit card, they were golden. As such, Nancy fit right in with us, and even though she and I were so different physically and in our backgrounds, I embraced her as a sister.

Charlie also liked the friend Nancy brought along on her visits— Deidre Shaw, the daughter of actress Angela Lansbury. Her celebrity kid status didn't matter to us very much, but I'm sure the possibility of her mother's money also appealed to Charlie. Personally, I hadn't had much experience with theater, television, or movies, but what I liked about Deidre was she was my age, had a sports car, brought us donuts, and was generally fun to be around. I got to know Deidre before I really got to know Nancy, who later also called herself Brenda. She treated me like a friend and an equal, driving me around with the top down, walking on the beach, or taking me to her mother's house when she wasn't around. At the time, her mother was touring with the hugely successful play *Mame*, and while sometimes she was in Los Angeles, for the most part she was on the road.

Deidre's striking home was on the beach side of Malibu along the Pacific Coast Highway. When we hung out at her house, it was clear that Deidre was proud of her mother, showing me pictures of her with all kinds of famous people that I didn't recognize. Still, the fact that they chose not to live in Hollywood said something about how her mother wanted to raise her. Her life in public school could have been normal, but because her mother's star was constantly on the rise, the lack of supervision made it easy for Deidre's exuberant personality to lead her into her own brand of independence.

Walking through her house, Deidre seemed to understand how out of step her life was with ours. The salty air of the nearby ocean permeated the house, and porcelain teacups lined the tables. The unpretentious style of the house reflected Deidre's parents' British sensibilities, but there was still an understated extravagance totally unlike life with the Family. Like the rest of us, Deidre listened to Charlie's speeches about how belongings owned you and not the other way around, and she seemed to dig how we shared everything together in a big cosmic lump like our clothing box. Perhaps because of that, she appeared almost apologetic as she showed me her enormous closet filled with stunning clothes and began to pull out things she thought would look good on me.

"Try this on," she said, handing me a silky shirt. The fabric was soft and I knew it was expensive. "It looks lovely on you," she said, sounding a bit like a movie star herself. She told me I should take it back with me. Then she picked out a bunch of things, including a pair of sneakers, giving them all to me.

Deidre would come and go but would get high with us and share our meals. Eventually her visits became sporadic and stopped all together. I missed Deidre, but I can see why Charlie didn't fight for her to stay. He didn't use any of his typical persuasion and did not seem offended. Deidre was underage and would not have had even her parents' tacit permission to stay with us. Her parents were famous, and even though she was a latchkey celebrity kid, she didn't have a note in her pocket saying she had permission to be on her own. Deidre would have been more trouble than Charlie would think she was worth, especially since there was no additional advantage to him.

On the other hand, Nancy began staying with us more and more. She was so into Charlie and his music that she began to follow Charlie around like the rest of us, ultimately staying with us for good. Her personality was a good fit for our group, and her father's money funded us in a way that reinforced the illusion Charlie was providing us what we needed.

Having well-off people like Nancy in the group only added to the mystique that Charlie could conjure whatever he wanted for him or for the Family, as their money enhanced his ability to "postulate" and appear as though he could make almost anything happen. The end result added to the mythos that he was somehow magical. As he had all along, he would "think about" what we needed and send it out into the ether. Then it would just show up, as if by magic, making it seem that simply spreading his love through his words and his music caused the universe to respond in kind. As Charlie put it, we were on a Magical Mystery Tour and the world was ours simply by asking.

Of all the different things that Charlie did, of all his manipulations both big and small that made me believe in him, this charlatan's ability to ostensibly transform his wishes into realities was perhaps his most effective tool for convincing me that he possessed actual power. Looking back now, I find it easy to view his behavior as that of a skilled con artist who understands how to create the perception of something, creating an illusion that matches a set of facts. Charlie wanted us to view him as powerful, so he would find ways to make sure we viewed him that way. He wanted us to put our faith in him, so he designed our reality in a way that would encourage it—asking the "universe" for things that he knew he could manipulate in his favor. He was remarkably effective, and when he was supported by money from people like Nancy, the illusion became that much more complete. More than any other aspect of my indoctrination—the pressure of the group, the mantras, the songs, the drugs, the sex—this rhetorical sleight of hand persuaded me that he truly was someone with special powers and ultimately made it nearly impossible to walk away.

Charlie's more straightforward forms of brainwashing—something he would completely deny, of course—carried their own significance as well. He often used guilt to keep our minds and our belief focused on him. Whenever he could, he would remind all of us how much responsibility it was to take care of us. He wielded this guilt to make sure we understood no one else could take care of us as well as he could or love us as well as he could, and I know that I for one fell for this every time. He also emphasized that no one else wanted me and I had nowhere else to go. He and the Family were all I had in the world. He could hone in on one's deepest fears and emphasize that he offered the only true solution.

He also spent hours talking to us about his ideas, programming us through his speech. Many nights we sat in a circle as a group and either sang to his guitar playing or listened to one of his "talk-tos," which were like unpredictable sermons. Charlie might lecture us about life, tell us a story, or go off on a tangent about the future. No matter what the subject, we were expected to listen raptly. Breaking focus was a sign of disrespect and would have consequences, whether real or imagined. A slight, a rejection—we would even imagine the punishments for ourselves if none were forthcoming. Charlie's talk-to subjects would range from the more benign—communal love, shedding inhibitions—to ideas that were far more disturbing, such as Charlie's bigotry.

From early on, parts of Charlie's speeches were devoted to using fear about African Americans, a term that came into common use only in the late 1970s and official use in the 1980s, to support his prejudiced view of the world. His ideas would grow more extreme over time, but even in the beginning, he was indoctrinating us to believe that black people were going to rise up collectively against white people. While he wasn't necessarily framing it as an armed conflict initially, he talked to us in the Family about the blacks and whites and the coming insurrection. As he told it, he had been in jail with black people, and this was something he had heard from them.

It was an upsetting prediction of a future filled with racially charged violence, and both his vision and the racism embedded in it were totally foreign to me. Back in Minnesota, I'd been very comfortable with African Americans; my first boyfriend had been black and my parents had always thrived in a diverse group of people. From my own life, I knew no one who matched the descriptions of dangerous militancy and violence that Charlie crafted in his speeches. His words did not bear out the truths of my experiences.

And yet, though his words disturbed me, I also recognized there was a lot I didn't understand about the racial dynamic of L.A. in the mid- to late sixties. My parents and I had come out to California in the wake of the Watts riots, which had taken place in 1965, and L.A. was unmistakably more racially charged than Minneapolis had been. My experiences may have taught me to ignore his words, but because Charlie leveraged this racially tense atmosphere to spread his unique brand of hate, my youth and uncertainty about California lent them more power. And his time in prison gave him additional credibility. It wasn't that I believed every word that he said, more that I absorbed the general sense of fear he projected about racial issues in L.A., and when it came to racial issues, this fear was a crucial conditioning tool that he wielded over us. At the start, this fear was interwoven with all of his other ideas, but eventually, it became more of a focal point for him, as he used it to keep us in line. From my perspective, this fear was how his hateful views ultimately took root in a group of people purporting to be open-minded.

His talk-tos weren't always about racially motivated fear—often they were just a platform for Charlie to hold court and tune us into his ideas. As such, sometimes it was hard to follow the conceptual threads of his speeches, let alone focus on whatever his overarching points were. Acid always helped me do both these things during his talks. My mind would take in the information, twist it around, examine it, and contemplate the implications. But when I was straight or just stoned on a little grass, forget it—just looking at Charlie being all serious was too funny for me to ignore. Often I could not stop myself from having a giggle fit, which was me rolling uncontrollably on the floor practically peeing my pants at my own humor. I couldn't even explain to anyone else what I found so amusing. Needless to say, Charlie was not amused.

Nor was he amused by the fact that I could be a total smart aleck. People say this is a sign of intelligence in kids, but even if that happened to be true in my case, it was not the kind of intelligence that Charlie liked at all. Sometimes I would interrupt him or make a crack. My mouth moved faster than my common sense. Once he was teaching us how to act dumb with people so they wouldn't think anything about us. I blurted out, "How dumb should we be?" He glared at me, and I thought I was going to get a wallop then and there. New people joined us for these talk-tos, so it was even more important for me to be on my best behavior, but somehow I found it even more difficult to set a good example. I had heard Charlie's rap over and over, so on occasion I interrupted, interjected, and rolled my eyes, finding it difficult to repress my boredom with this part of group life.

But though I tested his patience at times, in the aftermath of being hit by him in New Mexico, I worked hard to study his expressions and gestures, and monitoring his moods became the key to my survival there. He was teaching us the tool of monitoring people's slightest expressions, so I took those lessons and tried to apply them to Charlie himself. He could be anything to anybody, but we were with him night and day, so it was easy to see when Charlie was happy, agitated, pensive, or downright angry. And if you were caught off guard, like I often was when I couldn't pay attention to something he considered important, it could result in a smack or at times a beating.

*   *   *

THE HIPPIE SCENE AT THE TIME WAS LIKE A SMALL TOWN—WE ALL KNEW one another. Even though more people seemed to be arriving from out of town every day, there weren't that many people who'd truly committed to the ideas of the counterculture and that made the community tight-knit. Because of this, I wasn't shocked to see my parents walk into the Fernwood house one afternoon.

This had been my longest stretch without seeing them since I'd taken up with the Family. They were still living at the Hog Farm, but knew people in Topanga who'd told them I was at the Fernwood Street house. As a long-haired guru driving a black bus that now had HOLLYWOOD PRODUCTIONS painted across its side, Charlie was well known, so it was not difficult to keep tabs on me. Whenever people who knew my parents would spot me, they would let my mom and dad know, so they could keep track of me without directly trying to control my choices. At the time, I would have assumed our occasional meetings were happenstance. It wouldn't have occurred to me after seeing them at juvenile court that they would have taken the time or had the concern to know my whereabouts.

As I greeted them, I didn't get the sense they were in any great need to have me back living with them—they were still heavily into their own trips—but an occasional visit like this might have made them feel they had done right by me.

The situation was different from the last time I had seen my parents outside juvenile hall. In this setting, they were just some more hippies hanging out with us. They asked how I was. I am sure Kathy and Danny missed me, but they seemed to be happy too. Charlie and my mom got along well, and I watched Charlie and my dad get into a philosophical discussion. There seemed to be an interchange, but for most of it I saw Charlie talking and my father nodding. It was funny because later Charlie told me he liked that my father was such a free thinker. I hadn't observed my father saying much of anything. I don't think Charlie was used to having someone close to his age and intelligence to rap with.

It wasn't that I harbored anger or resentment toward my parents for choosing the Hog Farm over me. Being with Charlie helped me see they no longer held parental roles in my life. I was a part of a different world, a place where I felt I belonged more than with my parents. Though my parents and I were both a part of the hippie scene in L.A., there was very little overlap. Of course I was under Charlie's control and fully swept up in the Family's gravitational pull, but also weighing on me was that I saw myself as a woman and not as their child. I'd stopped thinking of myself as a teenage kid because nothing about my life said that I was a teenager.

When my parents were getting ready to leave, they surprised me by asking if I wanted to go with them. Actually, it was my mother who asked.

I stared at them for a moment to examine my feelings. They didn't look like the parents I remembered. They were in full hippie garb—my mother without makeup, her long hair swept back in a braid; my father in overalls, his hair unkempt and wild. Had they been dressed as the parents I knew before we dropped out, I might have felt differently. They appeared to be playacting the roles that allowed them to no longer be my parents. My mother was still beautiful, but she seemed to be following in my father's shadow. There was nothing solid for me to hold on to. I knew the second the question left my mother's mouth that there was no way I would go with them. My parents had given me my ticket to freedom, and I was not about to give it back to them unless they provided me with a good alternative, which they did not. I was committed to Charlie and the girls and felt loyal to them, but at that early point, I wasn't so lost that I couldn't imagine a better life with my real family. It wasn't always fun sleeping on the floor and not knowing where our next meal was coming from. But with my parents, there was no actual home to return to. No family dinners or backyard. No house in Santa Monica, my own room or friends. If I'd had something to return to, I would have returned; instead, all they offered me was the Hog Farm, an attic, and their own misguided quest for some meaning to their lives.

"It was so nice seeing you," I replied. "Thank you for the invitation, but I am happy here with Charlie and the girls."

"I can see that," my mother replied, but she seemed distressed. For that moment, I felt a pang of longing but dismissed it right away before it could take hold.

"Take good care of yourself," my father said. My heart jumped a little as I searched his face for a sign that he was unhappy without me. There may have been a second of connection, but it faded. He handed me five dollars and walked toward the van. My mother held me, and that felt good. Then I stiffened when I glimpsed Charlie watching me. I didn't want him seeing me missing my mommy. And I didn't want to feel vulnerable or confused.

I kissed her cheek and waved to my father even though I don't think he had seen me.

"Maybe I will come visit you sometime," I blurted as I watched my mother leave. I knew I never would.

THERE WAS SOMETHING AKIN TO A HIPPIE TELEGRAPH SYSTEM THAT would alert us to abandoned houses. The next place Charlie found was on Summit Trail, way back in Topanga Canyon, so there was more room to park the bus. "You don't need all these things," Charlie said when he would tell us to unload stuff we were accumulating. "We got each other, and whenever we need something, we will have it."

Each place we lived became something to love. We talked about the houses as if they were living things that did us a favor by putting a roof over our heads and giving us a place to spread out in. Nestled above a creek, with trees all around and a stone staircase inside, the house on Summit Trail was a special, cozy place for me. Early in the morning I would sit outside on the back porch to listen to the crickets. I have heard people say that if you slow down the sound of crickets chirping, they are singing in a harmony that sounds just like angels. This became how I measured my days, as Charlie had instructed us to get rid of any watches or clocks so we could live in the eternal now. We dropped acid at least once a week in this new house, and increasingly I had no sense of responsibility, because Charlie took care of everything. We had no connection to the world outside of what Charlie told us. We were isolated but becoming stronger in our connection with one another.

One day we were all sleeping off an acid trip and lovemaking party when Charlie roused us.

"We need some bread," Charlie said as he pulled blankets off everyone. He must have been awake for hours. He was pacing. "Get up. I said get up! Get dressed, all of you, in something that will attract attention," he ordered.

"Rise and shine." The Summit house had plumbing, but not a lot of hot water. We all got ourselves cleaned up so we would be presentable and took turns brushing or braiding one another's hair. Most of us had long hair now. Charlie insisted we not cut it because he said women were supposed to have their crown of glory. After we were all bathed, we helped each other dress in the items from our shared box and closet. I grabbed my favorite loose-fitting maxi dress. Whenever we had to get dressed up, I always reached for it first. The rest of the time I usually wore jeans or shorts. But I liked the way the cotton of this dress rested on me in the right places. It made me feel sexy. We never wore underwear. I don't know if it was because it made it easier for us to have sex whenever we wanted to or if it was because of hygiene. We would have had a lot of pairs of underwear to keep clean.

"Get a move on!" Charlie bellowed. He was not particularly patient and today we were becoming difficult to herd.

We piled into a red truck that Charlie had "borrowed" or might have been given by a friend and headed to Fernwood Market. Charlie would often take us into the local shopping centers and play his guitar to attract a crowd. His talk-tos in public were different from those when we were alone. He projected his voice to attract people to listen to him. He would start like a preacher sermonizing to his flock, and we would sit in our circle watching him to show people that we were interested in what he had to say. It was like Tom Sawyer painting a fence. We made it look like we were all in a rapturous state of consciousness raising and that would attract others. Or Charlie would play his guitar and we would sing harmonies. After a short while others would join in the circle and listen, mesmerized, by him. Charlie could have read the phone book or spouted nursery rhymes and his audience would think they had just heard the Sermon on the Mount.

For Charlie, music at that point seemed more of a means to an end than an actual focus in itself. Though his music had become a huge part of our lives and our routine as a group, it seemed constructed more around his ambitions to gain followers in settings like these than around any larger ambitions to be a rock star (those would come later). Like many others of the moment, he recognized that music was one of the most powerful ways to amplify a cultural message—whether it was to a group outside a market or to an even larger audience. He played in front of crowds and had even played at a club before I met him. His songs brought people together and brought us together. Music was a hook, a way to draw in bystanders and turn them on to his ideas. He wasn't playing covers or music that was already out there—only his original material. The songs he wrote and sang were all about his philosophy, but there was a cleverness to them that drew people in and made them catchy and easy to remember.

If he did have larger ambitions for his musical career at that point, then I didn't hear him talk about them. I never got the impression that he was out to get discovered, because if he had been, I think he would have performed in many more public places. I remember once Lynette said that "someday everyone is going to know Charlie's songs," but comments like that seemed more about the eventual spread of Charlie's ideas than about his becoming a huge star because of his music.

The songs in public places like this were also a chance to pick up some money. While Charlie played, we would panhandle. Sometimes we would just leave one of our hats or the guitar case open for people to put money in. Or we would go around to people asking for any spare change they had. We were polite and learned the balance between getting their attention and pushing them away. We got a lot of money that way because people were used to hippie panhandlers in the communities. We weren't repulsive street people. And we were offering entertainment and enlightenment at the same time.

Then we would put Charlie's postulating and recruitment into action. Charlie would punctuate his speech with rapturous intonation and the girls would scan the crowd to see if anyone seemed to be nodding in agreement. Charlie might spot a likely candidate and subtly nod in that person's direction after catching the eye of one of us. We would then know to sit next to him or her to strike up a conversation. We each knew our roles and we carried them out smoothly. It wasn't difficult to talk to people about Charlie and how important he was to our lives because I truly believed it. He made everyone feel as if he was talking directly to them and could see into their hearts.

"I am a reflection of what is inside of you. And I see and feel love. Do you feel it?" Charlie exclaimed as he looked right into the eyes of a young woman sitting in front of him. "If you don't feel the love, it is because of your own programming," he added, turning his gaze to

Ten months old in Minneapolis, where I was born.

With my younger brother Danny in 1955; I was just over two years old. I became a "mini momma" to Danny, and later to my younger sister Kathy, when they were born.

In 1959. I had just turned six and Danny was four when Kathy was born.

When I was in first grade, in 1960, my parents bought this two-story house. A year later, they traded this house for a trailer.

We had a garden in the backyard of our house; you can see our neighbor's greenhouse in the background. I'm playing with my mother at the age of seven.

My mother in 1960 with her precious sewing machine, which she lost when we traded our house.

ABOVE: This was taken in 1961 at the trailer park we moved to when my parents traded our house.

RIGHT: With Kathy in the front yard of the house we lived in when my father was working for his patron of the arts.

After my father left us in 1963, we moved to the projects in Minneapolis.

With Danny and Kathy right before I entered seventh grade. We'd only moved to Santa Monica a short time earlier, so my parents could be together again.

Relaxing in the backyard of our house in Santa Monica in 1965, when it still belonged to us. A little more than a year later, our house would become a center for other Oracle families to gather.

ABOVE: The fireplace in the living room of our Santa Monica home.

RIGHT: My father, Clarence, in our Santa Monica

ABOVE: At my sister's eighth birthday party in March of 1967, before my father cut off the table legs.

BELOW LEFT: After my father cut down our table and chairs in 1967, he also put red, yellow, and green lightbulbs in the light fixtures. (Kathy is on the far right, my mother is in front of the mirror, and Danny is looking up.)

BELOW RIGHT: My parents hosted family dinners with the Oracle; I'm at the head of the table.

My father is holding a joint in this picture, which was taken after my mother had introduced him to drugs.

ABOVE: This photo of our family was taken not long after we reunited in Santa Monica.

LEFT: Inside the geodesic dome that my father built in the backyard of our Santa Monica house in 1967. My father is holding a joint here too, and this was taken right before our family dropped out.

VOL.1 NO.3
1967 JUNE

LEFT: From the Southern California *Oracle*; my father's name, Clarence Lake, is in the masthead.

BELOW: A page from the Southern California *Oracle*.

Master Coordinator: Joe Dana
Editor: Stan Russell
Associate editors: Herb Petley
   David Ossman
Warmth & groove: Cosmo
   Kenny
Business Coordinator: Ed Ward
Liason Coordinator: Richard Norris
HiP Job Co-op: Love Ranger
Advertising: Bob Ardon
Indian affairs: Chesley Milliken
Tribal messenger: Craig Carpenter
Benefits: John Carpenter
Rock groups: Decky Lee
Editor Emeritus: Tom Schulz
Photography: Teddy Tubbe
   Rob Franz
Subscriptions: Debbie Burr
Contributing editors: Nat Freedland
   Lawrence Lipton
   John Wilcock
Soothsayer: John Hammond
Editorial assistants: Betty Dreebin
   Liz
   Joanne Davis
Art Director: Nearly everyone
Artists: Mike Stalm (cover)
   JD
   Fred Adams
   Brian McBean
   Bob Wilson
   Grady Jones
   Jerry Mermis
   Sandy Petley
   Clarence Lake
   Larry Altman
   Freddy
   Linda
Our thanks to: Bruce Deeton
   Sharon Alban
   Ralph Leverson
   Susan Fredericks
   Sue, Harriet,
   Gypsy, Hope
   Ardys Aronson
Copyright (c) 1967 by the ORACLE of Southern California. Executive offices at 840 North Fairfax Avenue, Los Angeles, California 90046.

UAL promiscuity," a middle-aged, plump housewife from Inglewood gasped out, with a sigh of relief at having done it. Other areas of concern were riots, poverty, disease, anarchy, drugs, and blown minds. One lady had a sheaf of clippings from the Los Angeles Times, a paper not known in the past for its concern for the interests of minority groups. All the clippings had to do with the Haight-Asbury district in San Francisco, from which our spiritual sistereminates, The San Francisco Oracle. The clippings described over-crc___ indiscriminate drug use___ ep-idemics, ___ of the ___ THIS v___ city of ___ Fifty r___ pies ___ city ___ and h___ have ___ of ' ___ mo___ tab___ it ___ be___ b___ e___ (

THE GREAT NON-GATHERING

A few weeks ago the entire Oracle Tribe - some 19 people ranging in age from 2 up into the 40's, with many beards and much long hair, bells, beads, incense - met together with th Los Angeles County Human R lations Commission in the ba' room of the Oracle mansion.] purpose of the meeting was explore ways of creating be communication between wha' commission termed "hipp and the "establishment." commission consisted of f or so very conserva' dressed mostly middle men and women. One man, a dignified, kindly his 50's, Tobias Kotzir duced the commission are the establishment. come to better under people. Frankly, so are worried!" This a three hour exchar us, representing the and them, speaking tablishment." It develo many people had expressed their ___ about the Easter Sunday

WIKIUP

WIKIUP, LESS COLOR-FUL BUT OFTEN MORE PRACTICAL, COVER WILLOW FRAME WITH THATCH, BARK SKINS, CANVAS, RUGS, BLANKETS, TARPAPER, REED MATS, ETC.

TOP VIEW
BASIC FORM

HOW TO BUILD A TIPI

12 FOOT TIPI CAN SLEEP SIX ADULTS AND REQUIRES: 30 YARDS OF 40" MUSLIN OR CANVAS, 14 POLES, 14' LONG, 20' OR 3/4" ANCHOR ROPE, 11 OR 12 STITCHING PINS 1½ BY ¼, 12 GLASS HEAD TACKS (OR TENT STAKES). CAN WATERPROOF, HIGHLY INFLAMABLE SO USE FIRE RESPECTFULLY. IF YOU NEED ADDITIONAL HELP, CONTACT CRAIG 2ORACLE.

FACE RISING SUN

26" MORE ROPE

COVER R DOOR TO T FACE

IMAGINARY LINE, FOR LAYOUT PURPOSES ONLY.

2" HEAVY CORD SEWN INTO REINFORCING PATCH

REINFORCING PATCHES

POCKET FOR SMOKE FLAP POLES

SMOKE FLAPS SEWN ON FROM LEFT-OVER SCRAPS

ROWS OF DOUBLE HOLES FOR 11 1/2 STITCHING PINS

LAY 13 POLES INTO THIS BASIC TRIPOD, TIE THEM TOGETHER AT 12', COVER AT 12' AND ON 8TH POLE AND LAY IT INTO PLACE, STITCH TOP WITH THE 6' ADJUST POLES TILL TOP IS TIGHT, TACK OR STAKE TOP DOWN, SECURE ANCHOR ROPE W/CENTER STAKE OR SECURE TREE FOR HIGH WINDS

Two wee___

ABOVE: This is the bread truck that my family drove around in when we dropped out.

LEFT: A group of Family members at Spahn Ranch. Catherine Shar is in the bottom right corner, Squeaky is in the striped shirt and Cathy Gilles is to the left of her. At the top left looking away is Sandy Good.

Larry the ranch hand from Spahn Ranch.

The present-day remnants of the Fountain of the World sect that Charlie tried to infiltrate to win followers.

Nancy Pitman with Zezo, Susan Atkins's son.

Lynette taking George to the restroom at Spahn Ranch.

Barker Ranch as it stands today.

Ballarat, California. Though a ghost town today, this was the last hint of civilization before Barker Ranch.

Death Valley on the way to Barker Ranch; this is Goler Wash. It's hard to describe how isolated Barker Ranch was in the 1960s. Charlie's plan was to make sure no one could find us.

This is the property where I camped out with Tex, after his confession that he had participated in the Tate murders.

The Olancha irrigation ditch where Tex and I were caught skinny dipping.

This is the truck I learned to drive on with Tex Watson still sitting on the Barker Ranch property in Ballarat.

The toolshed at B Ranch.

The nook in Bark liked to sleep.

My school photo, 1970, fr
tenth grade when I was l
Gardiners.

Outside of Jack Gardine

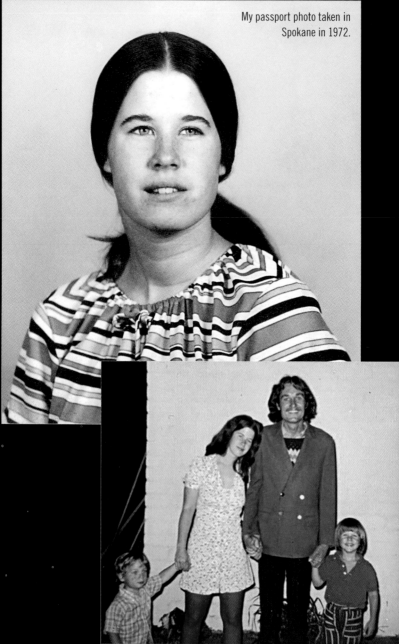

My passport photo taken in Spokane in 1972.

My father walking me down the aisle at my wedding to Todd in 1979.

Our wedding day in 1979. It was because of Todd and our children that I was able to heal the scars of my time with the Family.

Cutting our cake on our wedding day.

Me in 1960. This photo was taken in my parents' bedroom in the house we traded for a trailer, at the start of everything.

Me at Spahn Ranch in 2017.

a boy in the back row, "Young loves, your ego is what your parents made you. Your ego is what society taught you. Your ego is anything you acquired after your birth because at your birth you were a perfect person, no hang-ups just innocence. Now your ego is all the things that you fight against and are afraid of. But there is nothing to fear. You can free yourselves from this ego prison through love."

This is what the kids wanted to hear. Coming from a man over thirty who was validating their desire for change, Charlie's message was powerful.

"Isn't he groovy?" Susan said to a girl sitting next to her. The girl nodded in agreement.

"Charlie is love. He is everything. His love will set you free."

This was how the morning progressed, and we were sitting in a circle on the grass near the Fernwood Market when I recognized Jan and Joan's older sister's car. I couldn't help myself and completely lost my concentration on Charlie's rap as I looked over and saw Jan and Joan. Like a vision from a dream, my best friends were there, looking just as they had before my family dropped out. Without thinking, I jumped up from the circle and ran to them.

We, the three of us hugged and jumped up and down like we used to when we got together. I started talking a mile a minute and didn't notice Charlie glaring at me. In fact, I didn't notice anything except my friends. It felt as if I had just seen them the day before. Suddenly I was thrust back to my Santa Monica life with them on the beach, in my home, and at our favorite head shop. For a moment, I was a kid again.

"How did you find me?" I squealed.

"Our friend saw you with Charlie. She was picked u

ing by some of the girls and stayed with you all for a fe

I looked over at the girl and she didn't seem famili

"She recognized you from school and told us yo

went up to the house first but were followed by a

est, Dianne, he told us not to go up there like there was something wrong." I had my back to the circle, but I saw Joan's expression change.

"Oh, non—" I started to reply. The guitar playing had stopped and hackles rose on my neck. Charlie had come up behind me—I could feel it. If there had not been a crowd, he probably would have grabbed me by the hair and dragged me off.

"Dianne, get in the truck!" he said slowly and coolly. "Wait there until I tell you." I lowered my eyes from my friends but could feel them watching me walk away from them without so much as a goodbye. They would have to understand. I didn't want to anger Charlie any more than I already had. He would tell me that I should know better. I should know better than to leave the circle like that no matter what. What he was saying was important, and once again I couldn't pay attention like he wanted me to.

I watched out the window of the truck as Charlie gestured wildly to the girls. They were shouting at him.

"We are here to see our friend," Jan said.

"You don't belong here, little girls," he shouted back. Then he turned to the friend. "Look at you. You have your mother all over your face." I knew he was referring to the makeup she was wearing. Charlie had a thing against makeup and the painted ladies.

She yelled something back at him. He seemed to realize they were just kids looking for their friend because he lowered his tone and softened his expression. They didn't know anything about him, so he seemed to give them his rap, but whatever he said, they didn't seem to be buying it. Eventually Charlie made what was likely a menacing face at them, and they ran back to their car.

They turned to look at me, and as Joan closed the door, I could see she was upset and crying, but I couldn't understand why. I lifted my hand slightly to wave at them but in a way that Charlie couldn't . As emotional as I was about the whole display, I knew I had to ⸻ul to hide my feelings from Charlie.

Watching them pile into their sister's car, I wanted to tell Jan and Joan about the miracles around Charlie, about how anything we wanted would show up. But somehow I knew that they wouldn't understand about our life together. It wasn't about the sex or the drugs—though they probably wouldn't have understood those aspects either—it was more that they wouldn't understand my devotion to this man, or the fact that I lived solely according to his rules. It had been less than a year since I'd said goodbye to Jan and Joan when my parents dropped out, but it felt like a lifetime ago. I was such a different person now, and though I couldn't say exactly how, some distant part of me understood it wasn't for the better.

They had a home to go back to, a place to sleep with clean sheets. As they drove away, a flood of memories and nostalgia swept over me. The pages of *Seventeen*, boys at the beach—it all blended together in a powerful rush, and I felt overcome by the loss of so many things. Even school. Though I never would have admitted it, I missed schoolwork. Throughout the disruptions with my parents, school had been the only place that made sense to me with its definite schedule and expectations. Even when I'd started hanging out at the head shop, I never stopped loving school.

Unlike the run-ins with my parents, this left me shaken. As I'd come to understand, I felt very little for my parents, but Jan and Joan were different. Jan and Joan had known me before all this, when I was just a relatively normal kid with a family and a house. Their sudden appearance produced an alternate reality of my last year, one in which we'd been playing on the beach and going shopping together. Instead I was wearing secondhand rags from a communal box.

But though I was devastated to see Jan and Joan leav it was a sign of how far under Charlie's control I'd fallen that turned my attention to his mood, feeling relief that he tion anything about my transgression. He didn't hit m across the face as he'd done other times to discipline I seemed to get away easy.

"Your friends won't get our trip," Charlie finally said on the way home. "You can't stay tied up in your old world or you won't get out of that program. They are your old life and this is your life now."

Charlie often told each of us to give up our ties to our past, that we had to be loyal to one another because other people would try to pull us apart, but I had never thought about what he really meant until now. I crouched so Charlie wouldn't see my face. I didn't want to show any signs of homesickness because that would make me look weak in his eyes. I didn't want him to know what I was thinking—he always seemed to understand my thoughts even better than I did. In this moment, I didn't want to hear his lecture about outsiders or listen to him insult people who mattered to me.

As our bus turned toward home, I couldn't shake the look I had seen on Joan's face as she got into their car—a look that has haunted me ever since. Her sadness was clear, but there was something else—fear, as though she recognized the nature of the mess I was in in a way that I could not. Together Jan and Joan saw the things that I was unable to see. While they never could have anticipated the true dangers to come, they could see our group for what we were—a bunch of ragged girls following around a wiry, aggressive man—and in that, they saw the threat that Charlie represented.

I've thought back to that look often over the years because it was a warning, one of the few true warnings I received. Jan and Joan were genuinely afraid for me, and it turned out they were right to be.

13

SNAKE

WE STAYED AT THE HOUSE ON SUMMIT TRAIL FOR OVER A MONTH. IT WAS
March and the air felt like spring, a time of renewal and rebirth.
It was good that we were not on the road because Mary Brunner,
who had become pregnant with Charlie's baby sometime during the
summer of 1967, looked ready to pop.

"No one woman will fill his head with lies," Charlie repeated as
we all waited expectantly for the birth. As was true about so much of
his mind-set, he expressed his bitterness toward women and his own
mother in his aphorisms and passed these words on to us. Charlie
believed that children were the true kings and queens of the world,
and he was constantly lecturing us about how they were our teachers
because they were not yet programmed with societal illusions.

"You should watch and learn from the babies," he insisted. "They
know the truth."

We would gather around Mary at night and sing to her and her
belly. She wasn't comfortable at all, so we tried to take care of her
and make her happy. We all looked up to Mary because she was
the first one and we were all the sister wives. I don't think any of us
felt jealous of Mary for Charlie's attention, or at least that is how it
seemed. I felt happy and excited.

While we waited for the baby, we found ways to entertain ourselves. We all wanted to stay healthy and beautiful for Charlie, so we
would try all kinds of ways to cleanse our bodies. Charlie said that
eating food was a thought construct, and if we were really in tune

with ourselves, we wouldn't buy into the belief that we had to eat on a regular basis. He might have said that when the food supplies were low, but he also believed in fasting as a way of learning discipline over the physical. This little house was surrounded with lemon trees, and someone had also given us some jars filled with honey, so a few of the girls and I decided to take the lemons, water, and honey and go on a fast.

After more than a week of consuming nothing but lemon honey water, on a particularly warm day I went out by myself to explore the hills around the little house. I felt light-headed, but it was different than tripping. My body was filled with energy and my senses were heightened. I liked how I felt with an empty stomach and imagined that all the poisons accumulated by impure foods were leaving my body. I was becoming whole. I lay down and stared into the sun. Then I closed my eyes and the warmth penetrated my eyelids. After some time like this, I rolled over onto my belly and looked around. I was at eye level with the grass, which sprouted in little thickets. I imagined what it might be like if I were a snake slithering between the blades of grass and the rocks under the beaming sun. I wasn't on acid or dehydrated—I was simply allowing my mind to wander.

When I got back to the girls, I told them about my imaginings. Charlie must have overheard our conversation because he began to laugh.

"That's a good name for you, little one," he said. "From now on, you are Snake."

The other girls laughed and Susan Atkins tousled my hair. "Yeah, Snake."

I wasn't sure how I felt about this. I didn't like snakes enough to make them my totem and now my nickname. Things have a way of sticking with you even long after a moment in time—like tattoos. But as I thought more about this, my resistance evaporated like the dew on the morning grass. I liked having a separate identity that could sever any remaining ties that I had with my past. Maybe this was why my father changed his name. There could be something to it. Since my run-in with Jan and Joan, they had been invading my dreams, and it made me sad. Now I would become Snake, and that would be someone completely different from the person I used to be.

Though I got my name because of a lemon honey fast, it's quite amusing to me how minute details have become the things of legend. As the many stories and accounts of the Family have evolved, there have been persistent rumors that I got my nickname because of my sexual performance. The thought of that always makes me laugh. I wish everything about my time with Charlie could be explained away so simply. Unfortunately, most of it was as complex and bizarre as the legends have it. But the origin of my nickname was one of the few things blown all out of proportion.

Besides fasting and spending time at the house, we were limited in what we could do while Mary was resting up for the birth, but Charlie found things we could do at home. We had been having sex with one another at different times, but one afternoon he called us in for what he called a bonding experience of total love.

Charlie told us to take off our clothing. Since our first group sex session, he had been working with us to overcome our inhibitions. I was growing in my confidence as a lover, loosening up, learning to enjoy myself, and becoming quite comfortable with my body. The Summit house had a bathroom with a mirror, and one day Charlie made me stand in front of it completely naked for about an hour, just looking at myself from all angles.

"When you decide you are as beautiful as any other woman, you can come out."

I could see that my body was still more rounded in places than the older girls, but I also got used to that. My breasts were coming in nicely and I cupped my hands on them to see that they were now big enough to constitute a handful. Granted, my hands were small, but in my mind, that still qualified. I'd begun to love the freedom of nudity.

On this evening, Charlie had us sit in a circle. Seeing everyone else's nudity awakened my body even before the LSD was passed around. With the combination of LSD and nudity, I could be someone else altogether. Now I was Snake, and Snake enjoyed sex and was becoming good at it.

Charlie was providing the "sacrament" when there was a knock at the door.

"Brenda, Snake, see who that is," he said. I went to grab a towel and Charlie stopped me. "Let whoever is at the door see you just as you are. This is our Eden and you can be naked if you want to be."

Brenda and I skipped to the door and opened it wide. At the other side of the door was a handsome but totally confused young man with a backpack who was carrying what appeared to be a musical instrument.

He asked for a friend whose name we didn't recognize. I could see he was trying not to stare at our naked bodies, but he couldn't carry it off and was blushing as well. We pretended we didn't even notice we were naked just as Charlie told us to.

"Would you like to come in?" we asked. We must have sounded like a divine chorus of muses.

"My friend used to live here and told me I could crash with him if I was ever in the neighborhood." The guy, who told us his name was Paul, was awkwardly shifting his weight from one foot to another.

"Well, we live here with Charlie. Come in and we'll introduce you."

Paul followed us into the living room where the other girls were lounging. Susan was stretched out sensually and I felt a little bit of competitiveness. I was glad Charlie sent me to the door first. Susan always wanted first pick of any new boys who came around, and with her moves and experience, she usually got what she wanted. There were also a few other guys with us that night. Charlie had passed out all the acid and was now getting ready to play his guitar.

"Hey, man, I'm Charlie, Charlie Manson. You are just in time."

Leave it to Charlie to portray this uncomfortable situation as a sign from God. At this point I think Paul probably thought his prayers were answered too. He had walked into every young guy's sexual fantasy. He probably thought he was already tripping.

"Here, have some root beer." Charlie always liked to give people root beer. He felt it was as special a sacrament as the LSD or the zuzus. Then he handed him a lit joint. "Come join us."

Paul took a sip and passed the bottle back to Charlie, who gave it to Patty. She put it on the floor in the corner so it wouldn't spill.

"Hey, Paul, why don't you go ahead and sit between Brenda and Snake? Those are the two lovelies who met you at the door to our kingdom. This is all my love and so it is also yours. We all share it."

Paul put down his stuff and sat in between us.

Charlie gave us a nod and Brenda and I began the slow, sensual process of separating Paul from his clothes. He was a small man like Charlie, but only in height. His skin was soft and his body muscular; we opened his zipper and slid his pants onto the floor. We put his clothing in a pile with the rest of our garments.

The room became electric and Charlie guided us to breathe together. We joined hands and felt the current pass around the room through us all. Then Charlie orchestrated who would be with whom. Of course he assigned Brenda and me to our newest friend and Charlie seemed to send the telepathic message "Make this man happy. He belongs with us."

We each worked on him from our own side, moving from his forehead to his earlobes to his chest and finally to where he wanted us to be all along.

Paul was not going to forget this experience if I could help it. Charlie would expect something from him in return, but that was not my concern. I had one goal, to make him feel he was a part of us—the group, the Family, the greater whole we became when we took acid together. Charlie was love and we were love and now Paul was part of that love too. When we were all spent, we fell asleep together in a cluster of bodies. The cool breeze came in through the open windows and wafted across our skin.

The next morning as we were waking up, I noticed Charlie walking with Paul outside. I couldn't hear the conversation, but I was sure he was sharing his rap and his deep observations of Paul and his need for us. Charlie seemed quite interested in having Paul stay. I had never seen Charlie take to a man as he did with Paul. The other guys would come and go. I think Charlie kept them around to ease the burden of "taking care" of the needs of all of us women. That could certainly tire any man out.

Much to my disappointment, Paul decided not to stay. Charlie didn't say anything about it, but I knew he wasn't happy. It made me feel that I had failed in my seduction and recruitment. I know Charlie thought we had sealed the deal and he would have another addition to the family. And Charlie had given freely of his love and his women. Even though he never said it, there was always a sense of quid pro quo. It would only be a matter of time.

MARY WENT INTO LABOR ON APRIL FOOLS' DAY, 1968. THE HOUSE WAS buzzing with energy until things took a turn for the worse—something was terribly wrong. She was in agony and the baby didn't seem to be moving in the right direction. We brought over a neighbor who had either a background as a midwife or a nurse, and she confirmed the baby was in breech position, which sent everyone into a panic. Charlie grew quiet in a way I had never seen before—so scared he seemed almost in tears.

The neighbor told Mary to squat to help the baby move through the birth canal. She got into the position, and Mary delivered the baby with his feet first not long after. We all cheered once it was clear she and the baby were safe.

"Charlie, it is a boy," the neighbor said as she held the newborn up to Charlie. She asked Charlie to cut the umbilical cord, and then she washed the baby off in the sink and wrapped him in a blanket. Mary was exhausted but looked radiant. Stepping back from the scene, I couldn't help but imagine what it would be like when it was my turn to give Charlie a baby.

We propped Mary up as much as we could on a mattress and handed her the baby who hungrily latched on to her breast. She gave the baby the name Valentine Michael Manson after the main character in the book *Stranger in a Strange Land*, and Charlie heartily approved, though I don't ever remember calling him that. From the time he opened his eyes, he was everybody's Pooh Bear.

Pooh Bear was not only her baby, he was our newest family member, and now that we had a baby with us, Charlie talked openly about the importance of keeping his family safe and protected. Charlie reminded us that he already had two children that he likely would never see again—one from his first wife, who ran off, and the other from a prostitute he'd been trying to pimp out who became pregnant and left without telling him she was going. This time, with Mary giving birth to his son, he wasn't going to allow the child to be taken away without a fight.

Charlie felt the biggest risk to our family was that we were a target for what he called "misunderstandings by the man," and one of the best ways to protect ourselves was to be untraceable. Charlie had a friend from prison who was supposedly an expert forger. This man could help us out by creating the IDs. (Charlie always seemed to have the right friends for whatever he needed, a perk of the prison system.) If we had aliases and fake IDs, it would keep our true identities under the radar, and it would also eliminate the obvious problem of some of us being underage. I was in no hurry to return to juvenile court, so I was ecstatic.

When the guy came to give us our fake IDs, Charlie had fun creating our aliases.

"You are all now going to be different people. You, Snake, are going to be a married lady named Dianne Bluestein. How does that sound? And you are twenty years old, so you better act like it." He smiled when he said this, which pleased me immensely.

Maybe more than anyone else, I had the most to gain from the fake ID. Unlike the people at the Hog Farm, Charlie clearly felt that free love applied to me too, even though I was underage. He possessed none of the double standards or hypocrisy that I'd encountered there, which back then made him seem open-minded to me—one more social taboo that Charlie had jettisoned as he shed his inhibitions. Of course what I understand now is that, as with his openness toward two of his girls having sex, his inviting attitude about my age probably had more to do with my sexual value to him. He knew that some men would be interested in sex with such a young girl and he wanted to exploit that, something he didn't hesitate to do as time went on.

He didn't treat my age as a deterrent to enjoying the era of free love, although it was something he was cautious about because he knew I posed extra danger. While I falsely believed the note from my parents giving me independent status magically made me an adult, Charlie knew it was just paper. It was nothing more than a note that said my parents were not going to parent me and I could be on my own—nowhere near a legal document. And so keeping me around meant I was Charlie's risk to bear. He would tell me to avoid getting photographed or noticed when we were out in public, warning me against drawing attention to myself for any reason. That is why there are so few photographs of me from that time, even though I was there, a witness just beyond the frame. He'd tell me not to show my light in public because it was too bright, something I always took as a compliment back then, but now understand was simply about mitigating the threat my age posed to him.

My fake ID was the insurance we hoped would keep us both out of trouble, and from here on out, I didn't have to think about Bonnie Jean or Hugh anymore. I had two new identities. I was Snake and the married woman Dianne Bluestein. My husband was a guy in the group named Bruce, whom we now called John Bluestein, but this was only for the purposes of the fake IDs—he and I didn't hang out together. In fact, Susan was into Bruce, so I stayed far away from him. They gave Ella the name Cinder Ella and Susan Atkins the name Sadie Mae Glutz. I think that was because she was always showing off and trying to be more sophisticated than all of us. This name seemed to be a good way for Charlie to knock her ego down a little bit.

The fake IDs came in handy right away. After the baby was born, we got evicted from the Summit Trail house, so we rolled up the mattresses and packed them onto the bus. Until we found something more permanent, the bus would be our home. We drove through Ventura and stopped to camp near a place called Sycamore Canyon. There was a campground there, but we drove the bus farther back away from any people. The bus got stuck in some mud, but when we got out to push, we only managed to squish it in deeper. We ended up grabbing blankets and sleeping bags and hiking farther in to find a dry place to sleep for the night. I was in charge of our stash, which consisted of about four tabs of acid for the group.

We went far off the road in the woods and kept on walking until we reached a clearing. I gathered some kindling while the other girls made a circle of rocks so we could build a campfire. After the fire was burning and sending out some heat, we spread out our blankets and sleeping bags next to it and close to one another. We took off our clothes and snuggled in for the night. We thought we were deep enough in the woods so no one would see us or care that we were there. The baby, Pooh Bear, was just over a few weeks old. Mary held him close to her and I fell asleep to the sounds of him happily nursing.

The next thing I knew, a whole bunch of cops were shining lights into our faces. We all hopped to our feet, grabbing whatever we could to cover our bodies. We knew that the cops would jump to conclusions, and indeed they did. Some of the camper families must have seen us go into the woods, or maybe they were spying on the hippies. The cops weren't rough with us, but it was clear they thought of us as dirty hippie weirdos.

I was starting to get worried I'd end up back in juvie when I remembered the stash. That would really have gotten me in trouble. I was always warned not to toss your stash on the ground by where you were caught because the cops were trained to search around. I did the next logical thing I could think of: I popped all four tabs of acid into my mouth and swallowed.

While the acid was slowly taking effect, the cops asked to see our identification and I expected them to laugh or say something at our obvious poor puns. The IDs weren't bad when taken separately, but together, the ridiculous names were a definite tip-off. At first we all thought they bought it, but apparently they didn't, because the IDs were confiscated. The cops told us to put on our clothes and then took us to the station, where they booked us. What most people don't realize is the famous iconic photo of Charlie is the mug shot from that night. I don't even think he was on any drugs. He was more put out that his sleep was interrupted and we were arrested for sleeping in the nude and having the fake IDs.

I wasn't thinking about the consequences of being booked because now I had a bigger problem. The acid was kicking in. I had never taken that much acid at one time and don't know how high the dose actually was. I know I don't remember everything that happened that night except I began to sing every one of the Beatles songs that I had ever heard.

"I want to hold your hand," I sang at the top of my lungs. "For the benefit of Mr. Kite."

I tried to imitate all the musical sounds I heard in my head. I am sure I would never have remembered all the words to the songs if I hadn't been tripping so hard, but I think it ultimately helped us. The others ended up singing with me, so we simply seemed to be counterculture hippies out to annoy the establishment, which I suppose in a sense we were. More important, though, we didn't seem like a threat to anyone. I certainly wasn't a threat to anyone. I thought everything in the world was funny and colorful and filled with Beatles music. I never gave them my real name, but the next day they let us go anyway.

As we walked away from the station, we all thought we were obviously being protected by Charlie and his magical powers of postulation, but more likely, it was either dumb luck or the cops had bigger things on their minds. I often wondered if they ever put together later who we were. There was a big article in the *Los Angeles Herald Examiner* the next day, April 22, 1968, with the headline:

NINE NUDE HIPPIES ARRESTED;
FOUND HUDDLED AROUND BONFIRE

A bunch of us were arrested, including Charlie; Bruce Hall, my supposed husband; me; Nancy Pitman; Susan Atkins; Mary Brunner; the baby; a new girl who had joined us named Stephanie Rowe; Ella Jo Bailey; and a guy named Mark Damon. I don't remember him well, but I think he was nicknamed Motorcycle Mark.

The sad thing is they took the baby from Mary and accused her of child endangerment. I remember thinking that they were endangering the baby by taking him from his family and his mother. I guess they'd found the baby uncovered and cold, and that probably coupled with the look of us made them think that Mary was not taking good care of him. At the time, I didn't understand why, but in hindsight, I would have been horrified if I were the cops.

Because we all took turns caring for Pooh Bear, his absence impacted us all. Eventually Mary got him back, but the run-in with the cops left us all a bit shaken.

*   *   *

AFTER THE ARREST, WE STILL NEEDED A PLACE TO STAY, SO WE CRASHED with one of Charlie's associates, a guy named Harold True who was one of the first people Charlie met when he got out of prison. Charlie had roomed in prison with a man named Phil Kaufman who had contacts in the music industry. Although I didn't know about this, some accounts say Charlie came out of prison with at least eighty written songs that he hoped to sell. He even listed his goal during his transition meeting before parole as wanting to have a job as a musician. I enjoyed Charlie's music and thought it was sexy and special, but it wasn't until later that I realized the importance it held for him. Harold was Phil's good friend and may even have been the one to pick up Charlie when he was let out of prison as a free man.

Harold True was a physically big man who was a student at UCLA. His status as a student didn't in any way lessen the fact that he consorted regularly with ex-cons, drug dealers, and other unsavory characters. For the most part, the people I met through Charlie were like we were, grooving on Charlie and his music and expanding our consciousness with LSD and Charlie's words. Harold True was different, and I felt it from the moment I met him. True shared a house at 3267 Waverly Place, which was next door to what later became the site of the murder of Rosemary and Leno LaBianca. Perhaps a part of me was simply anticipating the future.

Our acid parties were mostly with our group, but to repay Harold's hospitality, Charlie set up an LSD trip and made it clear that it would include group sex. Now at this point, making love with the people in our inner circle felt like a beautiful thing, and to be honest, I enjoyed it because I trusted them. LSD and sex are very intimate partners. You become completely vulnerable to the other person or people, and for me at least, it is like joining souls. It was far more than sex that you might do for fun just because you feel like it. For that reason, I was happy when he invited Paul to join us because I instantly liked Paul and was turned on by how much he seemed to want us when we brought him into the group.

Harold True was a different story. I simply did not like Harold True—he scared me. This may sound ironic, given Charlie's eventual crimes, but there was something about Harold True that repulsed me. He was a very big man; to me, he was fat. I was used to being with our men, who like Charlie were often of small stature and handsome. They were typically baby-faced and were gentle lovers under Charlie's tutelage.

For some reason, Harold wanted me by myself that night. Like many men, he probably liked the fact that I was underage. Or maybe Charlie had presold him on my special skills, those I had learned on our trip to San Francisco. Either way, much to my horror, I was the one that Harold chose.

I didn't want to sleep with Harold True, especially away from everyone else. Everything in my body and my mind rejected the idea. It was an involuntary impulse. I didn't like the feeling of Charlie's passing me off to this man. Generally I was overlooked when it came to seducing men, and it fell to someone like Sadie. But when Charlie asked us to do something, he made sure that we did it so that no one else would think there was any special treatment. And on this night, he asked me to be with Harold True. I felt sick and tried to talk Charlie out of it, even resorting to tears.

Charlie went into a rage, grabbing me by the hair and pulling me into the bathroom out of the earshot of Harold, who was waiting for me in his bedroom.

"Do not disobey me, young woman. I told you to take care of that man. Do what you are supposed to do and don't backtalk me."

"Please, Charlie."

Charlie raised his hand to strike me but pulled back. He wiped the tears that were flowing down my cheeks. "It won't be too bad. Just get it over with and I will give you some zuzus."

His offer only infuriated me more. I thought back to the day in the bus with Lynette and how he gave me candy after showing me how to give a good blow job. On that occasion and on this, he was doing exactly what he said parents did with their children: They bribed them with candy. The realization made me incredibly angry, but I talked myself out of it. The other girls did what Charlie wanted, no questions asked. I usually got away with not having to perform, and I much preferred the zuzus to a wallop across the face.

I did what was asked of me that night, allowing him to pass me off to a man I was repulsed by as a gift because I wanted to please Charlie. Because I knew it was my responsibility as part of the Family. Because I was afraid of what would happen if I said no.

I brushed off these memories and tucked them deep inside. I try to repress the anger I feel as an adult woman looking back at myself as a teenage girl. I wish I could say it was the only time it happened, but that wouldn't be the truth. There would be other nights and other men. Instead of it being the only time, this was the first instance of a new, disturbing role for me in the Family. From here on out, my age would always be an asset for Charlie in this regard— that is, until it became a liability.

14

SPAHN RANCH

THE NEXT PLACE WE MOVED TO BECAME OUR BASE FOR MUCH OF MY
time with the Family: Spahn Ranch.

Spahn Ranch has become so deeply connected to the stories of
the Family that it's hard to separate what it actually was with what
it has come to represent. When our bus first drove through Chatsworth and the Santa Susana Pass sometime in late May 1968, I was
concerned that we were moving farther and farther into the middle
of nowhere. As much as I enjoyed nature, I didn't like the feeling
of being so far away from civilization. Lynette must have seen my
expression or was tuning into my thoughts because she smiled and
said, "Oh, it won't be so bad. It'll be fun."

When we pulled into the dirt drive, it was like moving through
a time warp. The place looked like something out of an old Western. If you didn't look behind the facades you could imagine yourself as a pioneer, part of the real America expanding its territory
after the Civil War. The best part was, the facades were attached
to buildings. They weren't just false fronts supported by wooden
posts. I forgot all about my concerns as we got out to look around.
The place had a boardwalk and horses roaming free. Charlie disappeared into the main house to talk to the owner of the place while
the ranch hands regaled our bus full of mostly young girls about
how at the height of its usefulness the ranch had been the setting
for the TV shows *Bonanza* and *Zorro*. I tried to visualize it as it
must have been, but as we surveyed the landscape, it looked run-

down, as past its former glory as its blind cowboy owner, George Spahn. The ranch was no longer used for the movies and television, except on a few occasions.

Charlie came out of the house with George, a big man with a Texas drawl that may have been created for the role of ranch boss. He wore a cowboy hat and dark glasses to protect him from the sun he likely hadn't seen for many years. It was obvious that George Spahn was not a weak, vulnerable man. He was cowboy smart, and it took all of Charlie's charm and con-man know-how to convince George to let us stay there. Charlie told him we were a musical group in search of a place to crash, but he purposely didn't tell Spahn how many of us there were or how many more there would be. Still, I am convinced Charlie didn't pull anything over on old George. George knew what he wanted to know. Charlie offered him girls to help take care of him, and built into that offer was taking care of whatever he wanted or needed for himself. Old George might have been old, but he was still quite interested in the kind of help Charlie offered.

The little house was separate from the other buildings, and when we walked in, it was clear that between the layer of dust on everything and the unmistakable odor of old man, the place lacked a woman's touch. I found a bucket in the back of a pantry closet and filled it with hot water. Lynette and I were the first to get to work on the place. Luckily there were some stiff rubber gloves that sprang to life when wet. I could clean anything as long as I was wearing gloves. I found some pine cleaner and poured in so much that the bubbles overflowed. There were no sponges, so I ripped up an old T-shirt I found in a drawer and used it as a rag. The first thing I did was wipe out his refrigerator. This was always one of the jobs I preferred. I would take on all the chores other people wouldn't think of doing, like keeping the toilets clean. When I finished, the water and the T-shirt were completely black.

Of course, cleaning refrigerators was not the only kind of help

Charlie offered him. Surprisingly enough for Lynette and me, not only could George get it up, but he was very interested in both of us. Thankfully Lynette grew fond of George, so my work was mostly dedicated to the housekeeping. In fact, it was George who gave Lynette the nickname Squeaky.

"Aren't you a cute old man," she squealed.

Then he gave her a pinch on the ass. He might not have been able to see, but he could still find his way to what he wanted. She let out a squeak and that is how she got her name.

Squeaky became George's number one girl both in the bedroom and out of it, but all the girls would take turns sleeping in a real bed with George; his house had amenities that weren't in the other buildings, since they were upon closer inspection more like shells with facades. But Squeaky would do most of the cooking and caretaking for George, which also enabled Charlie to keep track of George's comings and goings. Charlie had his eye on what we called the back house on the ranchland. There was another group of hippies already living there when we arrived, but Charlie quickly started postulating ways to get them to move on.

In order to secure our welcome at Spahn Ranch, Charlie knew that he also had to appeal to Ruby Pearl, who ran the place for George. Ruby was a sunbaked, leathery woman who always wore either a bandanna or a hat. A weathered old horsewoman, she was younger than George, but she looked as if she'd packed a lot of living into her years. It was common knowledge among the ranch hands that George had once had a wife and eleven kids before he left them all for Ruby. But Ruby wasn't just some temptress; she was strong and capable and didn't seem afraid of anything. A sort of latter-day Annie Oakley, Ruby'd had a show business career before getting involved with the ranch, old George, and the buying and selling of horses.

Charlie always made sure that Ruby was happy by offering her our help with the horses. The way George kept the place running was by renting out the horses to people who wanted to play cowboy or cowgirl for the day. Most of the horses were so well trained any idiot could ride them, and these trail horses knew the way out and back. All of the guys in our group pitched in with the mucking out of the stalls and the tacking of the horses for all the tourists. In this way, they were able to keep an eye on a different part of the ranch life.

Crashing at Spahn with others around meant we all had to be aware of what was going on, and Charlie made sure that all the training he'd been giving us about reading people was put to good use. Though we had the run of Spahn Ranch, we lived in the main area of the movie set, staying primarily in the saloon and in the jail, where we put mattresses on the floor. We also used the kitchen down the boardwalk to prepare our meals. But by setting up in the middle of everything, we were fairly exposed to everyone, so we had to be careful. Charlie didn't like anyone outside of our circle knowing too much about our business. It wasn't clear what our business was, something I didn't think too much about at the time. Charlie was firm about us not trusting outsiders unless he said they were okay, so that's what we did.

IN MANY WAYS, SPAHN RANCH WAS THE PERFECT BACKDROP FOR OUR acid-fueled fantasy world. It really was a land of make-believe, where we could pretend it was 1865 and we were living on the American frontier. I loved staying in the saloon, which was covered in wood paneling and had a huge wooden bar with a mirror behind it. We dressed in costumes we would assemble from our communal clothing box and acted like different people. And when we were outside, we would go riding and explore the woods and trails.

The people working the ranch all had their own colorful stories. Everyone there was really on the way to something bigger and better, at least in their imagination, and many of the ranch hands traded work for housing, food, and cigarettes. Their housing was ramshackle, but truth be told, so was their work. George had a soft spot for cowboy drifters, and in return he got their gratitude and loyalty. A stunt man named Randy Starr worked the horses but was always waiting for his next big break. He was a little bit bowlegged, which made him suited to cowboy and stunt work and not much else. There was also a guy named Shorty Shea, who didn't like us very much, and a guy named Juan Flynn, who hung around with us some of the time.

Whenever I could, I would volunteer to help out with the horses, mostly by mucking out the stalls. I was usually on child-care duty, so working with the horses was a welcome change for me. Ruby and Randy Starr worked with the horses and trained them. They made it look very easy. They were also always joking about the tourists who didn't know how to ride a real horse. Starfire was a real horse. He was completely white with a cream-colored mane and tail. He snorted as I made full eye contact with him. Randy was pulling on his rope and yelling for him to settle down. Starfire was full of life and didn't want to be led around by a bowlegged cowboy. I was leaning over the fence when Starfire pulled his way over to me. He pawed the ground with his hoof, which I took as a challenge.

"You like that horse, do ya?" Ruby asked with a mischievous grin.

"I really do. Can I ride him?"

"That is too much horse for you, Red."

In my mind she was calling me *yeller*, and in the frontier, them's fighting words. "I can handle it," I insisted.

"It's your funeral." She laughed.

I went to get a saddle. The horse had settled down and was calmly snorting at me.

"You don't need no saddle," Randy Starr piped in.

"Randy, don't you butt in," Ruby said with a glare.

Ruby gave me a leg up and handed me the rope reins attached to Starfire's bridle. I felt steady and confident as we rode on the path toward the trail.

"Now don't you go too far."

"I won't," I called back.

The air smelled wonderful and I loved seeing the ranch from the back of a horse. Starfire was steady and seemed to know what he was doing. We were halfway down the path toward the back of the ranch when Starfire turned into a beast. I don't have any idea what happened. The next thing I knew, he had executed a 180-degree turn and started whipping through the brush and the trees. I held on to his mane until that white devil purposely ran so close to a tree that he scraped me off like a barnacle.

I held on to his neck and mane as I slipped farther into the path of his legs. His powerful legs pummeled me—bump, bump, bump—but I wouldn't let go. He never slowed down. The sand and gravel sprayed my face and went into my mouth as Starfire tried to leave me in the dust. As I was underneath his chest, his sweat mixing with my own, he came to a full stop. My fingers were stiff from holding on so tightly and ached as I let go of the reins. I spat out the dirt and slid out from under him. I slowly got to my feet and noticed that instead of showing concern for me, Ruby and Randy were laughing.

"Ya wanna go again?" Ruby laughed.

"No thanks!" I hated admitting defeat, but the horse had gotten the better of me. I probably should have gotten right back on that white demon, but I recognized I was outmatched. Starfire was beautiful and compelling but dangerous.

When I wasn't trying to break horses or having them break me, my days were filled with keeping the place and our stuff clean much as I had always done. Charlie seemed to like that I was quite good at domestic duties. No one could clean and tidy things like I could.

The other girls got lazy when they were stoned. I would get energized and would make whatever hovel we were living in shine. This was my contribution and I liked doing it.

We washed our clothes in a creek behind the ranch, much as I imagine they would have done in the actual Old West. The twisted branches of the trees created shade and seclusion from everyone. There was a flat area near the creek bed perfect for camping or daydreaming, the latter of which I did a lot. We hung up a rope hammock and I would lie in it listening to the creek water. Sometimes Patty would come with me to help me hang the wash. She and I kidded around, but sometimes we could really talk to each other. I liked listening to her as she painted pictures with her words, and I trusted her more than I did Sadie. Sadie might have been telling the truth when she spoke, but there was always something slippery and self-serving in how she presented things.

"Oh, Sadie is all right," Patty would say. "Charlie says she just needs attention. Sometimes he purposely embarrasses her so she won't need it so much." Patty laughed, but her observation made me wonder how much of what Charlie did was calculated to teach us things. It made me nervous to think that his reactions were part of some bigger plan to mold us.

"Snake, Charlie changed my life," she said one day when we were washing clothes.

"How did he do that?" We all knew one another's stories, but we didn't all speak about our feelings. Charlie did most of the talking for us.

"I hated myself when I first met Charlie." Patty pinned a shirt to the makeshift clothesline we had set up by the creek. That was surprising to me. Patty was like an older sister and always made me feel safe when she was around. The six years between us made me realize what I had been for my little sister Kathy. For a moment, I felt a sentimental pang.

She opened her blouse and showed me that she had a lot of hair on her chest. I had seen her naked but had never really given it a second thought.

"Can't you see that?"

"You mean the hair?"

"Yes, I have never been able to get rid of it."

"How come it's there?" I asked innocently. I didn't want to embarrass her.

"I guess I must have an endocrine problem. I have always had it."

"Oh, that must have been rough." I remembered my Big Bertha Butt nickname. I couldn't imagine the bullying she had to endure.

"When I met Charlie and we made love, he made me feel beautiful for the first time in my life."

This made me think about the first time I made love with Charlie. He made me feel safe and loved. I didn't really care about feeling beautiful.

He gave both Patty and me what we needed. This seemed so selfless of him. Patty showed no possessiveness of Charlie and helped me see that he had enough love for all of us. I thought it was wonderful that he gave each of us what we needed to make us whole, because, however misguided I was, I honestly believed he loved me best. I had no idea that Patty was also harboring the desire to be Charlie's only girl, and that he misled all of us to believe that this was possible. If we had ever bothered to compare notes, our selfless love for Charlie and for one another would have devolved quickly.

When it came to the girls, we all fell for his con in different ways, drawn to disparate pieces of his act, but the idea that we were each his favorite was the lie that kept the group together.

EVENTUALLY THERE WERE ENOUGH PEOPLE AROUND THAT WE NEEDED more resources. Some people brought money and donated it to our common coffers, but most of the drifters were simply more mouths to feed, and we could no longer use Patty's credit card. Brenda's family had also gotten wise to where her resources were going and had put a stop to them.

One day Charlie called us together to the front of the saloon. "You girls don't know the best-kept secret in our society."

And with that, Charlie piled us into a truck he borrowed from one of the ranch hands and drove us through Chatsworth into Simi Valley. Simi Valley was the next town over through the Santa Susana Pass. When we got there, he drove behind a store called Lucky's.

"Take a look, girls." He jumped on top of the Dumpster.

I looked on with more than a little horror. I was expecting to see dead cats and other disgusting things. I was also worried that someone would see us. Charlie bent down, and when he sat up, he had a complete box of fruit.

"Look at this," he said, picking out a few oranges that looked bruised and handing the crate to Squeaky.

"Oranges!" she exclaimed. "They are beautiful."

"You try," he said to Sandy, Patty, and me. We were all watching him dig in the Dumpster. I looked inside and was surprised to see packages of food that looked perfectly good. I was hungry. We had been living on a very plain diet of oatmeal and raisins. I was really craving fruits and vegetables.

"Why is this all here, Charlie?"

"It is because the rich people don't like to eat their fruit or vegetables if it doesn't look perfect."

"The stores just throw this stuff out?"

"That they do. Can you dig it? They throw out food that doesn't look perfect, just like they throw out people," he laughed.

We spent the next half hour finding all kinds of foods that were still good to eat. We even found a container of potato salad that was still cold from having been in the cooler. We smelled it, of course. We found dented cans, but none of them were swollen like my grandmother taught me to watch out for. She always said if a can is swollen, the stuff inside is dangerous.

When we'd found everything edible, we put the haul in the truck and got ready to leave.

"What about this beauty?" Charlie pulled out a cabbage with some brownish leaves that we had left behind. He pulled back the leaves to show a perfect cabbage underneath. "See here? This cabbage that nobody wanted will make a great soup."

To add to the food haul, Mary Brunner had a friend who worked at the Helms Bakery. She persuaded him to come to us at the end of his shift to give us all the leftover pastries and breads that would be otherwise tossed. We didn't have to worry about going hungry.

We made a big feast on the first day of our garbage run, and afterward we got together by a campfire. Charlie played some of his songs and then started to speak.

Charlie's voice was soft and thoughtful. He wanted to teach us something, as if the music and the guitar and his speaking were all spontaneous and connected to one another. He would tell us things like how we were products of our parents' thoughts, that we needed to be free from their programming or we'd never know who we are. He told us that death and time were illusions and even told us we wouldn't have to eat if we didn't believe we had to. He described us as free souls trapped in society's cages.

Charlie ranged from one topic to the next. His meditations on death were always a bit trippy for me. I thought back to when I was under Starfire's legs—a brief moment where death seemed very real to me, not something that had been taught. But Charlie's voice was so convincing. (Years later, I'd learn that he had cribbed most of his views about the malleability of death from Scientology, among other places.)

Charlie was singing along with his guitar chords and continued to strum softly while he spoke. He liked to say that he learned at an early age that he was so smart he knew he was dumb. He said it was good he didn't have education because our schools teach people what they can't do. Eventually we all went to sleep, with the stars twinkling overhead, as if we really were back in the Old West, starting new lives on our own new frontier.

For the core of us at Spahn, these became our routines and our lessons. Chores, acid, talk-tos, Dumpster runs, horses, sex, and most of all, Charlie. Charlie kept a close eye on us and we kept an eye on him. At least I know I did. Even though our world expanded on the ranch, where there was more to do and more people around, we were still isolated and everything revolved around Charlie more than ever. He was our culture and the rhythm to our days. People interviewed after the crimes said that all they saw of us was we slept a lot, smoked a lot of dope, and ate garbage. That is probably what it did look like to them. Maybe that was the truth of our existence. But to us, it seemed like much more. We were living free and outside of the establishment with its focus on materiality, and Charlie was showing us the way.

As a fifteen-year-old living with Charlie and the girls, I didn't think about what was forming around us or how Charlie was molding us. Perhaps it was because I also had the example of my parents' efforts to seek a higher truth, but at this point, we weren't much different from the other communes of the day, all of which were trying to eschew materialism and live off the land in a communal setting. The biggest difference as far as I could tell was that Charlie was the center of everything for us, but even that wasn't strange in itself. Charlie's form of guruism was in the California air, and all up and down the coast there were men—they were almost always men—leading groups like ours and espousing many of the same things he was. People were looking for guides to the counterculture's promised land, and there were more than enough people out there who appeared to have the answers. In that regard, Charlie, as criminal as his instincts were, was fairly unexceptional, simply another false prophet taking advantage of the moment's uncertainty.

And then he met Dennis Wilson.

15

BEACH BOY

AFTER WE'D BEEN AT SPAHN RANCH ABOUT A MONTH, ELLA AND PATTY were hitchhiking along Sunset Boulevard in Los Angeles and were picked up by Dennis Wilson, the drummer for the Beach Boys, and invited back to his house.

Today, when you consider all the bodyguards and gatekeepers surrounding entertainers, it sounds unlikely that Dennis Wilson, as well known as he was, would have picked up two random young female hitchhikers and invited them back to his home. The Beach Boys were one of the biggest musical sensations of the decade, and though their cultural influence was on the wane by summer of 1968, they were still incredibly popular—their mark on Southern California culture indelible. But as unbelievable as this kind of casual encounter seems now, that's how it was back then in Los Angeles. In general, musicians were more accessible, and many treated their homes like crash pads with an open-door policy, inviting strangers over to hang out, do drugs, and have sex—a casual attitude which Charlie and the murders put a decisive end to in August 1969.

Unbeknownst to Ella and Patty, when Dennis picked them up, the timing couldn't have been better for Charlie. Some people have said that Charlie purposely had us hitchhike in places where he thought there might be people in the music industry driving by, but I am not sure of that. From my vantage point, the music was the message, not Charlie's key to fame. Charlie undoubtedly hid many backstories from us. We were his disciples and his built-in entourage. We weren't encouraged to question him and figured things out only if we were observing with an element of objectivity; something I lacked. I believed everything exactly as I saw it unfold, with the interpretations given to me by Charlie.

When Ella and Patty told Dennis about how Charlie was their guru, sharing some of Charlie's teachings with him, Dennis was more than polite, he was receptive. As it turned out, Dennis already knew a thing or two about gurus.

Just a few months earlier, in December 1967, the Beach Boys had met the original major celebrity guru, Maharishi Mahesh Yogi, in Paris. The Beatles and such notables as Mia Farrow, Elizabeth Taylor, and Richard Burton were already open followers of his teachings, and all of them, particularly the Beatles, were publicly associated with him in newspapers and magazines. While the Beatles came to be most closely associated with the Maharishi for introducing him to the Western world, the Beach Boys, like their onetime UK rivals, were also quite excited about the Maharishi's teachings. Despite the Beatles eventually severing their ties with the Maharishi, he went on to tour with the Beach Boys who ended their tour with him in May 1968 after news of the guru's health problem broke.

Now sans guru, Dennis had returned to his home on Sunset Boulevard. What that meant for Charlie and the Family was that when Dennis Wilson picked up Patty and Ella hitchhiking shortly after he came off tour, not only was he without a steady guru, but he'd been perfectly prepped for this unusual date with destiny. That was just Charlie's luck, since unlike the Maharishi, Charlie's brand of guruism clearly did not require adherents to give up sex and drugs, but rather encouraged them.

Dennis was vulnerable to Charlie's charm for many reasons. I recall he had just gone through a difficult divorce from his first wife, leaving their two children with her, and he was also a man of many appetites for escape, including drugs and alcohol. He was considered the most handsome and was the only real surfer in a group famous for the California beach sound of the early sixties. I think this went to his head, and also think it made him crave constant female attention. As I would later learn, perhaps Dennis's greatest vulnerability came from his relationship with his highly manipulative and abusive father, Murry Wilson, who would constantly tell them they would never amount to anything.

And if Charlie and Dennis had postulated for each other, Ella Jo and Patty became the gateway for the next stop on a mystical journey. The girls were trained to reel in a likely candidate and would have spent the car ride intensely focusing on Dennis to determine his needs. This was a big fish, so they would have flirted heavily, oozing pheromones while turning Dennis on to Charlie and his teachings. With Dennis's guru vacancy, he was presold by the time he dropped the girls off at Spahn Ranch. An introduction to Charlie was a must.

That Ella Jo and Patty could manipulate him was not surprising. Dennis might have been famous, but we were all becoming con artists in Charlie's image. We were difficult to spot as we grew in our expertise. Charlie used every opportunity and teachable moment to show us how to obtain the things we needed from others. The key to it all was to become good listeners. I discovered that people were not that difficult to read if you paid attention. If you listened carefully, you could anticipate almost anything someone else might need and then could reflect it back at them. Charlie understood that people were usually most interested in themselves, and if given some feigned empathy, they would talk way too much about things they shouldn't. Charlie had a finely calibrated recall for things he heard—almost like an auditory photographic memory—and if he heard something once, he could remember it. He'd tuck a seemingly random piece of information away in his memory and then use it to manipulate someone later, pulling out that obscure fact after weeks or months had gone by, long after the person had forgotten he or she had even shared that private detail with him. By deploying that sensitive information in this way, Charlie cultivated their trust in him.

Charlie emphasized that we should become what the other people wanted or needed. When we met strangers, I watched Charlie size them up, decide what he wanted out of them, and then become what they wanted him to be. If he encountered someone he considered a potentially useful follower who could bring something of value to the group—money, cars, skills, or connections—he would be the fast-talking con. He would pour on his rap and flash his otherworldly eyes, spinning a web around anyone close enough to listen to him. He could convince people to part with things before they would ever notice they had been had. Or he would pour on the all-knowing hippie guru trip that would make someone feel good about giving up whatever it was that Charlie wanted from them.

If the prospect was a manly guy, Charlie could put on this macho trip. He would act like we were nothing but broads to him and would make sure to ask us to service him either by doing whatever he asked or by being available to the men as objects owned by Charlie. He could even look like a greasy biker, making sure to show the tattoos on his arms. He could talk beer and broads, but I never saw him drink anything.

Similarly, he prepared us for different situations, such as how to act if we were stopped by the police. "If the pigs stop you, you are not to be yourselves. You will want to mouth off, but don't do it. You play dumb and innocent to the point that if there is a bag of weed in your hand, you say you don't have any idea how it got there."

Playing dumb was actually one of Charlie's most regular acts, because it made people underestimate him. If he wanted to be invisible to others or didn't want to engage with them in any way, he could become a dumb hick. He could have you believe he didn't have an ounce of intelligence or the ability to find his ass with both hands. In other words, he played it really well.

"Uh, I don't know, man."

"Whatever, I don't know."

"Like I said, I don't know, man."

He could look like a drifter just barely making it, putting up a shield of invisibility. It was like Charlie could turn on or off his own inner light and charisma to use it only when it suited him. He could get out of any situation by fitting in and mirroring what the other person wanted to believe about him. It even worked on the ranch hands, despite the fact that Charlie knew about as much about horses as he did rocket science.

When it came to the ranch hands or the other men who came to the ranch to ride horses, first, we were to read people to find out what they needed and then become that. We could put on the employee hat: "How can I help you?" or "It's a great day to ride horses." Or we could pour on the sexual flirtation if it seemed like the man would be receptive. Every encounter with the outside world became an opportunity to put Charlie's teachings to use.

Combine Charlie's agenda with these skills, and we were primed to be useful when Charlie needed to get things done. For Charlie, the best part was that none of us needed convincing, so when it came time to persuade others of Charlie's greatness, it wasn't an act—we were all true believers, which made us the perfect vessels. None of us felt we were complicit in a con or in something illicit, because everything we were doing was in service to Charlie.

Charlie's uncanny ability to access a person's needs now has many labels such as a type of cognitive empathy, this ability to read others and know them better than they know themselves without the emotional empathy to go along with it. Charlie provided scientists with a prime example of this type of pathology.

When Dennis pulled up to Spahn Ranch that day to drop off Patty and Ella, I have no doubt that Charlie instantly sized up the situation and understood the opportunity that Dennis's presence signified for him. Like the rest of us, Patty and Ella had been trained for precisely this kind of situation, and they'd delivered in sterling fashion. Dennis represented a direct line to a level of fame and influence that had long been inaccessible to Charlie—and the best part was that he'd been delivered right to Charlie's doorstep.

Dennis and Charlie hit it off right away, which is not surprising, given Charlie's skills at ingratiating himself with strangers. Dennis, in no rush to leave, hung out for a while, smoked some pot with Charlie, and listened a bit to Charlie's songs. It was obvious from the start that Dennis liked the girls and admired Charlie's harem. We sat at Charlie's feet and looked at him lovingly as he sang and played guitar. We made sure Dennis saw how much we idolized Charlie—we knew that was our job, without Charlie even having to tell us. Dennis seemed drawn to the idea that he was just another person around us, and though we were flirtatious, we were not groupies. I tended not to be starstruck, and for me, the real superstars were the Beatles; the Beach Boys felt a bit over. Drugs and particularly acid had changed everything.

Dennis was legitimately interested in hearing the new and different sound that Charlie was creating with his music. This is what made it so exciting. Charlie played guitar well enough, and Dennis, a self-taught drummer, hardly played at all, so Charlie began to show him how. Watching them together, we could see they'd connected with each other. Dennis's good looks gave him the kind of magnetism perfect for Charlie, but as it turned out, Charlie quickly keyed into his soft spots.

Charlie likely understood immediately that Dennis needed someone who wouldn't tear him down emotionally as his father had throughout his life. Though none of us knew this about Dennis at the time, the truth about his difficult upbringing and his damaged soul were confirmed in later accounts. Dennis responded to the stress by becoming an adrenaline junkie—he loved fast cars, motorcycles, and anything that would give him a rush—and he'd often let off steam by sneaking off to Manhattan Beach and surfing. Throughout the rise of the Beach Boys, Dennis had played the drums with his style and passion, breaking drumsticks and attracting women. Unfortunately, he was also the black sheep of the family. And into that void stepped Charlie, who was more than happy to become a father figure, a guru, a friend, a confidant, and a great procurer of drugs and women.

Charlie strummed his guitar and sang a chorus of "Look at Your Game, Girl," then stopped and gazed at Dennis. After enough time to make anyone uneasy, Charlie said, "You know, man, you got your father in you. He took over your mind, and that's why you don't believe in your own music." Dennis was visibly shaken with Charlie's insight. "You got to give up all that. That's nothing but a reflection in the wrong mirror."

We'd only just met Dennis, and we had no idea what kind of a person he was or what he was all about. But as he sat there staring at this small man surrounded by adoring women and living in an abandoned, semi-derelict movie set, it was evident he thought Charlie was onto something. Like most of us, Dennis probably had no idea what that something was, but at some point during the course of that evening, he decided that he too was curious enough to find out.

BY THE TIME DENNIS LEFT THE RANCH AFTER THAT FIRST VISIT, HE'D made an arrangement with Charlie to have a few girls come with him to go boating at a family cookout on the Colorado River. I don't know whose idea it was or how the decision got made. Dennis could be a bit wild and impulsive—he may have been looking for company or he may have been more interested in freaking out his family. I'm not sure if Charlie picked which girls would go or if Dennis requested specific ones; all I know is, I was selected to go on the trip.

Three of us went—Ella, Nancy, and me. Important as this trip was for Charlie, he didn't burden us with too many instructions—he knew he'd trained us too well. All that I recall he said was "make him happy." This meant to do whatever he wanted—sex, drugs, whatever it takes. Be friendly. Be a good listener to determine his needs and provide for them. Focus on him.

It was the end of May when Dennis came by the ranch to pick the three of us up in his Rolls-Royce. All we took with us were the clothes on our backs and our bathing suits. I wore cutoff shorts and a short blouse and had put some flowers in my hair. Dennis was handsome, with thick, layered hair flowing past his shoulders, and wore nice clean clothing. He looked like a man even though he was only in his early twenties. He smelled good.

Before heading out to the river, Dennis swung by his house to pick up a few things, and we got out to look around. Dennis was living in a beautiful estate at 14400 Sunset Boulevard that used to belong to Will Rogers. In a strange twist of fate, his house was right outside Will Rogers State Historic Park, near the beach which had been one of my family's first stops after we dropped out less than a year earlier. As I stepped out of the car to stretch my legs, I took it all in.

The scene felt surreal, a remarkable contrast with the dusty landscape of the Spahn Ranch, which had come to feel like my whole world. Dennis's property felt like a park—green grass, towering trees, a tree swing connected to a limb high off the ground by a long stretch of rope, and a deep blue pool nearby. The main house itself was a luxurious cabin made of huge pine logs, elegant but manly. The decor inside wasn't overdone. It was the kind of place where it felt okay to sit on the furniture—rustic and comfortable. A pair of French doors led to a huge kitchen with a bathroom off to the side. The fireplace was so big that I could stand up in it.

The other girls and I were quiet as we wandered from room to room, each of us awed in our own way. We were very mindful not to touch anything or to be overly familiar. Even now, all these years later, I remember how enchanted that space felt. We'd gone from one fake Western frontier at Spahn Ranch to another in the former home of Will Rogers. Both were movie sets in their own way, but whereas Spahn Ranch was merely a collection of facades, Dennis's home was quite real.

Soon we were back in his Rolls, speeding toward the Colorado River to hang out with the whole Wilson family. We arrived at dusk right near the dam in Parker, California, always a happening place, with bikini-clad women, people drinking beer, and barbecue grills on the beach. Dennis was waved through the gate, pulled up to a house near the water, and jumped out of the car with each of us on his arms. I don't know if this was a place the Beach Boys, their respective wives, and their extended family owned like a private compound or if they had rented it for the holiday. What I remember most was the immediate vibe of disapproval as Dennis brought his stray hippie arm candy into an invitation-only affair. We weren't the only ones who received death stares. The eye-rolling revelers were equally as put out by Dennis as they were by his guests. At first I felt sheepish, but then I caught on that this was the reaction Dennis was hoping for. This was no spontaneous act but rather a carefully choreographed thumbing of his nose at his family. I knew how to play along, as we had been well trained by Charlie to fit into any scenario. Dennis's flaunting of his inappropriate girlfriends was likely a script he had acted out many times before.

Dennis surveyed the landscape and waltzed us right up to his family, with me, flower behind my ear, on one arm and golden-tanned Nancy on the other. People looked us up and down but didn't say anything to Dennis about us.

We didn't hang out for small talk. It was awkward, but Dennis seemed to be enjoying himself. He grabbed our hands and took us over to where the food was being cooked.

"Have as much as you want," he told us, and we hungrily filled our plates with hot dogs, baked beans, homemade potato salad, and sweet corn. He procured some bottles of orange soda, and we all sat together near the dock.

People lounged on boats and appeared to be having fun, but no one came over to talk to Dennis or to us. I noticed people glancing over and whispering to one another, talking about how crazy Dennis had brought these strange hippie girls to this family gathering. How we were not classy girls, and he was just finalizing his divorce. Much as I didn't like being talked about, I'd learned to tune out people's judgments of me based on my appearance. I was living a free life, and if they had a problem with how that looked, it was their problem, not mine (though having a plate of free food in front of me made it easier to ignore them).

We had a hotel room for the night, but we never bothered to go there. Instead we slept out in the sand by the lake looking up at the stars. It was late spring, and the nights were still chilly, so we all cuddled up to Dennis to keep warm. I don't remember having sex with him, but I do remember having a good time.

We were there for a couple of days, hanging out with his family, who remained uneasy in our presence but lightened up as they got to talk to us. We were polite and well mannered and thanked them for their hospitality. Dennis was affectionate and playful, splashing with us in the water and having a good time. He seemed very aware if people were watching us and made sure to draw their focus to us if they weren't. For all his fame, Dennis couldn't get enough attention. He was funny and always on. Even with his closest family and friends, he was always performing.

Dennis took us out on a boat and I lay out on the deck in the sun. Then he started whooping and hollering, driving the boat faster and faster, kicking up the wake. He seemed to have to keep moving faster than the water beneath us. We went boating and swimming for the better part of the day, mostly keeping to ourselves. At some point, his family allowed us to sit with them, drinking soda and eating hot dogs as kids ran around.

I felt embarrassed that his family didn't really want us there, but I also felt remarkably at ease with Dennis. As superficial as he was, he was fun to be around and very energetic. He was always in party mode when we were with him and rarely seemed comfortable with us one-on-one. He also didn't like to stop partying, so it was not surprising that our ride home held one more adventure, clearly Dennis's idea of fun.

As we were leaving Parker headed toward home, Dennis spotted a rocky outcrop with a thirty-foot-high cliff. We were all a little stoned and feeling mellow when Dennis pulled the car over.

"What are you doing?" I asked.

"Don't worry, it will be fun."

Dennis looked determined, so we all silently followed him through a trail that led up the cliff.

"Look at that beautiful view," he said, and then suddenly, before we could respond, he jumped off the cliff into the water. I was stunned, but one by one, Ella and Nancy followed until it was just me. I walked to the edge of the cliff and stared down at the water below. I couldn't move.

"Just do it," Dennis yelled up at me. "It's a gas."

The other girls goaded me on. I didn't want to do it just because they all had, but as I saw them bobbing in the water, they seemed fine. The drop was so high—every time I told my feet to move, they just stayed in place.

"Are you coming?" he shouted. "We don't have all day."

I looked back over my shoulder, running my eyes over the way we'd come up. Climbing down from the cliff was going to be as treacherous as jumping off it, so I counted to three and leapt.

And when my body hit the water, I wanted to do it again.

IT'S HARD TO SAY HOW OR EXACTLY WHEN IT HAPPENED, BUT NOT LONG after we came back from the Colorado River trip, several of us basically moved into Dennis's house. At first we went back and forth between his house and Spahn Ranch constantly, but somewhere along the line it became clear that he expected us to stay. There wasn't a real discussion, it was simply understood that we were living at Dennis's house full-time now.

If Charlie was impressed by Dennis or his home when he first saw it, he kept it to himself, but I'm sure Charlie had a hand in the decision to move us there. After all, he'd been giving Dennis his speech about how meaningless material things are if you are empty inside, and Dennis was nothing if not generous.

"All my love is yours, Dennis," Charlie would say as the two strummed their guitars together.

Perhaps so as not to overwhelm our host, Charlie strategically cut down the number of us that moved in. He decided we should split up for a while, sending Sadie, Mary, Ella, Patty and the new girl Stephanie Rowe up to Mendocino in the black bus to explore some connections up there. Mendocino, another hippie enclave in Northern California above San Francisco, might have been a good option for us as well as a place to find new recruits. Meanwhile, he took Squeaky, Nancy, and me with him to Dennis's house. He also brought along a new member named Sandra Good, whom I initially dismissed as a privileged prima donna. She came from money, had allergies to this and that, and was always complaining, but she went on to become one of Charlie's most devoted followers.

Needless to say, living at his house full-time was a huge shift for us. To go from the comparative squalor of Spahn Ranch to a life of rock-star luxury was a dreamlike turn that none of us expected. Over the course of just a couple of weeks we went from sleeping out in a dust bowl and eating garbage to enjoying clean sheets, warm beds, hot meals, and indoor plumbing. Dennis had a housekeeper and a pool guy; there were people in charge of making sure the property was maintained. Even Dennis's soap was expensive and fragrant.

But beyond delighting in the obvious comforts of wealthy living, I became more and more aware of the charmed nature of the house itself. I'd never been to a place like this before—swimming in the pool, walking in the trees. While the log cabin Oracle house was large and probably had been impressive at one point, by the time we started hanging out there, it was a fairly run-down hippie hangout. Dennis's home represented total luxury, if not in the decor, then certainly in the lifestyle. It felt like a privilege to be there.

Dennis was very generous with us and invited us to stay; it seemed to me that he adapted quickly to having us living with him and enjoyed our company. Meanwhile, we took good care of his needs—cooking, keeping the house clean, catering to him, and always staying upbeat and cheerful. He'd give us money to go to the store, and we'd spend it carefully, always trying to be thrifty, not wasteful. He'd order pizza and buy spumoni ice cream. He shared everything he had with us, leaving us in the house alone and never worrying about us stealing his stuff (which we didn't). We'd drop acid at least once a week, and each night we'd play music or have group sex. There was no agenda or schedule, so like so much of our existence together, each day easily blended into the next.

We were taking care of everything for the men to keep them happy. Charlie made sure if Dennis needed some loving, we were there for that too. Dennis had been going through a problem with his ex-wife—some kind of custody battle that meant he didn't see his two children as often as he liked—so Charlie asked us to keep him from thinking about it. Even though I didn't sleep with him one-on-one, it was easy to sense his loneliness.

To avoid showing these feelings to people, Dennis kept himself busy with visitors and distractions. Dennis's house was a place where people would show up unannounced to party. There were always musicians coming over to jam, and Dennis treated Charlie as an honored guest.

"This is Charlie," Dennis graciously announced to his friends. "He is the wizard, man. He is a gas." Charlie would nod to the people and allow Dennis to take center stage as if he was responsible for some great find. Charlie did things like this on purpose to make his host feel good and to give other people the illusion of his importance in everyone's life.

When other people came by, whether they were Dennis's friends or other bands passing through, they often didn't know quite what to make of Charlie. He was this odd little man, but Dennis clearly thought he was cool, so people were generally reluctant to put him down. And we did our best to sidetrack the visitors anyway—dancing, singing, often having sex with them. For many people who passed through Dennis's house, we were a novelty act, a singing family group led by Charlie who loved sex and drugs, and whatever misgivings they may have had about Charlie didn't stop them from joining in too.

Charlie was pulling Dennis into his orbit, and it encouraged the wild side of Dennis, the part that liked to do drugs, jump off cliffs, and do the unexpected. Dennis was intrigued by the idea that people could live without money, and Charlie emphasized to him that his material things were simply trappings covering over a deep need for love. He seemed to buy into Charlie's "what's mine is yours" philosophy and his rejection of consumerism, even as Charlie stood to benefit the most from Dennis's wealth. Charlie easily manipulated people like Dennis, who were trying to find their place in the era's new way of thinking. And unlike many of the current gurus, Charlie could make his nonsense make sense.

"Dig this, Dennis," Charlie boasted one day, "my girls can make you a feast out of the things you rich folk throw away."

"Prove it," Dennis laughed and took up the challenge.

That is how we wound up driving in Dennis's burgundy Rolls-Royce to the back of a grocery store and showed him the art of Dumpster diving. We all piled into the car and went to either a Ralphs or an A&P. The chain supermarkets always had the best items because they bought in volume. It wasn't as big of a loss to them to toss away items that were technically still good because they had better margins. We were experts by this time in knowing when to look for good food and knew how to pick what was still edible. Some items were still cold, which meant they were just recently taken out of the refrigerators because of some arbitrary sell-by date. The food was perfectly good.

We all laughed and sang all the way to the Dumpster, dragging Dennis by his hand. The best thing we found on this run was a flat of strawberries. After culling out the bad ones, we had enough to make him a strawberry cake complete with fresh Cool Whip. Charlie was leaning against the Rolls watching as we showed Dennis how it was done.

"Dennis, do you know how much good food is thrown out in America?" he shouted.

One of the girls popped a fresh strawberry into Dennis's mouth and we all hopped back in the car.

That night the girls and I made an entire meal with the produce and other discarded food. Then we presented Dennis with his cake.

"Hey, man, this is a rebirthday cake for you. You were blind, but now you see." Charlie laughed and we all joined in.

Dennis shook his head but dug into the delicious-looking cake.

"Got to admit it, Charlie, this cake is good." He took another slice and shoved a huge bite into his mouth. "Mmmmm, you girls can make this for me every day."

Beyond Dumpster diving, Dennis was also buying into Charlie's ideas through subtler moments. Dennis had a nice brand-new stereo/radio/turntable combination in a wooden cabinet. The sound quality was incredible—unlike any stereo I'd ever heard. One night, not long after the album *In-A-Gadda-Da-Vida* by Iron Butterfly was released in mid-June 1968, Dennis decided to put the record on, and we all got up to dance. The music was perfect to groove to if you were on acid or stoned, and we had been smoking pot all day and had a great buzz on. But as we started to dance, Dennis moved stiffly and awkwardly. Charlie had taught us all to dance with abandon. When Charlie danced, he changed his movements with every part of the music. He never did the same thing twice. It was the same way he made love.

After a few minutes of watching Dennis move like an automaton, Charlie couldn't take anymore. He wanted everyone to dance and move gracefully and fluidly.

"Hey, man, Dennis, loosen up," Charlie said.

"I am loose," Dennis insisted.

"You got to lose your inhibitions," Charlie insisted. "Like with sex. Make love to the music. Let it penetrate you."

As Dennis followed Charlie's words, his appearance changed from a man with each muscle taut to that of a man who had burst through his shackles. It was simple yet transformative, and we all witnessed the difference. I think this is what Dennis liked about us as a group. It was humbling for him to have Charlie teach him guitar and how to dance. He could be himself with us because we weren't starstruck. We liked him for who he was.

But more than just employing philosophical double-talk and liberating Dennis from his inhibitions, Charlie used his charisma to make Dennis feel important, flattering him that he was smart and talented, and perhaps most important, making him feel special. And when Charlie worked to make people feel special, they found it hard to dismiss.

At the same time as I saw Dennis being taken in by Charlie, I began to fall in more deeply as well. For months I'd been listening to Charlie talk about himself in religious terms—reciting that message of him being "Man son" and using other kinds of messianic language about himself during our acid trips. While I hadn't ignored these messages, I hadn't given them the full commitment of my belief.

The unexpected arrival of Dennis in our lives, however, began to erode those lingering doubts for me. It wasn't that the presence of Dennis's money or the comfort of our lifestyle suddenly made me think Charlie was God, not directly at least. It was more that Dennis and his home seemed to be the epitome of all that Charlie had been postulating for, the vision that he'd been cultivating finally coming to fruition.

For over six months, I'd been listening almost nightly as Charlie told us that all we had to do was ask the universe for what we wanted and it would be presented. In the connection with Dennis Wilson, it appeared that was precisely what had happened: Charlie had led us to the communal promised land—everything he'd asked for had come to pass. We were living free of hang-ups, with no more worries about where stuff was going to come from. Our anti-materialism and practice of living in the now were working. Charlie's beliefs, which themselves were an extension of ideas I had heard from my parents, were being validated more and more each day. Just the fact that he'd been able to captivate someone as famous as a member of the Beach Boys was proof enough. All at once, things felt special, like we were going somewhere. Ever since I'd joined the Family, our existence had been building toward this, gathering steam, but after Dennis connected with us, the momentum became tangible.

Of course, the irony was that rather than demonstrating Charlie's power, his relationship with Dennis instead revealed the full extent of his con; Charlie's opportunism amplified how empty his philosophy actually was. We were in the lap of luxury, yet supposedly were leaving material things behind. We were living in the moment and being free, yet one person alone was footing the bill for our freedom. While I felt our presence there was proof of Charlie's higher power, in truth, all it did was demonstrate the innate hypocrisy of everything he put forth.

Unfortunately, I could see none of this at the time. Looking around at this fairy-tale-like landscape that Charlie had supposedly turned into a reality for us, I came to believe that Charlie was as powerful as he purported to be. And once I opened the door to that possibility, it proved nearly impossible to close.

AS WE GREW MORE COMFORTABLE IN DENNIS'S WORLD, THE FAMILY kept getting larger.

In late June, although at the time I would have been completely unaware of the date, a young girl named Ruth Ann Moorehouse and her father Dean joined us. From what I later learned, Charlie had actually met Ruth Ann back in 1967, when he was hitchhiking and her father had picked him up. At the time, Dean was a minister and was probably looking for some poor soul to proselytize. He had no idea that Charlie would turn everything around on him and see Dean's dark-eyed, virginal young daughter as worthy prey.

After that ride, Charlie had sex with her and cast his spell. He didn't even try to hide it from Dean, who became so enraged he threatened to kill Charlie. While Dean flew out of control, Charlie made secret plans with Ruth Ann for her to marry someone else (definitely not Charlie), whom she would then leave for Charlie. Like so many of Charlie's ideas, somehow this struck her as a good one, because that was exactly what she did.

In the meantime, Charlie, probably in an effort to avoid being killed by an irate father, turned Dean on to LSD. I have no direct idea what Charlie said to Dean while he took his first LSD trip, but afterward, not only were they friends, but Dean became so enamored with Charlie and LSD that he left his wife to pursue higher consciousness.

Ruth Ann left her husband, thinking it made her legal, and she and her father showed up at Dennis Wilson's to reunite with Charlie. Although I didn't see it personally, people say that when Dean showed up, he bent down to kiss Charlie's feet, which must have made a huge impression on Dennis.

"Are you ready to die?" Charlie is supposed to have said. As Dean nodded yes, Charlie gestured for him to rise up saying, "Then you shall live forever."

Another person who joined around that time was Brooks Poston. As Brooks later explained to the Inyo County sheriff in a 1969 interview, he had originally come to Los Angeles from Texas seeking a better life. He was only seventeen and a self-described hayseed, but somehow he'd met Dean Moorehouse and dropped LSD with him. Dean told him about this great man named Charles Manson and brought Brooks with him to Dennis's to meet up with Charlie.

I remember Charlie sizing up Brooks, but he didn't invite him to stay right away. However, Brooks gave him his mother's credit card, which bought him some time with us. Dean and Brooks wound up spending the summer at Dennis's working in the garden and pretty much staying out of Charlie's and Dennis's way as they worked on creating music. I saw Charlie walking with Brooks outside, giving him some serious rap. Brooks later said in his police statement that Charlie talked to him about women.

"You say you want to be with us, but I have an important question for you, young blood."

"Anything, Charlie."

"Do you think you could make love to a woman in front of twenty-five people?"

"With all of them watching?" It was obvious Brooks was shy and didn't have much experience with sex.

"When you can do that without inhibitions, then you might be ready for us."

"I haven't been with too many girls," he said. This probably meant none.

"It is your job to know how to please a woman," Charlie continued. "Don't you know that all women are good for is receiving the man? If you do it good, they will do good for you. Think about that."

Bobby Beausoleil showed up at Dennis's on occasion. He was someone who floated around the music scene in L.A., in and out of places you might find Charlie. Bobby had met Charlie in 1967 when they played in a band Charlie briefly put together called Milky Way. The band played only one show, but Charlie and Bobby had become friends and saw each other every now and then.

Bobby was someone Charlie respected, so he never pressured him to stay with us for any length of time. Instead, Bobby would come and go as he pleased. Bobby didn't seem to need Charlie in the way the rest of us did—he always had his own thing going on—and because he was a good-looking guy, he always had girls of his own. He had these smoldering droopy eyes that reminded me of Paul McCartney and his lips with a slight pout like a young Elvis. And of course his "I don't really give a damn" attitude toward his women only made them want him even more.

After a few weeks living with Dennis but intermittently going back to Spahn, I was driving with Nancy to do a garbage run when we spotted Paul on the side of the road. We picked him up and brought him to see Charlie. This was exciting because I knew Charlie really wanted Paul with us, and it seemed preordained when we found him out of nowhere.

We hadn't seen Paul since our one group sex trip with him, and this time, Charlie wanted to make sure he stayed with us. He pulled me aside and told me to put on a nice dress and go spend some time with Paul. He wanted me to work my magic and I was only too happy to oblige.

"Make him feel welcome, important, and desired," Charlie said. "Seek him out at every opportunity. Tell him how happy you are he is back and that you missed him terribly."

Charlie gave me conversation starters, suggesting I ask him what he had been doing since we had seen him last. Had he written any new songs? Charlie told me to touch him when I spoke to him; to hold his hand, kiss him, and of course sleep with him.

"Snake, go make love with Paul. He digs you. Make him feel important. Fuck him good."

I did as I was told. It wasn't difficult because I liked Paul and we had a connection. He and I spent hours in the woods at the ranch talking and kissing and making love.

Charlie added to the incentive for Paul to stay by taking him to meet Dennis. It was status by association, and Charlie knew Paul couldn't resist. Charlie was preoccupied with his music and with Dennis, but bringing Paul back into the fold made me see that I could still be important to Charlie. For that I was grateful.

16

A LITTLE MONKEY

WE STAYED AT DENNIS'S HOUSE FOR MOST OF THE SUMMER OF 1968.
Charlie and Dennis would go off and do things together while the
rest of us would lie around, swim in the pool, make love, and smoke
pot or drop acid.

The more time they spent together, the clearer it became that
Charlie's relationship with Dennis didn't flow in just one direction;
Dennis was changing Charlie as well, albeit in very different ways. If
only a few people were about, Charlie and Dennis would talk about
Charlie's philosophy, but if there were a lot of strangers, they would
play music. The more Charlie played, the more it seemed people
were into Charlie's songs, and we all noticed—Charlie most of all.

To me, this was where Charlie's musical ambitions truly took
shape, where he went from having a more utilitarian view of music
as a vehicle for his ideas to focusing on the music as a way to further
himself. Sure, he'd always played for groups of people, and had even
tried his hand in that band before I knew him, but if he'd been
harboring more grandiose ambitions for his music prior to meeting Dennis, he'd been quiet about them. Dennis changed all that.
While I don't believe that Charlie saw Dennis as anything but an
opportunity, there's no doubt that Charlie took Dennis's attention
to his music as a compliment, probably the biggest that Charlie had
ever received. Dennis's encouragement filled Charlie with bigger
hopes and dreams, and because the support was coming from Dennis Wilson, the door seemed open for Charlie to capitalize. After all,

Dennis was a star—and if he believed in Charlie's music, that meant other more influential people likely would as well.

Though Charlie didn't talk to me about any of this, those of us in the Family could see that he was growing more ambitious. Looking back, there was clearly a shift. When I first met Charlie, his thing was to live without money and just be humble. He got a taste of wealth after living with Dennis. Dennis started to feed Charlie the idea that he could really do something with his music, that his songs had potential. It didn't hurt that Dennis was also going around telling everyone what a cool and wise dude Charlie was. Meanwhile Charlie became focused on wanting to make a record, mostly because of this encouragement from Dennis. They played off each other, getting into a rhythm, and this back-and-forth built up Charlie's expectations beyond anything I'd seen previously.

While Dennis was encouraging Charlie's music, he was also taking care of us at the house. Though he was young and had a reputation for being wild and irresponsible, he was also surprisingly nurturing and caring. He took us to dentists to make sure our teeth were healthy. While we were somewhat ragtag, Charlie stressed good hygiene. He wanted us clean, which was why I think he was so angry at Sadie when he surmised she'd brought gonorrhea into our group.

Despite how sexually active we were—to this day I have no idea why I never got pregnant—we were a pretty closed group. Sadie was the exception. She would pick up guys and sleep with them. She may even have been prostituting herself because she seemed to have money to bring into the group. It upset Charlie because word would get around about our not being clean.

Unfortunately, we all ended up with gonorrhea, and Dennis kindly took us all to his doctor to get treated. There were at least eight of us, and the nurse, in her starched white uniform and clean white shoes, surveyed the room from one person to the next. I followed her eyes and her crinkled nose and wondered if any of us smelled bad. We had all taken showers or baths. Charlie had insisted upon it and we never ran out of hot water at Dennis's house.

There we were in the waiting room, most of us wearing blue satin balloon pants that we'd sewn out of some of Dennis's sheets, waiting our turn. Ruth Ann Moorehouse and I were flipping through a magazine and we kept commenting on how boring the clothes we saw were. None of us could sit still, and the doctor clearly wanted us in and out as quickly as possible. Even so, our decorum rapidly disintegrated. Charlie made some monkey faces at us and sang the chorus of one of his songs, "I Had a Little Monkey." We all started singing and banging on our chairs as one by one the nurse in the white shoes took us in to face the doctor. I was laughing so hard I could barely breathe.

"Miss Bluestein," she called. "The doctor will see you now." I no longer had my ID, but no one questioned Dennis about us. I figured he must have been a good customer. She led me into a small private examining room and didn't even ask me to get undressed. The doctor used a tongue depressor to check my throat, listened to my lungs, and wrote out a prescription. He didn't even ask me any questions.

"Give this to the nurse at the front desk and she will see that it is filled," he said without even looking at me. "Make sure to take all of the pills."

That was it. In and done. I was the last one to go in, so when I came out everyone was pretty quiet and ready to go. Charlie grabbed a handful of candy from a dish on the reception desk and gave me a lollipop. We left the office singing another chorus of "I Had a Little Monkey."

Those months at Dennis's were such a happy time for everyone. Charlie was relaxed and carefree. We swam in the beautiful crystal clear pool, laughing and passing around joints. We lit huge roaring fires next to picture windows overlooking the views of the park. There was no tension—only music and each other.

To keep busy, I embroidered my orange bathing suit with flowers and other curvy paisley designs. Then we took a vest from a three-piece suit and decided we should all embroider a piece of the vest to represent our love for Charlie. We considered it like his coat of many colors. We wanted to honor him with something made by our hands. That vest went with us everywhere for the next year as each of us added our little piece to it.

Charlie also led us in acid trips, much as he had at the Topanga canyon houses or at the Spahn Ranch. We would trip—sometimes we had group sex—and then Charlie would speak to us extemporaneously about how there is no death. There is no time. There is no right or wrong. We wanted to embrace this way of thinking, and it was repeated to us in every sermon Charlie gave, whether we were on acid or not.

This world that we were inhabiting at Dennis's wasn't just changing Charlie, it was changing me as well. With Dennis around, I tried to be on my best behavior. I didn't roll my eyes or interrupt. I was no longer sarcastic or dismissive when Charlie became serious. I was no longer simply pretending to listen—not only was I really listening, I was *believing*.

In hindsight, this was when I fully gave myself over to Charlie's beliefs. More than any of his other tricks or manipulations, this time at Dennis's became the ultimate postulation. The comfort, the ease of our stay at Dennis's house seemed to validate everything about Charlie's message in a way that felt irrefutable. Whatever counterarguments I'd made in the recesses of my mind collapsed under the weight of this apparent proof. Dennis's house was perhaps his most convincing argument, a backdrop too perfect to ignore, the convergence of everything in Charlie's con—the drugs, the sex, the ethos. It all combined to transform Charlie into something godlike, someone who had real and tangible power, who had chosen us as his apostles.

There have been many false prophets besides Charlie, but even now, all these years later, I find it hard to explain what it was like to actually believe that he was a kind of messiah. It's an incredible concept, totally impossible to fathom: that the person you're standing next to or having sex with is somehow related to God. It's preposterous, hard enough to say out loud, let alone to acknowledge that at one time I felt that way. But that's what it means to be in a cult: You lose a part of yourself to someone else or to a group, so that your entire mind no longer belongs to you. If you are fortunate, as I was, it all comes back eventually and you realize just how disconnected you'd become, how far you would have to travel before you could reconnect with yourself, and how close you'd come to losing it all for good.

There are no obvious analogies to what it's like when someone has that kind of a hold over you. It's not necessarily idolatry or worship—that is too simplistic. You simply have an unwavering faith that the person has a power that no one else on earth can possibly know or wield. And when you look at someone and honestly believe that person is related to God, and that person looks at you and tells you you're special, that you matter—it gives that person a power over you that's unlike any other. The feeling is impossible to describe, and thankfully, it's impossible for me to re-create it.

The fact that drugs were heavily involved in my belief that he was Jesus doesn't make it any easier to dismiss, because it wasn't as though I stopped believing this when I wasn't high. The acid may have amplified my feelings, but it didn't create them. Charlie was growing more grandiose by the moment, and I syphoned that newfound energy into what felt like faith. Today, as a churchgoing woman who has been a faithful Christian for decades, I find it hard to admit this to myself, let alone admit it to the world. But this was how I felt in that moment all those years ago.

I'd come to the Family because I'd wanted to belong, because I was looking for a place in the world. I was gradually drawn in until I couldn't see how lost I'd become. No one chooses to be in a cult; no one seeks it out or strives for it. Being in a cult is not something you notice as it is happening—it doesn't matter if you're incredibly self-aware or if you're a teenager who can't see past her own emotions. With a cult, you believe you're on solid ground until you discover—usually much too late—that not only is your footing shaky, but it's already given way.

But that doesn't take agency away from any of us. As compelled by him as we were, we were all still people who'd had separate identities when we first joined him. We had morals, with a sense of right and wrong. True, we formed a cult with Charlie as our leader and we followed him blindly, but we were all humans with free will no matter how far it had waned. As it turned out, at least some of us were not too far gone to break the spell.

ONE DAY, WHEN DENNIS AND CHARLIE WERE JAMMING, DENNIS TURNED to him and said, "We should record this stuff."

In an instant, Charlie's mood shifted, and he got all excited. After that passing comment, he started to get serious about practicing and having us sing his best songs with him.

"It's happening. I could be bigger than the Beatles," he said as he rehearsed one afternoon. Ridiculous as the statement was, in our eyes, it didn't seem like he was reaching too high. After all, if you think someone is the second coming, it's not out of the question that he might be bigger than the Beatles. As music took on greater importance for him, we now accepted that he had a divine mission for his music to reach as many ears as possible, that his music would change the world. There was no doubt in our minds that he could achieve this goal, and working toward it made him happier than we had ever seen him.

Dennis scheduled a recording session for Charlie at his brother Brian Wilson's house somewhere in Bel Air. Charlie brought a few of us with him in the car with Dennis. The house was a beautiful two-story place, with a state-of-the-art recording studio inside. While Charlie was jamming, he let us watch. He seemed nervous at first,

which I found unnerving. Dennis told him to relax and to show the
people what he had. We had been singing some background vocals
for him, but fairly soon Charlie signaled for us to leave. He seemed
to be having trouble getting into his groove. As we headed for the
door I noticed that someone who I believe was Brian along with
some of the others were stopping Charlie and making suggestions.
Someone suggested he increase the tempo of the song. I saw the slow
burn growing in his eyes. Charlie hated anyone messing with his
music. We could feel the tension rising as we went outside.

We ran into Mike Love, who was clearly avoiding the recording
session with Charlie. We made small talk and he was polite, but he
showed no more warmth than we had been given when we went
with Dennis to the Colorado River. I got the feeling he was not
happy about the recording session or the fact that Dennis was hanging out with Charlie. Having Charlie in the studio was going out
on a limb, but Dennis really believed Charlie had a new sound the
band could support as they tried to catch up with the new directions
in the music scene.

I moved away from Mike toward the people who seemed very
comfortable partying at Brian's house. It wasn't a huge crowd, but I
wondered if Brian knew all these people or if his house was simply
open to friends and their hangers-on. One of the men invited the
girls and me to go swimming. We didn't have any bathing suits with
us, so we went in without any clothes on. If the people were shocked
they didn't show it. The pool was refreshing and everyone was relaxed and doing their own thing. I don't recall Brian's wife, but there
have been accounts that she was not too happy with us being there.
Either way, it wouldn't have mattered to us. This was important to
Charlie, so we didn't care what she thought, but we probably didn't
care what anyone thought.

While we were sunbathing by the pool, I started to hear raised
voices coming from the studio and in the house, and we all sensed
that something was wrong. The studio was soundproof, so the voices

had to have been loud. When Charlie emerged, he was seething, muttering under his breath things like "Cocksuckers, they should leave it alone." His pupils were dilated and his energy had completely shifted. The group was dispersing, and Brian and the other musicians who had been in the studio with Charlie seemed shaken. I have heard accounts that Charlie had pulled out a Buck knife when he got fed up with the attempts to "produce" him as they would any other musician. That could have very well been the case, because the expressions on the faces I saw were a mixture of fear and bewilderment. As much as they had been involved with the drug scene, they probably hadn't encountered a real convict like Charlie, with his hair-trigger temper.

I didn't notice anyone else around when Charlie came outside. I was probably in the middle of talking with someone, but it didn't matter. Someone had insulted him and he was upset. The other girls and I were all watching him, waiting to see what he would do next.

"Get your clothes, girls," he demanded. "We're going." I was already halfway out of the pool before he even said anything. I grabbed my clothes and dressed hastily as we followed Charlie to Dennis's car.

Dennis was trailing behind but wasn't saying anything to Charlie. I am pretty sure Dennis let Charlie drive, which was probably not a good idea. I remember the smell of burnt rubber as we peeled out for at least a block on the way back to Dennis's house.

When we got to Dennis's house, Charlie paced around knocking things over. He was muttering about how they wanted to change him and he wasn't going to be changed. Dennis was trying to explain that they were producers and wanted to help Charlie be successful.

"Dig it, man, they want me to dress like you dudes. I ain't gonna wear no threads like that. That just ain't me!"

"Charlie, man, they are just trying to help. They didn't mean any insult to you."

"What about changing the words to my song? 'Cease to Exist' is 'Cease to Exist,' man."

Charlie was furious. Dennis tried to reassure him that there were other options. He talked about his friend record producer Terry Melcher, Doris Day's son, and how he might be able to keep things moving. Dennis was now dangling this connection to appease Charlie and to assure him that he shouldn't give up hope.

"Your stuff is good, man," he said. "These guys don't know you like I do." Dennis had another acoustic guitar but didn't give it to Charlie right away. It would have been feeding the dragon.

Charlie took off that night and left us all there with Dennis. We figured Charlie might be going to Spahn Ranch to check on the other Family members still holed up there. It was difficult to relax, but we made some food and all sat around smoking pot waiting for Charlie to cool off and come back. Though we all tried to distract ourselves, sinking into the couch and watching a movie, it was hard not to feel that this marked the end of something. After all of Charlie's enthusiasm for the music, his effort, the recording session, this represented a clear setback. But it was much more than that. It was one of the high points of my time with Charlie, and the highest heights must always be followed by a fall. Charlie obviously wasn't ready to give up. Somehow, he had decided that Dennis and the others owed him something. To him, encouragement represented a promise. In his world, a promise was a contract, and he was going to collect when the time was right.

THINGS BECAME TENSE AT DENNIS'S AFTER THAT. WHETHER IT WAS BE-cause of Charlie or the fact that Dennis was increasingly worried he would lose visitation with his kids was hard to say. But we all felt the shift—no one more than Charlie.

For one thing, Dennis became more anxious about things and clearly was not having as much fun with us. For another, Dennis would stay away more frequently, probably with his friend Gregg

Jakobson, leaving us alone in the house while he was out with other people. Charlie felt he was losing control of Dennis, and the loss of an important acolyte always made him angry. He went as far as suggesting we "snuggle up to him," a euphemism for seduction when we needed to bring someone back to the fold. Charlie would give him the gift of all his love, including his women, and there would be an expected return on his investment. Even though I wasn't asked, I decided to take it upon myself to help out in the best way I knew how.

Dennis was always nice to me, but I'm not sure I ever even registered on his radar. I spent my time cleaning up after everyone or cooking the meals. After a while I probably blended into the woodwork of the rustic log cabin. Although we'd both been a part of the group sex sessions, I'd never had sex directly with Dennis, or at least not that I remembered. But I had watched him during our group lovemaking sessions. He was experienced and the girls pushed their way to him to take care of his needs. The only way I knew to get noticed was to burrow into Dennis's bedroom to show him what I could do to please him.

One afternoon when Dennis was out, I made my move. I went into his bedroom, changed his satin sheets, lit some candles, and took off my clothes to wait for him. I thought about how this could help Charlie, imagining intimate pillow talk with Dennis about how badly the recording session went, and offering my explanation that Charlie just worked himself up sometimes. Then as I ran my hands down his taut belly, he would tell me about the troubles he was having with his ex-wife.

After Dennis got home, he sauntered into his room, jumping back in surprise when he saw me in his bed. I was trying to look my sexiest, as I had seen Sadie do.

"Hi, Dennis," I said with my best come-hither look. I was envious of Sadie and her confidence with the art of seduction. I knew what to do when things got going, but I never knew quite how to get started. I wasn't a natural flirt.

"Hi, Dianne," he said sheepishly. "It sure is sweet of you, but I am really kind of tired." I knew Dennis had a reputation for liking sex, so it was clear that he wasn't into it with me. If I thought about it, the girls he slept with were always older than me. Even I forgot that I was only fifteen.

"Are you sure, Dennis? I could give you head."

"You are so sweet to offer, but why don't we just rest awhile."

He got in the bed in his clothes and let me cuddle up to him. Soon we were asleep. In the morning, Charlie saw me leave Dennis's bedroom wrapped in a sheet. I was hoping he would jump to a conclusion so I wouldn't have to explain what really happened.

In a group defined by its open attitude about sex, I found it hard not to take this as a rejection, and it left me feeling down about myself, looking for someone to help. That someone turned out to be Dean Moorehouse, who most certainly didn't care that I was underage. He was always trying to get me into bed. He was old and out of shape, but at this point I wanted someone to desire me, so I slept with him.

I didn't think much of it, but a few nights later we all dropped acid together. Charlie was playing his music and we were singing as usual. I went into the kitchen to pour some juice and Charlie followed me. He put his hands on my shoulders and looked straight into my eyes. "I think it is time for you to go, little one, ya dig?"

I couldn't believe what I was hearing. What had I done wrong? I'd tried snuggling up to Dennis. I'd even made old Dean happy. I became panicky. I had no place to go. I had no idea where my parents were and didn't want to leave Charlie and the girls. It was actually Dean's desire for young girls that had put some heat on the house. However, this soon became a nonissue, because it was time for us all to go.

Dennis was the first to leave. He left us there at his house and moved into a place with Gregg Jakobson. Dennis's lease was up, but he didn't bother kicking us out. My assumption is he wasn't too keen on asking Charlie to leave. This way there wasn't a lot of conflict or discussion. We helped ourselves to the things he left behind and stayed as long as we could until we were officially evicted. I know that Charlie wound up with some of Dennis's gold records, but I am not sure if Dennis gave them to him as he was shedding himself of material wealth or if Charlie simply added them to what he felt was his due. There were many things happening behind the scenes that could have explained Charlie's attitude.

We headed back to the only place we knew had room for us, Spahn Ranch and old George Spahn. Squeaky had been keeping that door open for us.

Moving out of Dennis's house was hard for me, and I was one of the last of us to leave. Naturally, it was beautiful and luxurious, but more than that, it was a place where I'd lived a few months in a row, a first since my family had dropped out. Even though Dennis's house was in no way my own, it had started to feel like home nonetheless. I'd explored every tree and knew the slopes of all the hills. The smells of the freshly mown grass and the chlorine of the pool permeated all my clothes. Life there had been a fantasy, of course, but one that I'd been eager to embrace. I was despondent to the point that I contemplated walking to a neighbor's house to see if they needed a live-in maid. At least that way I could be nearby. As ashamed as I am to admit this, I actually contemplated offering sexual favors as part of my offer. I was feeling rejected so didn't have a lot of confidence that I would even be desirable. I knew street corner hookers had sad lives. You were at the mercy of bad guys, bad drugs and disease. I thought that to do that you had to be bottom desperate. It would have been jumping from the frying pan into the fire. It is ironic that I didn't see the similarities of my situation with Charlie. I thought I didn't know much about the relationship of pimps. I didn't feel like Charlie passed me out and around. Somehow being part of a family meant I was being protected and that I was different from these other girls out on the street. What I didn't realize was I knew everything about the relationship of pimps.

Charlie let me come along with everyone to Spahn. Dirty and dusty as it was at least I was not alone and adrift. There really was nowhere else I could go. If I went to anyone in authority to find my way into foster care I would be submitting myself to the machine and to society. This would be a betrayal of Charlie and my parents. In my heart, I was invested in the "Age of Aquarius" ideals and the search for a new way of life. I knew returning to Spahn Ranch would be troubling because once again we would be nomads, drifting without a home, belonging everywhere and nowhere. But there really was no other option—this was the life I'd chosen.

17

A DOOR CLOSES

IF CHARLIE WAS DISAPPOINTED ABOUT LEAVING DENNIS'S HOUSE, HE didn't show it. He seemed to see it more as a product of Dennis's moving than a rift in his relationship with Dennis. Dennis left, so we had to as well—no big deal. We resumed life at the ranch as if those months with Dennis had simply been a beautiful dream, but it was hard to shake the nagging feeling that something very real had been permanently lost.

When we got back, we tried to regain our hold on the ranch. Charlie again had his eye on the back house, which was a better place for us than the movie sets. He was becoming more concerned about our privacy, and the back house was a desirable spot, because not only was it large enough for all of us, it was remote.

"I just want us to be left alone," he said to all of us at one point or another.

With each new location, we became more isolated from the outside world, which made us closer as a unit. No one would be able to see us from up on the Santa Susana Pass, and no one would spend the time hiking the quarter of a mile or so back there to bother us. The only problem was that when we returned from Dennis's, other people were living there, so for the time being we stayed in the different movie sets.

Perhaps because he was trying to get us into the back house, Charlie made it clear that we were to do everything we could to make old George Spahn happy. As it turned out, George really liked

Ruth Ann, so that helped. Like Squeaky, he gave Ruth Ann, her nickname, Ouisch. That one stuck too.

Fun and down-to-earth, Ruth Ann fit in well and made for great company. Since she was close to my age, she still showed signs of being a kid. We had a lot of fun pretending and dressing up in the costumes that we had all accumulated. We got our chores done, but we also spent time exploring the ranch and relaxing together. It didn't even feel weird that I had slept with her father because she almost didn't seem related to him. They were so different. I didn't trust Dean Moorehouse—Ruth Ann was the opposite.

While my friendship with Ruth Ann was a great outlet that allowed me to behave like the teenager I was, acting like that still had its drawbacks with Charlie. After we got back to the ranch, I started getting in trouble with Charlie again. He seemed to get frustrated by my behavior, which he didn't always feel was appropriate. Sometimes it was small stuff, like when he let me take the truck on a garbage run. Spahn Ranch was located near some great grocery stores in Simi Valley that we frequented for our almost daily garbage runs. But Lucky's was always my favorite. It was a smaller chain but it always had good items in the garbage. We'd now compete for the best finds of the day. On this day, I took a whiff of a container of milk that had turned sour. Instead of putting it back, I handed it to one of the other girls anyway, a slight grin on my face. When she saw me smiling, she threw a wilted cabbage at me. Charlie was nearby watching us and shot me a look that prevented what could have become an all-out food fight. I was still into laughing and doing silly things, but increasingly he felt it was time for me to grow up and made sure to tell me so.

Harmless as the look from him was, he also showed his frustration with me in more disturbing ways. One night Sandy, Patty, and I were cleaning up after dinner along with some of the other girls, and I must have been daydreaming. Charlie was getting ready for the evening speech and sing-along, and I must have been taking too long to put the dishes away.

"Snake, what are you doing in there?" he called.

"Finishing up," I replied, still taking my time.

"Snake, move it!" he shouted more sternly.

"Be right there," I answered, rinsing off the dish I had just washed.

"*Snake, I'm talking to you. When I talk to you, you drop what you are doing.*"

Before I could respond, he pushed the dish out of my hands and into the sink. Then he grabbed a wrapped-up extension cord from the shelf and beat me with it.

I never saw it coming. There was no way I was going to cry. The more he beat me, the more I held in my tears and stared him down. I was really confused, but all at once, I saw his face soften—it even looked like he gave me a wink.

"Look what you made me do. When I talk to you, you do what I say immediately. None of this 'be right there' shit. What if that was an emergency?" The others stared silently as Charlie made an example of me. "Go put something on those welts." He turned to the others and said, "This is how all you women need to be. You need a father to tell you what to do, and you damn well better listen. A real woman submits to her man. Snake is near perfect."

The pain under my skin said otherwise.

As I walked over to George's to see if he had any ice, I heard Charlie and the others singing one of my favorite songs:

Your home is where you're happy
It's not where you're not free
Your home is where you can be what you are
'Cause you were just born free

*   *   *

FOR SOME REASON, CHARLIE DIDN'T SEE THE MOVE FROM DENNIS'S AS the setback to his musical career that it clearly was. The con man in him for once had conned himself, making him believe that somehow great possibilities remained.

It wasn't that Dennis was done with us entirely. In fact, Dennis may have moved out to get rid of us, but he still kept coming around to see us at Spahn Ranch with Gregg Jakobson. Charlie hadn't given up on his music, and both Dennis and Gregg continued to encourage Charlie and give him hope that his songs could take him somewhere. Dennis and Gregg might have been stringing Charlie along because they didn't want to upset him, but they genuinely seemed to care too. Dennis and Gregg were not members of the Family, but we certainly considered them our friends. Gregg would spend a lot of time listening to Charlie, not only to his music but to his philosophy. Their attention worked on all of us because we all held fast to the belief that Charlie was going to do something with his music. He had been working on some new songs, and our nightly sing-alongs around the campfire were becoming less free-spirited and more like rehearsals. He would even stop in the middle if he wanted us to do it differently. We wanted it to be perfect for Charlie, so we would redo a chorus as many times as he needed us to do it.

I know that Charlie had his fingers in a lot of things and was doing his best to cultivate contacts in the music industry who could help him become the success he believed he should be. He was reputed to be a drug dealer to musicians, but I never saw any of this directly. He was looking for ways to connect, and good drugs were always a draw. None of us had any concept how to break into this world that Charlie had set foot into but couldn't conquer. As was true of much of his life, he was on the outside looking in, not accepted, not respected, and it was beginning to wear on him. Even though he never said anything to us directly, I got the feeling he was no longer satisfied with garbage and flies.

Whatever Charlie's musical future was going to be, eventually it was clear that Dennis would not be a part of it. Though Dennis kept coming by for a time, ultimately his visits stopped altogether. At the time it seemed easy enough to dismiss—after all, people dropped in and out of Spahn Ranch all the time, drifting in and out of our circle—but there's little doubt that Dennis probably sensed the lack of stability in our scene and in Charlie. Whatever connection he'd shared with Charlie and with us, however much he believed in Charlie's potential, none of it was apparently worth the dangers that Charlie posed. I am not sure how this happened or why, but in September of 1968 the Beach Boys with Dennis on vocals recorded a version of Charlie's "Cease to Exist," renaming it "Never Learn Not to Love," changing some of the lyrics in the song, and making the bridge and the sound to be more pop. The song, credited to Dennis Wilson as the only writer, later found its way onto a Beach Boys album.

I am sure Charlie was outraged. There are stories that have Charlie visiting Dennis after finding out about the song and leaving a bullet at his home to send a not so subtle message. Dennis did not understand Charlie and might have thought this was a way of accounting for all the money he'd spent on us. He might have been pressured by his bandmates who thought he was a fool for being with us in the first place. Dennis could be easily swayed, only now Charlie was not the one influencing him.

What he didn't count on was that Charlie had a long memory. Dennis may have stopped coming around, but Charlie's impact on his life was not going to disappear quietly.

IN LATE AUGUST, WE FINALLY MADE IT TO THE BACK HOUSE AT SPAHN Ranch. I never knew how Charlie maneuvered the people who'd been there to relocate—whether he'd convinced George Spahn that the other occupants weren't doing it justice, or simply drove them out himself. But once we got the green light, we wasted no time, spreading out and covering the floor in mattresses so we could take turns sharing them.

Charlie had always been particular about those we brought into our group, but after we got to the back house, this tendency became more pronounced. During his talk-tos, he started to emphasize how special we were compared to the rest of the world. Instead of focusing mainly on loving one another and opening our minds, he spent more time issuing warnings and evoking fear.

Still new members kept coming. A handsome young man named Charles Watson joined us. While hitchhiking, he had gotten to know Dennis, and we had seen him and partied with him at Dennis's house. That is how he found his way to us, and Charlie invited him to stay. To avoid confusion between Charlies, Charlie nicknamed him "Tex," since that's where he was from. A quiet guy who became dedicated to Charlie, Tex became something of a big brother to me. Even though we had sex during the orgies, there was never anything romantic between us. He took the time to teach me how to drive his truck, understanding that if I knew how to drive, it would give me a much-needed boost in confidence.

Some of the ranch hands also liked to spend time with us. One of them we nicknamed Clem. He liked us so much he stayed with us. He would alternate between hanging out in the back house and helping out with the chores. Tex would work on trucks and cars while Brooks and Clem worked with the horses and mucking out the stalls. Clem was not the brightest guy, so Charlie nicknamed him Scramblehead. He needed Clem around to keep the women happy; there were, after all, quite a few of us. Clem was a welcome addition because what he lacked in brains he made up for in his endowment, which seemed enough of a genetic abnormality that, one time during an acid trip, the girls and I went so far as to measure it.

Charlie gave us free rein to come and go if we wanted to—at least at first—and sometimes we'd pick up guys in town and bring them back, but it wasn't always to recruit them. There were rules about who would be asked to stay and who would not. While initially the decision seemed to be based more on personality type, as we settled in at Spahn once more, it became apparent that Charlie was now openly allowing his deeply prejudiced nature to weigh in to this selection process. One evening, several of us brought a guy up to the ranch who was an albino, and Charlie made it known that not only did the guy have to leave, he wasn't even welcome to hang out with us.

Pulling me aside, Charlie explained to me that we were special and chosen and we would not contaminate our family with someone inferior like this. He said I should have known better than to bring a white ghost albino home with me. He wanted only beautiful people who were perfect to build our future. Charlie hadn't fully laid out what he planned for us. To me, we were gathering likeminded people who believed in a better world. What I didn't know was Charlie was looking to create a better world in his own image in response to an apocalyptic vision he had yet to share. We were to become his breeding stock and anyone coming into our sphere would be adding to the gene pool.

Because I didn't harbor Charlie's prejudices, his reaction surprised and upset me. I felt embarrassed for the boy Charlie rejected just because he had light eyes and white hair—I thought he was good-looking. I was given the job of sending the boy on his way, but I couldn't bring myself to do it, so Charlie took it upon himself. He had a way of making people very uncomfortable if he didn't want them around. He wasn't very subtle.

"You can't be here," Charlie said to him. "You don't belong."

The boy was taken aback but quickly lowered his head. "I don't want any trouble, man," he said. He left quietly, but I could feel how dejected he was.

In spite of my concerns over moments like this, I deferred to

Charlie, because that's what I did any time I had an issue with something he'd said. But that was my first realization that Charlie had a plan and it was hardly haphazard. He wanted to create an actual family in his own image. Seeing his bigotry rise to the surface, as it would more and more often after this, made this more real. I had been under the impression we were simply looking for a loving group to live out his philosophy rather than building an exclusive group. As I now understood, Charlie wanted to create a family not just by recruits but through procreation.

AS WE SETTLED BACK INTO LIFE AT SPAHN RANCH, CHARLIE DECIDED IT was also time to bring back the girls—Sadie, Patty, Ella Jo, Stephanie Rowe, and Mary Brunner—who had been living in Mendocino. Unfortunately, their bus broke down on the way back. Bobby Beausoleil was sent to help them out. Though he wasn't a member in the same way that I was, Bobby was the only man Charlie seemed to respect. He never tried to make Bobby stay with us, but he considered Bobby a brother. Whenever they needed something from each other, there were no questions asked.

When Bobby picked up the girls in Mendocino, they figured out that the bus couldn't be repaired, so they bought another one, painting it light green and taking out the seats. Also with the returning Family members, Bobby brought a couple of other girls back with him. One was Catherine Share, who was also known as Minon Minette. She had a very beautiful singing voice. It didn't take long for the girls to give her the nickname of Gypsy, because she was much more exotic looking than most of us. She had sultry features and dark wavy hair and was much more hip. I knew very little about her background at the time but later learned she met Bobby when they worked together in a soft-core port film called *The Ramrodder*, which is an odd twist had been shot at the Spahn Ranch.

Gypsy looked like a mystical bohemian, but her rootlessness was not by choice. She was born in Paris but was sent to the United States at the age of two after both of her parents, who'd been Resistance fighters against the Nazis in World War II, committed suicide. She had so much talent and charisma that in another life she probably could have been anything she wanted. Her father had been a Hungarian concert violinist before the war. She had inherited his musical talent and could sing and play both the violin and piano. Her gifts could not satisfy the hole inside of her, which made her the perfect addition to our growing tribe. Charlie loved that she could sing backup for him, and like all of us, he gave her a sense of security that had been missing from her life.

The other girl who came with Bobby and Gypsy was a pretty girl named Leslie Van Houten. Even though he was ostensibly married to a woman named Gail, either by consent or default they had an open marriage, and Leslie was his girlfriend of the moment. She was hanging all over Bobby when she came to us, but all of us knew that Bobby was not the kind to stick around very long for anybody.

I was glad when Gypsy decided to stay on with us, but when Bobby took off and left Leslie with us, I wasn't so sure. She looked too perfect with thick straight dark hair, a turned-up nose, and highly symmetrical features. When she smiled, she had perfect teeth that seemed to take up her entire face. She wasn't that much older than I was, but she had gone to high school and had been a homecoming princess. The story was that even before she graduated she was experimenting with drugs and had gotten in trouble with her family. They sounded to me like nice people who were just looking out for her, but she wanted to ditch the life they were living, so she took off.

After Bobby left her behind, I tried to be kind and not possessive, but Leslie rubbed me the wrong way from the start. And I don't think I was the only one who wasn't sure about Leslie. Sadie had always been considered the sexy one in our group, but now

Leslie, as the new pretty girl on the block, was real competition. It didn't help that Sadie was also visibly pregnant. She could still flirt, but she couldn't move around very well with what looked like a watermelon in her belly. Sadie carried differently than Mary had. During her pregnancy, Mary seemed to glow with the beauty of motherhood. Sadie was the opposite, resembling a seal with flippers flapping around a belly full of fish. She couldn't use her sexuality to gain attention, so instead she would whine that she didn't feel well unless she was doing something that a woman about to give birth shouldn't do, like riding horses or getting high.

In early September, Paul hitchhiked with Sadie, Mary, Ella, Stephanie Rowe, and Patty to escort them back to Mendocino for a court date on drug charges. According to the local newspaper and a hearing transcript, when the women had been in Mendocino, they'd gotten into trouble because they had given LSD to a minor. In an article in the *Ukiah Daily Journal* June 24, 1968 the girls were being called the "witches of Mendocino," and their aliases had been used in the newspaper, which infuriated Charlie. None of them used their real names, but he still didn't want this case to be traced back to us.

The charges were dropped for some of the girls, the court accepting their argument that they were simply in the wrong place at the wrong time, but Mary Brunner had to face the music to the tune of sixty days in jail. For her part, Sadie plead guilty to what was then felony possession of marijuana, and given three-year's probation with a suspended sentence of sixty days in jail.

On the way back, Paul was picked up by a girl we ultimately nicknamed Juanita. She had a van and an inheritance, so when she picked up Paul, he used his wiles to entice her back to the ranch. When she was introduced to Charlie, he treated her as though she was the only woman in the world. I had watched this act so many times by now that I could practically recite his rap by heart. But it worked—much as it always did, and as it still did on me.

Juanita joined us and decided to stay, and so did her money. This was a good thing because it bought more time for us with George. He owed back taxes on the ranch and we used Juanita's money to pay them. George was grateful, so he didn't pay attention to any of the complaints by some of his ranch hands. One guy in particular, a ranch hand named Shorty Shea, really didn't like having us around and spoke to George about us. He and Charlie would figuratively beat their chests at each other, but it all seemed harmless at the time.

IT WAS OCTOBER 7, 1968, WHEN SADIE WENT INTO LABOR. CLEM RAN TO find Charlie, yelling all the while as if he were Paul Revere announcing the arrival of the British. The labor was early and unexpected unless you considered that she wasn't practicing great prenatal care. Charlie seemed put out when he came running, wiping his hands with a rag. He must have been in the middle of a car repair because he was out of breath and covered in grease.

We all dropped everything and gathered around Sadie and got her onto a bed. A birth was a huge and exciting event, but whenever anything happened to Sadie, it took everyone's energy and created chaos. We made sure she was comfortable and warm. We all knew that this baby was not technically Charlie's. Sadie got pregnant by the guy we all called Old Bruce, who had been my fake husband John Bluestein. It didn't matter. This was our baby and was part of our extended family. Anything we did for Sadie, we were also doing for Charlie and our future.

Charlie took charge and told us to boil water and sterilize things such as a razor blade. We were all gathered around her on all sides while Charlie talked her through the delivery. Mary, Ella, Squeaky, Sandy, Stephanie, Katie, Ouisch, and Paul watched eagerly as the baby's head crowned. It felt like we were all giving birth.

After the baby whooshed out in a pool of fluids and afterbirth, Charlie told me to cut the baby's umbilical cord with my teeth, which felt like an honor. It may have been because he could sense a little jealousy between Sadie and me. I both loved and hated it when she treated me like a little girl. Charlie was always trying to ease any conflicts between us so we could all live in perfect harmony.

"This is how people have done it for thousands of years before doctors got involved," he said to ease my hesitation. I took my job very seriously and made sure to separate the baby from its mother with a clean bite. Charlie tied up the cord with what looked like a guitar string. The baby was small but really cute. After the baby was cleaned off and wrapped in a blanket, Charlie looked at his face and kissed his forehead.

"We should give him a powerful name."

"What about Caesar?" Paul quipped.

"Better yet, Zezo, a complete original." Then he added Zose Zadfrack to finalize the alliteration. "That is his name. Zezozose Zadfrack Glutz." Then we all joined in laughing. "No one else will ever have the same name as him."

18

ON THE EDGE

GIVEN THAT NEW MEMBERS WERE STILL FINDING THEIR WAY INTO OUR ranks, it's not surprising that Charlie was looking for a bigger and better place for us. He kept his eyes open for opportunity, and the strange commune down the road in Box Canyon was an ideal place for him to infiltrate. At the time I didn't think much of it, nor did I connect it to the uncertainty surrounding his music. It was hardly perceptible at first, but things were shifting. Charlie's tone had changed. His grandiosity, still ever present, was taking a darker turn.

Long before I'd met him, Charlie had created his philosophy, such as it was, by putting together different ideas he'd encountered throughout his turbulent life or in prison. Though he was functionally literate, the power of his auditory memory allowed him to recite things even if he'd heard them only a couple of times. He often quoted a mishmash of statements from the Bible and other sources, using them to support his speech as if he were a divine messenger. While in jail he'd also grown familiar with Dale Carnegie's *How to Win Friends and Influence People*, taken classes on the power of positive thinking, and learned the tenets of Scientology, pieces of which he wove into his rambling sermons. With each new idea, his focus morphed, which could make his messages muddled and confusing, but I didn't question any of it. In my state of mind, everything he said or did made sense, something that was supported every time I looked around at the circle and saw heads nodding in agreement with his words.

But just because he was leading his own group now didn't mean that he stopped absorbing new ideas from others, especially if they supported his own views. And so it's not entirely surprising that as Charlie tried to grow our ranks, he turned to the Fountain of the World, a compound nestled into a nearby shaded forest, not just to recruit them as potential members but to merge their ideas as well.

While I can't say for certain how Charlie found out about the Fountain of the World, because it was close to us, perhaps he and Paul simply stumbled upon it while exploring the area. After all, with an ominous aura that made it clear something strange existed behind the trees, it wasn't hard to spot. There were several buildings made of stone, some appearing to be built into the side of the mountain, but there were also some ruins that left evidence of their martyred founder.

The Fountain of the World was a religious order based upon the spiritual teachings of Master Krishna Venta, who lived from 1911 to 1958. Krishna Venta and his acolytes had formed a commune in Box Canyon in the Santa Susana Mountains near Simi Valley. They were dedicated to humanitarian service. The members wore robes, grew their hair long, and went barefoot; the women wore scarves on their heads. Barefooted and otherworldly, Krishna Venta and his wife toured England, and the Fountain of the World provided disaster relief when needed, such as assisting in firefighting and providing food and shelter to those affected by floods or natural disasters.

Or at least this was the popular image that people had of Krishna Venta. In truth, the California mystic was ahead of the guru trend that would emerge in the 1960s. Krishna Venta claimed that he was Christ, the new messiah, and claimed to have led a convoy of rocket ships to Earth from the extinct planet Neophrates. There were also plenty of overtly apocalyptic undertones to his message, including talk of a coming race war between blacks and whites.

While Venta himself was killed in a suicide bombing at his compound in 1958, parts of his message were still alive and well when

Charlie took us to visit the Fountain of the World. He brought us all there to listen, learn, and ingratiate ourselves over the course of several weeks. The women wore robes of different colors in accordance with their assigned roles in the community and looked like nuns. They were welcoming and invited us in for meals and shelter. They told us about the different artisans and scientists who were going to help the world. The women explained that they had nurses, carpenters, and craftsmen whose robe color matched their talents. Whenever one of the women would get me alone, she would discuss the rules they lived by and point out how much they were contributing to the world.

Still, beneath this sunny vision of their work, I found the place unsettling. For one thing, the Fountain of the World compound was spooky and dark even in the daylight. But even beyond the superficial, I didn't like the energy of the people, in spite of the members' outward warmth and kindness. Their excessive flattery also raised my suspicions. Maybe it takes a recruiter to know one, but I didn't trust them. Though the meals were far better than what we had been eating at the Spahn Ranch, I was interested in no one but Charlie as my guide and didn't want to hear about their martyred leader Krishna Venta.

Another unsettling thing was the cross they had on top of the hill. It was intended to look like the place where Jesus was crucified, and the women explained that once a year when Krishna Venta was living, he would reenact the crucifixion by staying on the cross. It was their holiest of days. Perhaps because of this, we weren't respectful of the cross. We dropped acid on the hill underneath it and made love with one another. We didn't include the Fountain members, but it is likely that they knew what we were up to. For all I know, Charlie wanted them to know.

While Charlie never seemed to buy into their belief system, he did have an ulterior motive for our presence. It was as though he and Paul were trying to stage some kind of takeover of the Fountain of the World. They had much nicer accommodations and an existing membership. Charlie probably tried to indoctrinate the remaining members of the Fountain of the World into believing that he had now picked up the mantle of the second coming by using his typical techniques. He likely tried to sexually seduce the women with his charms about inhibitions, failing to see that he was using a sixties approach in an attempt to influence a cult that had been formed around the values of the fifties. They were into purity and had no reason to give it up to Charlie. They probably saw through him and perhaps even considered him the devil. Perhaps they were right.

Either way, Charlie came to recognize that they had no room in their lives for a second messiah, especially when the first one was already a martyr. For all his arrogance, even Charlie knew he would never be able to compete with a memory.

We didn't leave the compound peacefully. There was definite conflict, loud yelling, and a great deal of chaos before Charlie finally told us to get into the bus to leave. We had been going back and forth there for several weeks, and Charlie was visibly unhappy that all his efforts led to nothing more than some meals and some new ideas to add to his rap.

This was the first time I'd witnessed Charlie get rejected like this as he attempted to manipulate people into joining him. While it didn't shake my faith in him or that of other Family members, it did elicit a change. We left the Fountain of the World in a hurry and returned to Spahn Ranch, where Charlie could maintain his leadership, but after that, he seemed more driven. Rather than dwell on the rejection, I think Charlie was inspired by and impressed with the devotion the Fountain Members had not only to their dead martyr but to a philosophy. The structure of their cause had generated a power that outlived Venta. As he did with everything, Charlie seemed to analyze what made the Fountain of the World successful most likely so he could incorporate it into our own growing cult. If Venta had inspired devotion to such otherworldly ideas, perhaps

Charlie could as well. Charlie was learning how to be a leader of a flock who would follow him anywhere, to any idea no matter how insane. The only question was where it would all end.

WHETHER IT HAD TO DO WITH THE FOUNTAIN OF THE WORLD OR HAP-pened by coincidence, Charlie's lectures took a definite turn toward the apocalyptic as we settled back in at Spahn Ranch. They also became much more racist.

Though Charlie had always shared his bigoted views with us about the tensions between white and black people, for the most part, he aired those beliefs only when it was just Family members around. Now Charlie brought these up more often, becoming more serious when he spoke to us and focusing on stories about black men he'd met in prison. He described how they were going to rise up from being oppressed. When he spoke about this, it sounded less and less like he was giving a sermon and more like he was addressing his troops. His tone was unnerving.

Even the acid trips became less fun. Before, our trips were about bonding and love, and we could lose ourselves in the music or focus on one another and the anonymous body parts of our group lovemaking—that had been the experience that resonated with me, that made me feel wanted and needed. Before, the whole point was to escape into our own world without fear; now fear seemed to be the goal, and I was definitely becoming frightened.

During one acid trip, Charlie led us into a bonding exercise with one another in which we passed energy hand to hand. I was definitely aroused, but instead of having us make love, Charlie grew serious and told us how important we were to the future of our race.

"What goes around comes around, and it is only a matter of time before the universe will balance itself out."

He went on at some length about the coming race war, and when he dismissed us, I went out into the woods away from everyone. My head was spinning from his warnings and prophecies, so I lay down in some grass to get into a better space. I struggled to keep things together and not give in to my fear of what Charlie was telling us, but it was hard to dismiss his words. The mind can find meaning in seemingly disparate events, especially on acid, and what I saw from my vantage point was a man whose own observations and increasing delusions appeared to connect the dots to something bigger than all of us. Confronted with the reality he was constructing for us, I didn't see him as a con man or a manipulator—I saw him as my protector, my guide, my lover, and my friend. I trusted him to bring us to safety, and if some kind of race war was brewing, he would be the one to show us how to defend ourselves or at least how to stay out of the line of fire.

The darkening of his rhetoric didn't change the way I saw him. I was in too deep for that. Charlie was still a light, someone who would protect us and would make things right even if the inevitable was to happen. I never looked behind the curtain to see what the wizard was hiding there—I took things at face value. Ridiculous as it was that there could be a race war between blacks and whites, the picture he was painting felt plausible, as did the idea that we would be caught up in the middle of it. By convincing us that racial tensions were driving us toward an inevitable conflict, Charlie shifted our focus to the only thing he had always understood throughout his life: survival. If I wanted to get through the inevitable for which Charlie was preparing us, I would listen and learn. And at least I was with people who could protect me. After all, Charlie seemed to have a plan.

While it's easy to see these new delusions as simply the product of a bigoted mind becoming increasingly disconnected from reality, disappointment over his stalled music career was almost certainly playing a role in his transformation as well. Nothing much was happening with his music, and the discussions around it became more about his frustration than about any kind of record deal. He was more concerned about his message being lost in the slow-paced wheels of an industry that wanted to mold and change him. He started talking about his music as a mission, maintaining that his words were important to the world. If only the music industry and those who played its game could see who he really was, they would stop being arrogant and broadcast his message. Although he would never admit it, I am sure Charlie felt the same sense of rejection that anyone would feel; this was heightened by his belief in a divine appointment. He wasn't about to dress the way they wanted or change the words to his music; these obstructionists weren't seeing what was coming down and they were going to be sorry that they didn't.

With this serious tone around everything, I tried to act more mature, but it bothered me that Charlie was changing from the apparently free-spirited creature he'd been when I first met him. He was no longer playful or fun, and the lack of companionship from him left me painfully lonely. I'd been living apart from my family for almost a year, and in that time, I'd replaced their presence in my life with the love I'd received from the group and from Charlie. But now we were no longer about love and sex, and I missed that affection.

I did my best not to become envious that Susan and her baby got all the attention, but I still felt resentful. As many times as I had sex, I had never gotten pregnant, and it had become a source of immense disappointment for me. As a needy fifteen-year-old, I believed that by getting pregnant, I could bring Charlie's favor back to me. Charlie had tried to impregnate me once, but it didn't take. What I didn't realize was that at that point I really couldn't become pregnant, since stress and malnourishment had caused my periods to stop almost entirely. Perhaps this was God's way of watching over me.

Charlie was also determined to add even more people to our group, especially women, so when Bobby would bring someone around or a new potential member would arrive, Charlie would shine his light of affection on her. If someone had asked me directly how I felt watching his dance of seduction, I would have told them I didn't care that Charlie was with other girls. But in truth, it was eating away at me. I loved the other girls, but they couldn't make me feel like Charlie could. When I would see him talking to someone else or playing the guitar, I couldn't help but fantasize that he still loved me best, even as it felt more like whatever purpose I'd served for him had passed. If he would just spend some time alone with me, I could once again feel as if I was the only person in his universe who mattered.

No one ever asked to be with Charlie. When he wanted sex, he would nod at you and signal for you to come with him somewhere. But I was tired of waiting. His withdrawal was more than I could handle. Maybe he was testing me to see if I was strong enough to ask for what I wanted. In my mind, I played back scenes of Charlie's telling me to speak up in the group. He hated it when I was silly, but he encouraged me to use my mind.

"You are no dummy, Snake—say something." I knew that I would hesitate before speaking. I never wanted to be wrong about anything. Then he would become impatient and move on to someone or something else.

In the end, I was less afraid of this mythic race war than I was of never being loved by him again, so I watched him and waited for the right time to approach. Unfortunately, this was a huge miscalculation on my part, not the first and not the last.

One afternoon I found Charlie sitting alone on a rock outside the back house. He seemed relaxed and lost in thought. This seemed like a good moment to make my move.

"Hi, Charlie," I said, cautiously trying to gauge his state of mind.

"What do you want, Snake?" I had his attention so I went for it.

"I want you, Charlie," I whispered in his ear. I also gave him a little kiss on the cheek. " I want you to make love with me."

"Oh, you do, do you?" I thought he was pleased with me as he smiled mischievously. He took me by the hand and we practically skipped into the woods. My heart was pounding with expectation. He was moving a little fast, but he seemed playful.

We stopped in front of an old gypsy caravan that must have been used as a prop for a movie or television show. It was nestled in the woods, so we would have all the privacy we would want. He helped me up and followed right behind me. I could feel him pressed up against me. Something about this excited him.

The gypsy caravan was a lot bigger inside than it looked. There were comfortable pillows and blankets strewn about, and you could stand up without hitting your head. Of course, I am pretty short and Charlie wasn't much taller, but it was roomy by anyone's standards.

Now that I had gotten Charlie alone, I waited awkwardly for him to make the first move. He liked to be in control, so I waited to see what he wanted from me.

I smiled at him but he didn't smile back. I didn't know what to make of his demeanor. He was like a changeling, switching from a soft loving expression to that of a storm about to touch down.

"You want me to make love to you?" I nodded but didn't say anything.

"*You want me to make love to you?*" he practically shouted at me, as if what I was asking was absurd. I hadn't seen this side of him before. He appeared enraged, like he would just as soon hit me as have sex with me.

He grabbed me by the arms and pushed me against the wall with my back facing him.

"Charlie, what are you doing?" I asked. This was not what I was expecting from him. I had done things I didn't enjoy with men because I felt I had to, but I had never felt frightened or in danger from anyone—until now.

"Little girl, you need to know that you can't always get what you want. You need to learn some serious lessons about life." He pushed my head forward so it hit the wall, ripped down my skirt, and entered me from behind.

I stopped hearing anything but muffled sounds as I tried to escape the moment. We had tried all types of positions, but I had never had anal sex before, and it hurt. My body automatically tensed to try to prevent him from penetrating me, but he was too forceful, pulling my hair back as he thrust inside. It felt like I was being ripped apart. Hot tears streamed down my face.

"This is what I got in prison. Is this what you like, little girl?"

When he finished, he pushed me down on the pillows and glared at me. I could barely breathe. He pushed his way out of the caravan and left me there, sobbing and gasping for air. I'm not sure how long I stayed there, but the first thought I had was that I wanted to die right then and there, to disintegrate into nothingness. My heart and my spirit were broken.

It was dusk before I gathered up the nerve to come back to the movie set jail where we kept some of our clothes. We also had some of our mattresses there. I was supposed to help with the cooking, but instead I went down to the stream and sat in a little trickle of water flowing from a few days of rain, my blood forming little rivulets of red in the runoff.

As if in slow motion, I climbed up on the cliffs overlooking the clearing where we had camped and had had so many fun evenings singing songs and dancing to Charlie's music. I walked to the edge and looked down. It would be so easy to keep walking right off the cliff to a thirty-foot drop. Then I would show Charlie that I understood the real meaning of death. I didn't feel afraid. I felt nothing.

The sun was setting and everything was going dark. I stepped closer to the edge and inhaled. As I lifted my foot to take the next step, something stopped me. I felt my heart lift and release the sorrow that had built up inside it. It seemed that someone or something was with me. The empty place inside of me was filled by a feeling I did not recognize. Here I was, so close to the edge that I kicked some dirt into the stream below. Then, as if someone took my hand, I moved back. Somehow I knew that it was going to be okay.

19

BAKING SODA BISCUITS

I WAS A LOT MORE CAUTIOUS AROUND CHARLIE AFTER THIS. I DIDN'T know what to call our encounter, because thinking about it made me sick. I knew it was not what I wanted, but it confused me. If I had asked him to have sex with me, could I really call what happened rape? Of course, now anyone would say it was, but back then I still didn't even realize that my grandfather's anatomy lesson had been a form of sexual molestation. I had no understanding at all that I was in any way a victim.

The rape and its aftermath had a profound effect on me. My sense of my place in the group, already fragile for weeks, was lost. The feeling of belonging that had drawn me into the Family almost a year earlier, that had grounded me and made me feel like a part of something bigger than myself, had been ripped from me. Just as Charlie had given me a home in the group, he just as quickly had taken it away. Not only was Charlie becoming more serious and intimidating in front of us, he was apparently also changing in private as well. The person I'd encountered in that caravan was not the man I'd followed all those months ago. I'd always known he was capable of violence, but I'd never thought he was capable of something like this. And now, in the wake of what happened, I had no idea what to do.

What it didn't do was force me to leave. Distraught as I was, it didn't take long for me to start rationalizing the rape much as I had the random beatings I'd suffered, thinking that he must have had his reasons, that he was somehow justified in his actions, that I'd deserved what happened. Difficult as this logic was to accept, buying into it felt like the only way I could move on—I had no other alternatives. I was fifteen and on my own, with nowhere else to go. I hadn't spoken to or heard from my parents in months, so I didn't even consider them as an option. I had no family to turn to other than the Family, which left me with no real choice.

My only strategy was to study Charlie's moods even more closely than I had before, making sure to do whatever I could to avoid provoking him. While it wouldn't necessarily save me from random punishments, it would hopefully allow me to stay in the Family. If I was included in the day-to-day activities, my role in the Family was secure. Belonging to something was all I really wanted anyway.

During this time, Paul was the one bright spot. While I couldn't tell him what had happened, he at least took my mind off things and gave me someone to hang around with. Because Charlie frowned on exclusive relationships, Paul wasn't like a real boyfriend, but he was someone I felt I could trust. We'd find time alone together to make love. He was playful and lighthearted, often playing the flute for me while we lay in the grass listening to the stream and the birds.

I did my best to put what had happened with Charlie out of my mind—a difficult task, but one that was made easier by the new buzz going around the ranch. Charlie had a new plan for our Family—he wanted us to go into the desert.

Like most things with Charlie, the plan had begun through random talk that he spun into something bigger. Ever since we'd moved to the back house at Spahn, it had been apparent that this still was not isolated enough for Charlie. As talk of the race war became more of a fixture in the evening sermons, he'd taken to focusing on where we should go next and how we needed to be able to retreat to different places once the race war broke out. Scary as this talk was, I could tell from watching him that he was looking to put something real into motion. When he wasn't preaching to us, Charlie was constantly lost in his thoughts; you could practically see the wheels turning in his mind as he plotted our next move.

Then, as if he'd postulated for her, a girl named Cathy Gillies showed up, and almost immediately she became the answer to the question that only Charlie was asking. When I first saw Cathy, I didn't think there was anything remarkable about her. In fact, she would have been just like any other girl who joined us, except that she had an idea for a place we could "retreat" to, a place in the desert where we could go to live away from everything. Her grandparents owned a ranch house in Death Valley in a spot so remote it was perfect for us. Cathy—dubbed Capistrano by George Spahn, later shortened to Cappy—fit our needs perfectly, and her serendipitous arrival seemed like further proof of Charlie's ability to manifest what we needed.

It was Halloween of 1968 when we all took our first trip into Death Valley to see Myers Ranch. Cappy's grandparents were part-time miners but were likely part of the migration during the Depression, when many families sought to escape the food lines by establishing claims to land they perceived as the last frontier. The claims were for mining, which gave people the legal right to build a home on government land. Some people used the homes as a potential livelihood, an answer to homelessness, or in later years as a retreat when they simply wanted to get away from city life. The mining life was not for everybody, which is why the home they called Myers Ranch was available.

The ranch was located through the Goler Wash near the Panamint Range, which forms the western barrier of Death Valley. We had no experience traveling in the desert through the canyons and dirt roads, but Charlie trusted Cathy to lead the way in one car while we followed her in the bus. It takes an amazing amount of fortitude and energy to get to this place. If Charlie hadn't trusted Cathy I don't think we would have had the perseverance. The terrain was treacherous, with the only sign of life being the occasional sighting of the wild burros that lived in this area. It was certainly in the middle of nowhere. The last connection to civilization was the little town of Ballarat, which was more a cluster of buildings than a proper town. Ballarat, now officially considered a ghost town, sits at the foot of the entrance to Goler Wash, the only direct path up to the ranch. We stopped in Ballarat to get soda pop and shoot the breeze with the few grizzled old miners who ran the small store there. All they had were a few candy bars that looked as ancient as they were and a rusted-out refrigerator that hummed loudly as it cooled down the pop.

I hadn't seen Charlie smile for a long time, but he didn't hide his pleasure as he surveyed the mountains, a king admiring his new kingdom. The desert would suit our needs, and now he had high hopes for the accommodations. We got as far up the wash as we could before we had to park the bus and hike in. We each grabbed as much as we could carry and trudged upward for several hours with nothing but the occasional jackrabbit to telegraph our arrival.

When we got up to the ranch, I was one of the first to run inside. It reminded me of the cottage Goldilocks might have discovered in the woods before the three bears arrived home, a place where you would expect a grandma to come out at any moment with a tray of cookies and a glass of warm milk. Cappy took me from room to room, and we both jumped on one of the beds, which was covered with a comfortable chenille blanket. Rather than chastise me for acting like a kid, Charlie watched and smirked, which caused me to relax for the first time in weeks. We were all relieved that something had lifted the gloom off Charlie's shoulders, if only for a moment.

The next stop was the kitchen, and it was love at first sight for me. In the kitchen was a Hoosier cabinet, filled with glass jars containing flour and other foodstuffs. Nancy Pitman, who had also come with us, had a look at the jars and then glanced back at me. We both burst out laughing and said, "Biscuits!" For the first time in a long time we could bake something warm and delicious for everyone. Charlie gave the go-ahead to get started. Before we began baking we all ran outside to look around the house. It was an oasis. There were pomegranate and fig trees, similar to the Garden of Eden.

The cottage was spacious and comfortable. There was a fireplace, a pool of some kind, and even a guesthouse. There was plenty of room for all of us, and it was very neat and tidy. As soon as everyone settled in, the other girls and I went to work to make baking soda biscuits. We rarely, if ever, had so many ingredients to work with. We made a feast, and most of us were able to sit at a real table for the first time since we were at Dennis's house.

"This place is a gas," Charlie told Cathy.

Being new to the group, she didn't seem to realize how significant it was to see Charlie hopeful about something. A free spirit who was fun to be around, Cappy was about three years older than I was, and before coming to Spahn Ranch, she had been a groupie who liked to hang with Buffalo Springfield. That was about all I knew about her because after she mentioned the desert cottage, that was all everyone talked about. She was a miracle for the group and the hero of the hour.

Perfect as the ranch seemed, our time there was short. After a week or so, Cappy made it clear that she didn't really have permission for everyone to stay *permanently* at the ranch and that there could be a problem if her grandparents decided to return. At another moment, this news might have been devastating to Charlie and caused him to explode, but he didn't react as I would have expected. Interestingly, he didn't seem upset at all and went on with business as usual. He and Paul spent time in Ballarat and looked around the desert while leaving us to relax and wait for our next move. As always, I was confident Charlie would figure something out.

A few days after Cathy's announcement, Charlie and Paul informed us they had noticed another place about half a mile away that was unoccupied. The Barker Ranch was built about the same time as Myers Ranch and with the same legal support—a home for a mining claim, even though the original owners never used it for that purpose. It was built as a hideaway, so in some ways it was better suited for our purposes. Charlie and Paul had investigated the place and found out through a guy named Ballarat Bob, who was the local keeper of town gossip, that it was owned by a woman named Arlene Barker. Mrs. Barker was now residing in Indian Springs, a nearby town, and had no plans to go back to the ranch, which was why it was going to seed.

Almost immediately, Charlie started working to secure the right to stay there. Charlie met Mrs. Barker with flowers in hand and a story about how he worked with the Beach Boys and was a musician who needed a quiet place to create. To prove his story, he gave Mrs. Barker one of Dennis Wilson's gold records. It was just the right kind of currency to seal the deal.

"We got the place," Charlie told us when he got back from Indian Springs.

"Yeah," Paul piped in. "You should have seen Charlie. He had Mrs. Barker eating out of his hand."

"Well, thank you, kind sir." Charlie did a fake bow with exaggerated hand gestures. He was back to his old happy self. Or so it seemed.

We all smoked some dope that night and sang. Charlie was too hyped up to make love to any of us, so we all just went to sleep.

"I been thinking about this," Charlie announced in the morning. He appeared like he had not gotten much sleep. "We should go back to town and get our things together. We also need supplies so we can make it through the winter. That also means money and vehicles that can handle this terrain."

We started rolling up blankets to put in our backpacks when Charlie announced, "Snake, you and Nancy are going to come with me to Las Vegas. We can get some supplies and see some friends of mine."

Charlie took Nancy and me with him, while Paul, Cathy and the others headed back to Spahn. I had never been to Las Vegas, so I was enthusiastic that Charlie had chosen me to go with him and Nancy to get the supplies. I was eager to see the Strip and the slot machines, and my eyes had to adjust to the lights as we approached the main drag of the city. We passed signs for two-dollar steaks, which made my mouth water. We saw women dolled up in fancy dresses, high heels, and makeup, their hands resting on the arms of men with gold chains around their necks.

Charlie, though, showed no signs of slowing down.

We whizzed right past them to a run-down motel on a seedy back street. I was hoping this was a shortcut to some other location, but Charlie pulled over and parked, telling us to wait as he went to knock on a door. The door was opened by a large man who seemed to know Charlie. I couldn't hear anything, but they were laughing like a couple of old friends. He didn't seem like anyone Charlie would know from San Francisco, so I figured he was someone from the joint.

After a few minutes, Charlie pointed to me as I slouched down in the back seat. I wasn't hiding really, just postulating that I would become invisible.

Charlie came back to the car and said, "Now, girl, you know exactly what to do."

"With him? Charlie, do I have to?"

Charlie glared at me, and I became really frightened. I started to cry.

"Now don't you go on crying. You agreed to go on this trip, didn't you? Well, this is part of it. You go on in there and do what Charlie taught you."

I held back my tears. "If you say so, Charlie."

The motel room had a cheap bedspread that was scratchy under my bare legs. The man had showered, so at least his shaggy hair was wet and not greasy. I tried not to look at his face because I was afraid I would cry. My body went numb, but I knew what the man wanted from me. Well, at least I was good at something.

He sat next to me, and I slipped onto my knees, hoping that he couldn't hear my sobs. Eventually, he turned me over and had sex with me. I tried to imagine I was on an acid trip and in the other room watching what was happening. That this was happening to someone else, some person that was not me. Nothing worked, so I just waited until the man was finished. I hated that I was doing this, but it was what Charlie wanted. I'd already learned what would happen if I displeased him. As soon as it was over, I went into the shower, turning the hot water on and sitting on the hard floor. I scrubbed until my skin was red, staring down at the blue tiles on the floor clustered in small square patterns that never repeated precisely no matter where I looked.

Charlie was waiting for me outside the motel door. The back of the car was filled with supplies and canned goods like vegetables and powdered milk. There were also bags of rice. He took me back to another motel room where Nancy was waiting for us. I wondered if she had to do what I just did. She got back in the car, and we took off for Barker Ranch, leaving the lights of Las Vegas behind. As he drove, Charlie handed me a sandwich and a soda. No one spoke for the entire ride.

WHEN WE RETURNED TO BARKER RANCH, IT BECAME APPARENT THAT this move to the desert was making Charlie's plans for us more complex. I started to realize just how much Charlie had going on.

Even before we'd left for the desert, I'd noticed that bikers from a club called the Straight Satans had started showing up at the Spahn Ranch. Charlie invited them to partake of our food and instructed some of the girls to be nice to them. Tex and the guys also hung out with them, and they seemed to have the job of acquiring vehicles at Charlie's behest. Vehicles and car parts showed up at the same time as the Straight Satans, so it was not difficult to figure out why they were with us and why Charlie wanted everyone to be nice to them. The biker men were intimidating and seemed dangerous. They even smelled different from the guys I was used to, a combination of nicotine, anger, and lust.

Once we were out at Barker Ranch, the relationship with the Straight Satans became a bit clearer as Charlie explained our greater need for vehicles. As I would later learn, the Straight Satans, including a guy named Danny DeCarlo and his cohorts, were helping to "borrow" dune buggies or other vehicles that could be retrofitted to traverse the rough terrain of the desert. What I didn't know was that Danny DeCarlo was also responsible for bringing guns to Charlie when he eventually felt we needed them for our protection. I personally never saw them or shot them.

Similarly, one day, as if by telepathy, Bobby Beausoleil showed up with some Dodge power trucks for Charlie before speeding out of the desert on his motorcycle. The trucks were crucial because Barker was so isolated—daily garbage runs were a thing of the past—and with so many of us living together out there, we needed ways of stocking up. These trucks would become fixtures of our time in Death Valley. (Even today, a truck that was probably the one Tex Watson drove remains in Ballarat like a ruin from a natural disaster.)

Even with the trucks, we still needed supplies, which after several weeks at Barker were dwindling. Charlie said it was time to go back to Vegas, which was the closest big city to Death Valley, and my stomach clenched. Thankfully he wasn't going along on this trip, which meant no visits to sleazy motels. Instead he sent Paul, Juanita, and me on our own, and away from Charlie's watchful eye, we were even able to go see the Beatles movie *Yellow Submarine*, which had just come out earlier in November. We dropped acid, of course, and just generally cut loose, which felt liberating after the heavy burden that Charlie had placed on all of us. The movie didn't disappoint, and right afterward, we drove to Las Vegas still tripping, as I re-played the images from the movie over in my head.

When we got to Las Vegas, we had a chance to utilize the skills Charlie taught us about postulating for what we needed, which naturally included some conning, stretching of the truth, and out-right lying. Employing charm and flattery, we went to different stores and asked for donations for the victims of a desert flash flood, walking away with some very generous contributions. The bulk of the haul was bags of rice and powdered milk, but we also scored ketchup packets. I guess people felt flash-flood victims needed con-diments. This meant we would be living on what the desert rats told us was called cowboy soup. At least it was something, and the price was right.

Perhaps in celebration, Paul gave us each an additional tab of acid, but this time I had one of the worst trips I had ever taken. Maybe being back in Las Vegas had triggered my paranoia, but for the first time during an acid trip, I was completely horrified. I got separated from Paul and Juanita and wound up wandering through a hotel until I heard someone in a room playing the flute. I thought the flute player might be Paul, so I went into the room and tried to hide under the bed. There was a strange young man in the room, but what was even stranger were the knives I thought I saw coming through the walls.

When Paul caught up to me, I was under the young man's blankets, sobbing uncontrollably. The next thing I knew, Paul had wrapped me in a blanket and led me back to Juanita's van. We slept in it overnight, and by the next day I had come down. Paul, con-cerned, asked me if I was okay, but I couldn't talk about my experience. This was the first time I felt abject terror. Unfortunately, it would not be my last.

WHEN WE GOT BACK TO BARKER, WE DISCOVERED THAT CHARLIE HAD changed the plans again.

"Snake, Paul, Juanita, and Brooks, you are all going to stay up here until we send for you or until we get back. We want you to fix it up and get it ready for all of us. We have some things we need to do in town until we all come up here together."

This was not what I was expecting, but what made it worse was that he changed his mind again and told Paul to come with him, leaving me alone with Brooks and Juanita, two people I didn't know well, in the middle of nowhere. While they were nice enough, they were latecomers to the group, and although I liked Juanita, I didn't know her like I knew the other girls. I couldn't understand why Charlie was singling me out—I'd done everything he wanted me to do.

"It won't be too long," Charlie had tried to reassure me before he left, but I didn't believe him. Maybe this was his way of getting rid of me.

Brooks, Juanita, and I were supposedly there to fix up Barker Ranch, which had been neglected for a long time. There was a lot of work to be done from cleaning to dressing it up. Juanita and Brooks spent time together exploring and getting high, while I created a path to the front door, using broken bottles and other pieces of glass I found strewn about the place to create a sort of mosaic. Although the desert was dusty and forbidding, the Barker Ranch, like Myers Ranch, was in an oasis, full of trees and wildflowers. It wouldn't be so bad turning the place into a home for everyone. I made a circle of white rocks around the base of one of the trees; it remains there to this day.

It was starting to get cold at night, so I had to make sure to keep the fire lit. Brooks and Juanita played cards a lot, but I wasn't interested. They seemed to like each other, which made me feel even more left out. I was bored and depressed, resentful that I was being ostracized. I found myself thinking back to all the times my parents had chosen something else other than me. This felt like that, only worse.

As if in answer to my prayers or postulation, Bobby Beausoleil showed up one day out of nowhere on his motorcycle and wanted some girls to go with him to help him panhandle. I am not sure if Charlie knew he was coming up to the ranch or if it was happenstance. Either way, it didn't matter to me. I jumped at the chance to go with him. I put on a jacket and hopped on the back of his motorcycle.

Bobby was steady on his bike as he took us the back way out of Barker Ranch through Death Valley. I held on to his waist, looking back over my shoulder as the mountains receded in the background. I should have been happy to be riding off to freedom, but knowing that I'd disobeyed a direct order from Charlie, I became overwhelmed with the sick feeling that I had made a terrible mistake. It was the same feeling of abject terror that I felt in Las Vegas on my acid trip, only this time, I was completely straight. This was no flashback. This was a flash-forward to something that wasn't right.

20

OUT OF SIGHT

BOBBY AND I STOPPED FOR A ROOT BEER AND SOME GAS, AND THEN sped toward Los Angeles. Bobby knew right where he was going, and apparently it wasn't to panhandle. Instead he took me to a little yellow house with two stories and pillars in the front and a guest-house in the back at 21019 Gresham Street in Canoga Park.

As Bobby and I pulled up to the curb, I held my breath for just a moment, wondering just which version of Charlie would greet me. It didn't take long to find out.

"What the hell are you doing here, Snake!" Charlie bellowed when he saw me get off the back of Bobby's motorcycle. "I thought I made it clear that you were to stay up in the desert."

"I—"

"You what? You didn't listen to me. I am going to find your parents so you can go home to them. I told you not to disobey me no more."

"I—" Bobby didn't say anything or come to my aid. He just went in the house, which would have been spacious had it not been for the number of people crowded inside. Charlie continued to glare at me as I stood frozen in the doorway.

"Get out of my sight. Go help Sadie."

Gypsy gestured toward the guesthouse, but no one said a word, so I skulked away before I could bring more of Charlie's anger upon myself. He said he was going to find my parents, and it sounded like more than an idle threat. I had no idea where they were but if Charlie wanted to find them he would.

Sadie was in bed in the guesthouse. She looked awful and jaundiced. Patty intercepted me, and before she let me in the room, she told me that Sadie had a contagious form of hepatitis and that I should give her some soup and make sure she was eating. Patty said to let her sleep, since that was what was best for her. When I was left alone with Sadie, I curled up on the floor and put my head on my knees. I tried not to cry but couldn't help it. I would get yelled at if I woke up Sadie and I didn't want anyone coming back here to see me like this.

Sadie partially opened her eyes and smiled weakly at me. "Hi, Snake," she said softly. I put a compress on her head and tried to feed her the soup. She didn't want it and rolled over to the other side. When she woke up later, she saw I was still holding the bowl of cold soup and tousled my hair. I wasn't sure if I wanted her to touch me in case I could get her disease, but I was happy at least someone was glad to see me.

"Sing me a happy song," she croaked. Her usually loud voice was hardly more than a whisper. I was scared that she was too sick to get better. I had never seen anyone I knew die. As much as Sadie annoyed me, she was a sister and a friend.

"Your home is where you're happy . . ." I started.

Sadie fell asleep to my a cappella singing, and I did too until Patty came in to wake me up. Patty was wearing a loose-fitting dress and had taken a shower. Her hair smelled clean. Mine felt dirty and I hadn't changed my clothes for several days.

"Hey, Charlie wants us all together. Come on, hurry up." She took a quick look at Sadie and said, "You shouldn't spend too much time in here."

"Charlie—"

"You don't want to catch what she has."

I followed Patty into the living room of the main house. Everyone was sitting on the floor or on the scattered pieces of furniture. There was a wide space in the front of the room where Charlie was pacing back and forth. He would start to talk and then would stop and look around the room to make sure everyone was sitting there and paying attention.

I looked around the room at their faces. Tex, Leslie, Ouisch, Paul, Mary, Nancy Pitman, Sandra Good, and Gypsy had all come to the house at Charlie's request. I don't remember if Squeaky was there or back at Spahn Ranch taking care of George. I took my place with everyone else and tried not to draw any attention to myself. Perhaps if I did everything right he wouldn't kick me out of the group.

Charlie's demeanor seemed very different. In his hand was a Bible, and nearby a record player was plugged in. It had been weeks since I had seen him, but just looking at him, I grew frightened. He wasn't the same person who left me at Barker Ranch; even his face looked different. It was wild-eyed and it was clear he had an agenda. The changes must have been building for a while, but after being isolated at Barker Ranch, they were immediately apparent to me. I searched his face for something familiar, but he was like a man possessed with a singularity of purpose that left no room for frivolity. For someone who'd showed us a thousand faces, this was one he must have kept to himself until now. It was terrifying and exhilarating at the same time. I had been there since the beginning and didn't want to be left out of what was now seeming more like a mission.

In the years since, I've thought back to this moment, seeing him address us at Gresham Street, as the point of no return. That hesitation I'd felt on the back of Bobby's bike, that sense of menace wasn't just about disobeying Charlie's order, it was a sense of foreboding, of what was coming down, of the shift that had been going on while I'd been isolated at the ranch. All was suddenly laid bare. From here on out, whatever Charlie was putting in motion, whatever his goals would be, they would bear no resemblance to the person he'd been or the Family that we'd been just a few months earlier. Whatever bound us together had dissolved and in its place was a darkness that none of us could clearly anticipate.

Charlie held the Bible up for everyone to see and began to speak gently. We all sat around enraptured by his presence and the importance of what he was saying. I had heard the story before, but today it felt like a revelation.

"Some of you already know what happened when I first took the sacrament of psilocybin." Several of us nodded, but kept silent.

"Mary, you were there."

Mary Brunner smiled and nodded. She was all but glowing with pride.

"In some way, you were all there. You know the truth. I am just reminding you in case you forgot. We were on a mattress and Mary, my Mary, my Mary Magdalene was at my feet. It was beautiful."

Then Charlie's voice got louder; it was booming. "Then I was on the cross. I was on the cross for all of you." He arched his back, looked at the ceiling, and put out his arms as if they were on the cross. "They nailed my hands, they speared me, and I wore the crown of thorns for all of you. And Mary wept as I died for you."

Mary Brunner was crying and we were all getting worked up into a frenzy.

"I fought it for as long as I could," Charlie added. "Then I shouted out in agony: 'God, why hast thou forsaken me?' Then it all became clear. I had to give up. To live, I had to give everything up and simply surrender to death. And that is what I did. I died for you all. And, after I died, I saw the world through everyone's eyes."

I looked around the room and everyone was crying. I was crying for Charlie, but I was also crying for myself. I didn't want to be sent away. I wanted to be good enough for Charlie. I no longer saw

Charlie as a mere man. Even in his cruelty and inconsistency, he had a reason. Maybe he wanted me to stay in the desert for my own sake because of how much he truly loved me.

Charlie walked around the room and placed his hand on the shoulders of each of us as if to impart God's love. I was overjoyed that this might mean he had changed his mind about sending me away. I overrode the fear I felt leaving the desert to absorb the joy of the moment. Unfortunately, that moment was short-lived, as it took Charlie only a few days to locate my parents. I would not be given a reprieve after all.

IT DIDN'T TAKE CHARLIE LONG TO FIND MY FAMILY BECAUSE IT TURNED out my mother was living in a house just a few blocks away from Gresham Street. My mom was now with a man who I had never met, and they were living with Danny and Kathy acting as house parents for an alternative school called Summerhill. In exchange for watching over some of the students, they got to live in the house. The crazy thing was their house was around the corner from Canoga Park. They were practically living within walking distance to Charlie and the girls, and I'd had no idea.

Charlie didn't tell me his plan to return me to my mother until we were in the car driving over. Upon learning the news, I didn't feel even a hint of relief; all I felt was rejection. The one promise I expected Charlie to keep was that ours was a family I could count on—and by returning me to my mother, he was breaking that promise. I sat sulking as he started in on me.

"I told you to stay in the desert and you disobeyed me. When I tell you something, you have to listen to me. There is some heavy shit coming down. I can't have someone like you doing your own thing all the time."

"Charlie, I said I was sorry. You left me there for a long time."

"Snake, I gave you an order. I had my reasons for leaving you up there. You disobeyed me. And you are underage. I don't need no underage kid hanging on to me like you do."

This made me start to cry, but he flashed me a look that stopped my tears. I held his gaze longer than he wanted me to because I wanted to memorize his face. This felt like the end. Once again, I had no choice about where I would be and with whom. In the moment when I thought I would be leaving the Family for good, I forgot about the beatings and the brutality. I imagined this might be what death feels like.

As I walked into the house, all my family members were surprisingly happy to see me, even my mom's new husband. Chance was also there. Evidently they had all become friends. My father and my mother's new husband even did some repair work together and named their company the Fixateers. Chance was teaching art at the alternative school and showed some unexpected enthusiasm when I arrived.

None of their warmth mattered to me. Once upon a time I would have loved nothing more than to come home to find my family waiting and ready to welcome me, but it had been too long—I was too damaged, too transfixed by Charlie, the group, and what the Family meant to me. I'd been in Charlie's orbit for too long—simply changing the scenery from the Family to my real family wouldn't be enough to deprogram me. A different setting alone wouldn't make me forget what I'd been through, what I'd shared, or what I was missing. All I could think about was Charlie and the Family and how I could return to them. I also believed I was part of a mission and was needed in spite of Charlie's displeasure and rejection.

I agreed to stay to check it out, but from the start I knew I would never really give it a chance. That first night was awful. I kept singing Charlie's songs to myself. Everyone from the alternative school seemed far from alternative. They were square and privileged. My first impression was that this was a school for rich kids whose parents were playing at being hip. I wanted to tell the students about Charlie's philosophy, to make it clear to them how they were playing follow-the-leader into an establishment trip. Instead I just kept my mouth shut and bided my time.

I lasted two whole days before I escaped and hitchhiked back to the Gresham Street house. I don't know if my parents were surprised or disappointed to find out I'd left. On some level they probably assumed that my visit was destined to be short-lived. At least now they knew where I was staying, even if I didn't want to be found.

I found the Gresham Street house easily enough. I'd tried to memorize the directions when Charlie was driving, but its bright yellow color was a dead giveaway to anyone in the area. The house had been nicknamed the Yellow Submarine, so when I described it to the person who picked me up hitchhiking, he knew exactly which one I meant.

When I returned to the Gresham Street house, Charlie didn't seem all that surprised to see me, but he wasn't going to let me get my way. This time, though, he didn't show his anger. Instead he just told me to get into the truck, taking me directly to the house of a man named Gary Hinman. Gary wasn't a member of the Family, but he was a friend. He lived alone in a modest house in Topanga Canyon and was the kind of guy who opened his doors to hippies and people he considered his friends no matter how little he really knew them. A chemistry major in college, at that point he was close to earning his PhD from UCLA in sociology. During the day, Gary taught music, worked at a music store, and was very good on the piano, the trombone, and the drums.

Bobby Beausoleil introduced Gary to us because Gary let him stay in his house when Bobby needed a place to crash. Gary was older than Charlie, with a receding hairline. He was effeminate, and I'd always thought he might be gay. That made me like him even more because he had a gentleness about him that seemed more female and nurturing. Though Gary never fully joined our group, we treated him like part of the Family and he was welcome to be with us and to have anything we had.

As we sat in the car outside of Gary's house, Charlie gave me clear instructions. "Snake, you be good to Gary so he will let you stay a while. You can't be around right now. I have too much to take care of and you don't listen very good."

I nodded, took my little bag of stuff, and went up to Gary's door. Gary didn't ask any questions. He simply invited me in. It was probably pretty obvious that I was an outcast and that Gary would have to watch over me until Charlie figured out the next move.

"What did you do to make Charlie so mad?" Gary asked me when I plopped down on his couch. He must not have seen Charlie really mad—this was nothing—but I was surprised he jumped to that conclusion. I downplayed the situation so Gary wouldn't think I was in any trouble, and immediately offered to make him some food. His apartment was kind of messy. All kinds of instruments, including a set of bagpipes, were strewn about his house, lying on top of his papers and books.

"I can make a sandwich for you," he said. "It's no bother."

Charlie had drilled into us that the woman's job aside from sex was to cook and take care of the man. I wanted him to get a good report about me, so I insisted that Gary let me take care of him.

"That would be kind of nice," he relented. "I am usually the only one here."

I made some peanut butter and jelly sandwiches with whatever I could scrounge in his refrigerator. I put some potato chips on the plate. I found some Oreo cookies too and added them to the menu.

Gary exuded none of the tension I had been feeling from Charlie and the Family at Gresham. As I unscrewed my cookie and licked the center cream, he showed me his prayer beads and explained about his Buddhist faith. He was planning a trip to Japan some time the following summer. He recited the Buddhist vow of Nam-myoho-renge-kyo to me which means to embrace one's Buddha nature to end suffering. From what I later learned, these were the words on his lips as he took his last breaths.

Things were quiet for a few days. I enjoyed the atmosphere and it was certainly better than being with my family at the alternative school, but I still wasn't where I wanted to be and we both knew it. After a few days and some meaningless but nonthreatening sex, Gary saw that I was unhappy and asked me about it.

"It's nothing personal, Gary. I really like you."

"The only problem is before Charlie brought you to me, he made it clear he didn't want you back at the house with all of them. Maybe that is better, even though it isn't what you think you want."

I pondered what he was saying, but the force pulling me back to Charlie was too great. This time I knew if I disobeyed him, there would be hell to pay.

"Where can I take you?" Gary was also not going to defy Charlie. Even though he was not an official part of the Family, he was someone averse to conflict. We decided he would take me to Spahn Ranch because at least Squeaky would be there and I could eventually catch up with everyone when Charlie wasn't mad at me anymore.

When I got back to Spahn Ranch, I was surprised that another commune had moved into the space where we had been living. There was no one that I knew, just a few faces I recognized from our time at Spahn, and it was unsettling to see a bunch of strangers in a place that had felt like home. Gary's car was long gone when I realized how truly alone I was again. After a while someone from this group noticed me sitting by myself on the boardwalk by the old fake saloon.

This commune seemed similar to ours. They were into psychedelics and shared everything. They had tried to live off the land, but they didn't know how to do it. So now they were making a deal with George as we had done, to help out until they could figure out their next move. There was a great deal of idealism everywhere, but people still had to eat. The communes that had been cropping up everywhere during this period were beginning to see the realities of life beyond the aphorisms. Unlike Charlie's Family nothing was holding this group together but a common interest in psychedelics and one another.

The members of this group were older than me, but they decided to invite me to hang with them. It was obvious I was underage, and for all they knew, I was a runaway. They had seen me with Charlie, so they didn't make a big issue out of my presence. We all dropped acid together and I had another terrible trip. Maybe it was all the confusion falling in on me or the fact that I was with strangers, but I guess I wound up sitting in a hammock, looking frozen. I wouldn't speak to anyone, so they must have reached out to Charlie to rescue me. They had no idea what to do with an underage catatonic who was not their responsibility.

And with that, someone from the Family came to get me, and once again I ended up back at Gresham Street.

21

PREACHING THE WHITE ALBUM

AS I WALKED THROUGH THE DOOR AT GRESHAM STREET, I HOPED I WAS coming home for good, but as I'd soon learn, there was little about our group that I recognized as home anymore. Even though it was the beginning of 1969, I had not even acknowledged that a new year had turned.

When Charlie saw me, his expression was one of resignation. He was clearly unhappy with me but signaled for me to sit with the group on the floor. As I scanned the room, I noticed a new dark-haired girl, whose name, I later learned, was Barbara Hoyt. She wore glasses and was more full-figured than most of us. She had left home after an argument with her father and was picked up by some of the girls when they saw her sitting by the side of the road. Charlie took her on a motorcycle ride and brought her into the fold.

It was already late afternoon and Charlie administered acid tabs to each of us. The last thing I wanted was another bad trip, but now that I was back with my family, I tried to relax and let the drug's power ease into my consciousness. Charlie was sitting in the front of the room with a candle to light up the book he was reading.

Charlie broke the silence and began to preach. "Dig it," he began. "It is time you all know the truth," he exhorted. "When Jesus came the first time, the Romans killed him. The establishment didn't recognize him, and God let him die on the cross. Well, God let me die for you too. Only now God is angry. He says his children have not followed his rules. He says we have been destroying the planet, we are bad to the young ones, and we hate the creatures of the earth. So he is going to make it right." Tears filled my eyes.

"That is why he sent me," Charlie continued. "He sent Man's Son to straighten things out. Blessed is the one who reads aloud the words of this prophecy, and blessed are those who hear it and take to heart what is written in it, because the time is near."

That made me shudder. It reminded me of something he'd said in the car when he was sending me to my mother's house, words I didn't fully understand at the time but that would later make sense: "There is some heavy shit coming down."

During my first night back at the Gresham Street house and for several nights after that, Charlie read from Revelations. Given that he wasn't a skilled reader, it was unclear how much of it he'd memorized and how much he was ad-libbing, but most of the time we would drop acid and listen to him talk for what seemed like hours. Then one night he did something different. He pulled out the new Beatles album, which was completely white on the cover with the exception of the embossed letters spelling out the group's name. This of course came to be known as the White Album.

He played the album over and over that night and for many nights after that, because he wanted it to penetrate our consciousness. The record quickly became a fixture in the background. He played it constantly, dissecting it in his mind and even playing it backward. He also started alluding, quietly at first, to the fact that the Beatles were talking to him through the record, though he didn't say precisely what they were saying, just that these four prophets of God were speaking directly to him through their music. All at once, the White Album became the soundtrack to Charlie's rants. Until one night the record itself became the prophecy.

Charlie was particularly agitated that evening, pacing back and forth and mumbling to himself. He signaled for us all to sit and listen, but I made the mistake of not going to the bathroom before taking my place in the corner. Once Charlie commanded us to sit, there would be no getting up without retribution.

Charlie stood in the front of the room, punctuating his speech with his hands. "The Beatles know what is coming down! They know and they have been looking for me."

He let the words sink in, wanting us to appreciate the magnitude of what he was proclaiming. He had been so intoxicated with this epiphany that he didn't take the time to prepare us with any sacraments of acid or even our usual joints.

"Dig it, the Beatles know all about Revelations and what is going to come down. And they have been sending me messages through their music. They have been looking for me. They know that Man's Son is here on earth to carry out this mission, but they haven't known who I am."

We'd been listening to the album for days, but this statement went far beyond anything he'd ever said about it. Before this night, the thoughts he expressed were more like mutterings and musing; nothing was fully formed. As odd as it might have sounded to those not in his group, Charlie seemed to be on to something. He was ecstatic and appeared irritated that the message, something he expected all of us to immediately embrace as his chosen recipients of the divine revelation, did not elicit the electric response he had hoped. He was almost jumping out of his skin, he was so adamant.

Charlie put on the White Album. I avoided looking at the others as the sound of "Back in the U.S.S.R." surrounded us, but rather concentrated on the growing pain of my full bladder. I tried to breathe softly to lull myself into a meditation. This time he turned the music up until it was so loud we could clearly hear the lyrics of the songs.

"I haven't told you the entire picture," he said. "It is time."

"What do you mean?" one of the girls asked. I didn't turn to see who it was. The pressure in my bladder was becoming unbearable and I was doing my best to talk myself out of it. When Charlie didn't snap at her for interrupting, I took this as a good sign that I could get up to go to the bathroom. As I started to rise, Charlie pointed at me and glared. His eyes were ablaze.

"Snake, where do you think you are going?"

"Charlie, I have to pee really bad," I implored.

"Then do it, but don't you dare leave when I am talking to you."

I couldn't hold it in. It was a combination of weak bladder control and terror at what he would do to me in front of everyone. I'd had my share of beatings and fists to my face, but something told me these would all pale in comparison to what would happen if I left in the middle of this sermon. I felt the warm liquid dripping down my leg and onto the rug. No one looked at me or said a word, but I was humiliated.

Charlie continued while the music played in the background, launching into his speech about the race war and blacks and whites; only this time he took it a step further. This time he made it about the Beatles and how they too knew what was about to happen.

Then when the album was over, Charlie played it again and told us all to listen carefully to the words. "This will tell you everything that you need to hear."

The first song he played was "Blackbird," and we all listened to the words.

"Don't you see!" Charlie insisted. "The Blackbird is the black man. It is as plain as anything. And now they are ready to arise."

Charlie then quoted from Revelations: " 'For the lamb at the center of the throne will be their shepherd; he will lead them to springs of living water. And God will wipe away every tear from their eyes.' This is why we have to go to the desert. I will lead you to the springs of living water and we will wait out the tribulation. It's happening and we have to prepare."

Charlie's expression was unrecognizable. This Charlie was so convinced that to disagree with him or question him would have been futile. It all made sense, at least to him. He was connecting the dots in ways that supported the reality he'd created.

As I sat in my own urine, but without the benefit of LSD, I forced myself to pay attention to Charlie's every word. In the past, it had been difficult to view the race war he was describing as anything other than an abstract concept. If I had been left to my own interpretation of the White Album, I certainly wouldn't have made the complicated connections Charlie now heard in the music. But because all his postulating had made him otherworldly, this grandiose direct link to the most famous musicians on earth seemed like it could be true. He had shown us he could be taken seriously by a member of the Beach Boys. When down is up and up is already down, it wasn't a stretch to add the Beatles to our reality about Charlie. He could guide us to see not what was there, but what he wanted us to see—whether it was finding edible food in the garbage or convincing us that the Beatles knew on a subliminal cosmic level that the lyrics to their song "Sexy Sadie" were really about our own Sadie Mae Glutz.

From this day forth, Charlie displayed a sense of desperate urgency. We were moving beyond concepts and messages in music; now he would be teaching us to survive. We were his Family, but we also became his soldiers—the only people who could validate his vision of the future. The problem was, Charlie's prophecy was a self-fulfilling one for us; cut off from the outside world, we had no way of knowing if the ideas he was conveying were in any way accurate. There was no other explanation of our world beyond the one Charlie crafted for us.

To be clear, I believed it much as the others did, but if any part of me had seen imperfections in his disjointed logic, I would have made excuses for them as I had for the other chinks in his armor. Every time he beat me, I bought into his rationale that I sought punishment as a means of attention, and that he was conditioning my mind with pain to prevent me from doing things that would hurt the others. When you are isolated by groupthink and told you are chosen and special, it is difficult to resist. As difficult and absurd as it is to admit, in this moment, I saw all he said about the Beatles as being totally plausible. I was guided by fear of Charlie and of an uncertain future, clinging to this Family, I believed, was my only source of protection.

AFTER THE WHITE ALBUM REVELATION, OUR ENTIRE ROUTINE CHANGED— whatever connection we had to the recent past ended. Everything became about actions and preparedness. We had to get ready. The rest of our time at the Gresham Street house was spent in indoctrination, drug-fueled or not, and exercises to help us rise above our fears.

"If you are afraid, you will not survive," Charlie repeated over and over as he had us show him how much pain we could tolerate.

One afternoon he called me to the center of the room where he had lit a candle. "Snake, hold your hand over that flame."

I obeyed his command and held my hand over the flame until I could smell the burning of my skin. I flinched from the agony and Charlie became enraged.

"Pain is an illusion," he said, his voice rising. "You feel pain because you were taught to feel pain. If you are afraid of feeling pain, you will never survive what is coming down."

More than rage, there was disgust in his eyes as he glared at me. All at once, he took a chair and smashed it into pieces. Before I could react, he took a part of the chair leg and beat me with it until I was bruised and bleeding. Then he pushed me to the side. He had everyone take a turn at the candle while I sat against the wall, trying not to cry.

When Charlie introduced the Beatle's White Album, the songs became his shorthand way to illustrate what was coming down. The song "Helter Skelter" became the key, because it sounded like chaos and destruction. From then on, that song title stood as our not-so-secret code name for the race war between blacks and whites and the coming apocalypse.

Then he decided that the Yellow Submarine house was too overcrowded. It had become very overheated with so many bodies crammed into a small space, and the tension was palpable. One of Charlie's friends knew that the group Iron Butterfly was going on tour, and he volunteered to break us into their now-vacant mansion. It was near a correctional facility, which is probably how the man knew about it. Charlie's friends often had the same questionable past as he had. Charlie had connections everywhere and kept track of them until he completely used up what they could do for him. This house gave us a temporary break, like a calm before a storm, and though it was not as luxurious as Dennis's house, it offered Charlie an opportunity to jam with people through the unwitting kindness of the Iron Butterfly, who left their expensive musical equipment behind.

After a few weeks, we all returned to Spahn Ranch, which Charlie somehow managed to reclaim. Everything was different. Gone were the whimsical days spent playing dress-up in the movie sets, making love, or singing by the campfire. When he wasn't training us, he was poring over massive topographical maps of Death Valley and the surrounding area that he'd managed to accumulate so he could plan different escape routes to the desert. Charlie was singularly focused on these maps, which he had taped together and spread across the floor of the saloon. Like a mad scientist plotting the path to Mars, Charlie insisted there was a direct route from Devil's Canyon to Death Valley. He spent hours studying the maps, so we left him alone and went about our regular chores.

In the middle of this descent into madness, there was a moment of possibility that could have changed the direction for all of us.

Even though he had stopped talking about it to me, Charlie had never given up on the thought that he could do something with his music. He had gotten a taste of recognition and in spite of Charlie's anger at Dennis he kept his connections in the industry alive. Finally, in the spring of 1969, after months of trying to arrange it, Charlie was able to get Terry Melcher, Doris Day's music mogul son and the co-producer of the Monterey Pop Festival, to come out to Spahn Ranch to hear him play. This was probably arranged at least partially as a way to appease Charlie, who was still outraged over the recording of "Cease to Exist."

Terry had actually been coming around for a while, though I wasn't aware of his presence or importance until we started preparing for this special visit. A part of the same circle as Dennis and Greg, Terry hung out with the Family for a while, presumably using our drugs and sleeping with some of the girls. A former producer for the Byrds who'd been heavily involved with the sound of the sixties music coming out of L.A., Melcher was exactly the type of person Charlie had been aiming to impress—the kind of guy who could launch Charlie's music career.

Whatever Charlie did to postulate for this visit didn't matter to us. We all prepared for Terry's visit by rehearsing, cleaning, and cooking. Charlie's mood changed, which meant that at least temporarily the sun could peek out from behind heavy storm clouds. A record deal would mean a lot of things to Charlie—recognition for his music, reward for his ideas, but perhaps most significant, income.

Terry arranged for us to record at a real studio. That is how I remember it. He listened to Charlie, first at the ranch, and then got our hopes up with an actual session. Brenda, Ouisch, Clem, Paul, Sandy, Squeaky, Gypsy, and I all backed up Charlie with our soulful harmonies. It felt as though magic could happen and that we were finally getting it right. I prayed for Charlie to get what he wished for because it always seemed to slip through his fingers.

"It's going to happen, Charlie, it is going to happen!" Squeaky shouted as we all danced together when we were finished. We all cheered and I know we expected the good news right away that would change everything.

As days passed with no word from Terry, Charlie's patience was brief. Because Charlie had nothing but time on his hands, he became more and more focused on leaving for the desert. It was clear we couldn't wait for Terry Melcher, as any day wasted would be a day we could be caught unprepared.

Charlie reached out to Terry to find out what was going on, but the answer was not what he wanted to hear: Terry simply wasn't interested in helping him get a record deal. Charlie was livid. He thought he had a deal with Terry and the rest was just details. Now it turned out that his last chance at music stardom was lost.

"Those motherfuckers don't keep their promises!" Charlie shouted.

He was of course irate, but there was also a disappointment I wasn't used to seeing in him. It was obvious he had been counting on this break and was not used to hearing the word no. Charlie always had things in motion, working other plans and other angles. This was the first time he'd hit a real dead end since I'd met him. As hard as he tried, nothing he could do would suddenly produce a record deal—it seemed his power, such as it was, did not extend to the music business.

For the next week, Charlie stayed by himself and barely spoke to any of us. He took long walks in the hills, as if he could find the solution to his problem up there. Terry Melcher may have been done with Charlie, but Charlie wasn't done with him.

THE END TO THE DREAM OF CHARLIE'S MUSIC WAS A FAILURE ON SEVeral levels, but it reflected a very real immediate problem for us: We needed money. The possibility of money that the record deal had represented had kept things going. Without that potential, we looked for new ways to fund our move to Barker Ranch. As it turned out, most of these were criminal.

We were all told to think of ways to bring in some cash. Tex and the guys continued to steal cars and work on dune buggies with help from the Straight Satans, who helped out by either doing the work or providing the stolen vehicles being retrofitted. Meanwhile Sadie, who had been earning extra money at a go-go club in L.A., suggested we create a nightclub in the saloon at Spahn Ranch. We named it Helter Skelter and decorated it with streamers, Day-Glo colors, black light posters, and a strobe light. Makeshift as it was, the club drew in people from Simi Valley, which in turn brought some heat from old George. We were attracting too much attention to the place and had to shut it down.

Though it didn't last long, the nightclub expanded Charlie's horizons. The road we were on was popular with a lot of motorcycle gangs, and they'd learned about us because of the short-lived nightclub and Charlie's reputation for good drugs and pretty girls. While we already had some of the Straight Satans helping Tex with cars, now Charlie doubled the effort and invited other bikers to become regular visitors. More unsavory characters than usual began showing up, and I did my best to avoid them. Danny DeCarlo, a Straight Satan, was one of the bikers who became a more regular member of our group. He stayed with us most of the time because of a conflict with his old lady, and because he was having an affair with a girl that we nicknamed Simi Valley Sherry. The bikers made me uncomfortable, but thankfully Charlie didn't push me to make them feel welcome. For the most part, the bikers had sex with whoever was willing. I was given more domestic chores, such as taking care of the children and doing laundry. From what I understood, Charlie was also using the bikers as muscle and protection in case we needed it. This was when guns started showing up at the ranch, along with additional dune buggies.

The Straight Satans were a help to Charlie, but they were also a huge red flag to the local cops that what was going on at Spahn Ranch was more than a bunch of peace-loving hippies. The cops raided us, but I escaped their attention by hiding in the shower. They took people in but let them go the next day. The cops came again, and this time I hid in the grass. I think it was my fear of Charlie that helped me avoid being caught. I didn't want to bring him any more trouble.

Perhaps in an effort to make money off drugs, Nancy Pitman made a tea out of belladonna, a plant that grew on the ranch, which was a poison but was also known to be a hallucinogen. Some people have said Tex or Charlie wanted to poison someone, but more likely they were looking for another drug they could sell to make some quick cash. The only problem was, Tex tried it out on himself. The next thing we knew, he was arrested for public intoxication. The arresting officers said he was slithering around on the ground terrifying schoolchildren. When we got him home the next day, I was put in charge of taking care of him. He was so sick he couldn't stand. When he came to, he had very little memory of what he had done or where he had been.

Consuming belladonna root wasn't the only questionable choice Tex made. He desperately wanted to please Charlie and bring in money, but Tex didn't share Charlie's street smarts. This became obvious with a failed drug deal that he embarked on, one that would become very problematic for Charlie. I know the details of the shooting of a drug dealer whose alias was Lotsapoppa only from later accounts, but I do know I witnessed a very angry-looking African American man confronting Charlie one day. This was not something that happened often, and I later heard that Charlie assumed he was a member of the Black Panthers. That may have been what he told us to keep us believing in the impending race war, but what was most certainly a sighting of Bernard "Lotsapoppa" Crowe added to our evidence that Charlie was telling us the truth.

From what I later learned, as Charlie was becoming desperate to raise money for us, Tex came up with a harebrained scheme to get some money from one of his outside girlfriend's drug dealers. I never knew the things Tex and Charlie were up to outside of the

Family, but accounts say that Tex planned to pose as a drug dealer. The scheme was to take the money from Lotsapoppa and not deliver the drugs. One of the problems that brought the man to the ranch was he knew that Tex's real name was Charles, so when he asked around about a Charles, someone directed him to Charlie and Spahn Ranch.

In spite of Charlie's efforts at appeasement, the dustup at Spahn didn't end the story. Charlie went back with Tex and a friend of the Family named TJ to work things out with Lotsapoppa. The plan was for TJ to shoot Lotsapoppa if necessary, but when TJ backed out, Charlie decided to do it himself, only to have the gun jam twice before he finally shot Lotsapoppa in the chest.

Not only did Charlie believe that he'd killed the man, but he also feared retribution by the Black Panthers, because he believed Lotsapoppa belonged to the militant group. As it turned out, he was wrong about both. In fact, unbeknownst to Charlie, Crowe survived the gunshot and emerged a year later, as a witness at Manson's trial. When a man Charlie thought was dead walked into the courtroom, Charlie was shocked, to say the least, but he whispered to Crowe that there were no hard feelings.

WHEN PEOPLE WEREN'T ENGAGING IN CRIMINAL ACTIVITIES TO TRY AND get money, Charlie continued testing our loyalty in other ways.

He had Paul steal a truck for him with a bunch of us tagging along, and we were all arrested. It turned out the truck had been stolen several times, so the cops let us all go the next day. They might have thought the truck had such bad karma that we weren't at fault.

After Nancy Pitman volunteered that her mother was rich and that we needed her stuff more than her mother ever would, Charlie sent some of the girls with Nancy to her mother's house to steal a bunch of things from her. When they returned, she handed us her mother's furs and other items she relieved from her mother's possessions. She didn't seem to care about what she had done, stealing from her own mother. Angry as I'd been with my mother at times, I couldn't imagine taking something that mattered away from her—it just seemed coldhearted.

We used the furs to decorate one of the dune buggies for Charlie. He was our leader, after all, and the girls wanted to make sure that his dune buggy was more than transportation—it was also his throne. We covered all the seats and the back of a dune buggy with furs and began embroidering his vest so it would be finished for him in time for whatever was coming down. As a present for Charlie, we all cut off the braids in our hair, which he tied to the roll bar. We each left one hank of hair that we could still braid as a symbol of our dedication. It was a way to honor him as our leader.

He also began to test us through the survival training he was giving us.

I didn't know what to do when Charlie handed me a Buck knife—my instinct was to give it back to him. I had always had a pocketknife, but it was for clipping flowers and plants or cutting up apples. Charlie gave each of us real weapons, and the first time I held the knife in my hand I felt sick.

"Don't be scared of this, Snake," he said. "This may be the only thing between you and some black man cutting your throat." The thought was unimaginable.

Charlie called all of us together in the back house away from prying eyes, and I realized each of us had been given the same weapon. The knives had blades that were about four to six inches. They were sharp and looked deadly. My hands began to shake, but one of the girls, Patty I believe, put her arm around my shoulder and told me to relax. Everyone knew that Charlie took out a lot of his frustrations on me, and this was not the time to make him angry. What I didn't know then was he had been terrorizing the other girls as well. We never talked to one another about Charlie's abuse. It wasn't until I became aware of testimony from parole hearings years later that I learned they were randomly beaten and threatened just as much as I was, but we all rationalized Charlie's behavior as part of the plan. He was making us strong and we had to be obedient.

Charlie called us all to attention and gave us our instructions. He began by showing us a thrust and jab. "Thrust and jab like you mean it."

Then he lifted the knife up. "If you're going to kill someone, you have to kill them. Start in their chest and lift up. This will kill them."

Thrust, jab, lift. He showed us and then we repeated the motion. Thrust, jab, lift.

"That's right. You are getting it. This is no time to be pussies."

He went around the room like a drill sergeant.

"Give it more push, Dianne. Use your focus and your strength."

Thrust, jab, lift. I followed his instructions and killed my imaginary enemy.

"If you don't want to be killed, you have to be willing to kill. Are you all willing to kill?"

We answered in the affirmative.

"When Helter Skelter comes down, this knife might be the only thing between you and your enemy. I guarantee you they want you dead."

"Aren't we supposed to go to the desert to wait it out?" I asked innocently.

"If we make it to the desert, we will be all right. But Helter Skelter is upon us and if it happens and shit comes down we have to be ready."

He stood in front of us and asked "If someone asked you to kill, could you?"

"Are you willing to die?"

Following his lead, we trained to kill our enemy.

"Remember to aim for the chest. If you are in a hurry, you may not hit a major organ. But if you do it this way you will kill them. Pull up," he instructed us. "No hesitation." I convinced myself that he was preparing us for something in order to avoid it. I believed that if we could show him that we were willing to do it, we would not be asked to. This was the "die to self" he was talking about.

"Keep these knives with you at all times. They are yours."

Despite the fact that I vividly remember that day when Charlie taught us how to kill or be killed, I have no idea what happened to my knife after that. In fact, I have no recollection of that weapon as existing beyond that day. I don't know if I held on to it, attached it to my clothing, or hid it under my mattress. When later asked about the weapons and Charlie's training, I tried to minimize what had happened by saying all men carried Buck knives at that time. But the truth is, I was given a weapon and trained how to kill or be killed if it came down to it. He fully expected us to be prepared for something real. We just didn't know what it would be.

22

A SIMPLE BAG OF COINS

IT WAS JULY OF 1969 AND EINSTEIN'S THEORY OF RELATIVITY WAS AT play. Time seemed to speed up or slow down according to our activity level and the urgency Charlie was projecting. We were gearing up for an exodus into the promised land, and Charlie was like a modern-day Moses leading his people from the bondage of societal servitude. He had us preparing to go to the land of milk and honey, where we could live until after the Helter Skelter race war. It just so happened that, according to Charlie, this shelter from the war was a big hole in the middle of the desert.

The notion of this underground oasis was loosely based upon Hopi Indian legend, Gypsy's favorite book, Jules Verne's *Journey to the Center of the Earth*, and snippets from the Bible. As Charlie told it, this place could be accessed through a hole in Death Valley leading to what he called the bottomless pit. Charlie intimated that he knew where the hole was by waving his hands over his topographical maps and changing the subject to what we would find there. This would be a sustainable world where we would never be too hot or too cold, where there was natural light, and where there would be enough food to last through this period of tribulation. Charlie showed us a line on the map indicating the Amargosa River, an intermittent waterway on the map known to have been running through the desert for thousands of years. Somehow his tying the underground oasis to a river on a map made his words as plausible as anything else we were hearing, since it meant that this underground world would have enough water and therefore vegetation to provide for our needs. Charlie also described more benefits of this mystical space, saying things like "None of us will age down underground. When we come up after the race war, we will be as strong and vital as we are now." While down there, we were supposed to have as many babies as we could, so our family could repopulate the earth with beautiful, strong, healthy people. And of course, though the whole idea was lunacy, we believed it because we were believing it together, and because it came from Charlie.

Other than this focus on the hole, talk around the ranch was about the need for scratch, greenbacks, or whatever slang term Charlie used to describe money. We were no longer simply postulating for the things we needed—we were seeking monetary miracles. One came in the form of a pretty blond girl named Linda Kasabian, who'd been brought to Spahn Ranch by Leslie. A hippie with a little girl and an ex-husband, Linda joined us, and to prove her commitment, she scored about five thousand dollars from her ex and his friend. She also came with a car and a valid driver's license, which would prove useful for Charlie but devastating for her future.

But not even Linda Kasabian's money was enough. Having used up most of his favors from everyone he knew, Charlie was actively scheming for additional revenue sources, which was what led Charlie back to Gary Hinman.

Although I don't think anyone can truly know how Gary's name and money were first connected, someone said they heard that our friend Gary had come into an inheritance. The rumor—although it could have been the truth—was that he inherited about twenty thousand dollars, which Charlie and the others assumed he would be keeping in his modest Topanga Canyon home. Some people claim that Gary was a drug manufacturer who sold the Straight Satans some bad synthetic mescaline, but this doesn't sound like the Gary I knew. When I was there, all he could talk about was wanting to take a pilgrimage to Japan to further explore his spiritual beliefs.

In late July 1969, the phone rang outside at the Spahn Ranch. I'm not sure why I was the only one in the vicinity of the public phone on that particular day, but it was ringing and ringing, so I decided to answer it. For all I knew, it was somebody's parent trying to arrange to pick them up after a horse trail ride. On the other end of the line was a very agitated Mary Brunner telling me to get Charlie. Something was wrong and she needed help. That was all I knew. I felt a little put out when I got Charlie to come to the phone and he yelled at me for answering it in the first place. Everyone always seemed to be yelling at me for something, so I walked away and went about my business.

Following the call, Charlie and Bruce Davis got into the truck and sped out, presumably to meet up with Mary for whatever emergency she was claiming. Charlie had been cursing under his breath, but he always did that when he thought we were bothering him with things he believed we should be able to handle ourselves. He had important business to supervise. The ranch was becoming more of a compound, with field phones throughout so the Straight Satans, acting as guardians, could alert everyone of intruders. I did my best to ignore what was happening around me. None of it was making sense, so I felt it best to stay out of the way.

Later that day Charlie returned with Bruce, still cursing about having to do everything himself. I heard everyone talking about how Gary was not giving us the money he owed us, so Charlie had to go over there to talk to him. The word was, Charlie had cut Gary's ear. I assumed it was an accident and Charlie never meant to hurt the man. That was enough for me to know and I tucked it away along with my childish interpretation of all the other criminal activity occurring right under my nose. I was sure Gary would be okay and all would be forgiven.

*   *   *

ON AUGUST 5, CHARLIE FOUND OUT BOBBY BEAUSOLEIL WAS PICKED up for something that had to do with a stolen car and put in jail.

Soon after Charlie went into a tirade. At the time, I had no idea what it was about, but he said things like: "That cocksucker. What an imbecile." Charlie paced and stomped around and kicked at anything in his way. "Motherfucker! Do I have to do everything myself!! When are you idiots going to get it right?"

My heart was racing. Charlie appeared completely out of control, but he soon threw his hands in the air and walked off. Everyone who had been standing around scattered, barely speaking to anyone else. I couldn't have been the only one who was becoming terrified. We all seemed to be monitoring Charlie's moods and doing our best to avoid awakening the beast.

The tensions continued to rise and more vehicles were showing up at Spahn Ranch. What we didn't know was that the local police were watching us. Police affidavits from as early as July 1 indicate that the police were aware of the stolen vehicles. The police were surveilling us from helicopters, taking aerial photographs of car parts and dune buggies strewn about Devil's Canyon. One report had a cop coming to the ranch and being told by Charlie that there were guns on him from all directions. Charlie may have known that we needed to get out of Dodge, but I was busy taking care of children, doing what I was told and keeping my mouth shut.

Charlie began to instruct the older girls in what they called creepy-crawly missions. He would have them dress up in dark clothing that would be hard to spot at night. Then he would send them to random houses with the mission of moving things around unnoticed just to play head games with those he called "the sleeping pigs" or stealing small items to contribute to the coffers. These creepy-crawly missions were not burglaries per se. Charlie said these were training missions, a way to help them overcome their fear and learn to be silent and undetectable. I was never included in these.

Though I didn't participate and was relegated to child-care duty, I was aware of what was happening each night. Charlie probably didn't ask me to go on the missions for a couple of reasons. The most obvious was, I had a history of disobeying his orders. As obedient as I was to him, there was still a strong possibility I might question or go against his request, and he didn't want someone who might challenge his words. A second reason was that even though the creepy-crawlies were ostensibly nonviolent, they had the possibility of leading to violence, and he probably knew better than I did that I would never hurt another human being. It never occurred to me that we would ever be in the position of perpetrating violence upon other people. Even the hypothetical violence of our knife training was difficult for me. If violence was a part of any plan, Charlie likely would not have relied on me to carry out his orders. Of all those in our family, I was probably the only true flower child.

Still, at the time, I was disappointed about not being included on the creepy-crawlies. While in hindsight, this non-inclusion was the best thing that could ever have happened to me, it was difficult feeling so separate from the group. I find it hard not to see the work of another force in moments like these. Though my obstinacy with Charlie and my aversion to violence most likely shaped his decisions, as was true in that moment on the cliff after he raped me, someone or something thought I was worth saving.

I HAD NO REASON TO THINK ANYTHING UNUSUAL ABOUT THE CREEPY-crawly missions immediately following Bobby's arrest, but they were far from ordinary. What I witnessed on those days would become important in the years to come, even though they seemed like random events at the time.

In the days after Bobby's arrest, Charlie was preoccupied and there were a lot of small gatherings of people that didn't include me—I was definitely being left out. I watched from the periphery and did my best to stay out of the way. I was aware of Linda, Tex, Sadie, and Patty going out on a creepy-crawly together one night, and there was a lot of talk going around the ranch the next day.

Though I didn't know the specifics, I didn't like the energy I was feeling from everyone. Things seemed wrong. Even the children were nervous, so I did my best to calm them. The next night Barbara Hoyt, Leslie Van Houten, a girl named "Little Patty," and I went to sleep early in the back house. The back house was a one-story wood building with a large living room, one large bedroom, one small bedroom, a long large kitchen and a bathroom. There were about four beds in the house and a screen door that allowed a breeze and for us to look out into the night.

I would have stayed asleep, but sometime early the next morning, I heard Leslie come in, probably around seven, judging by the light. She had been out all night.

She came in and dumped a bunch of things on her bed. She liked to sleep in the living room near the fireplace. She asked me to help her get some firewood which we used to build a fire. She took a rope off her bed that was with the pile of stuff and put it in the flames. She also added a brown purse and some credit cards which started to smell awful. We both turned and saw some headlights headed our way. Leslie begged me to help her out and pulled the rope out of the flames, ran into the bathroom and tried to put it out.

"Snake, don't let that man see me," she said. "He just gave me a ride from Griffith Park." Then she jumped into her bed pulling the sheet over her entire body and face. I knew not to ask any questions.

Three men in a peach-colored older model car pulled up to the front of the house but only one of them approached. He pushed his way partially through the door and asked about Leslie. I told him she wasn't in and he insisted that he had just dropped her off. He also commented about the field phones we had set up around the ranch so we could communicate with each other from long distances. I don't know why, but he also said we "had a lousy bunch of men." I tried not to look rattled so I just stared him down. In only a few minutes he got into his car and left. Leslie must have been holding her breath because there was no sign of movement until she decided it was safe enough to remove the sheet.

"Don't worry, Snake," she said and handed me some wood to build up the fire again. She finished burning the little brown purse even though it was difficult. It didn't catch very easily. The credit cards burned and then she took off the clothing she was wearing and burned that too. I watched the flames consume everything while she took a shower. I figured if she wanted to tell me anything she would.

When she got out of the shower she showed me a plastic bag of coins and dumped them on the table. We both counted about eight dollars without counting the Canadian nickels.

"Here, Snake, you can have these."

Coins meant snacks, so I gladly grabbed the bag and returned the coins. I thought it was a nice little haul. I had no idea that aside from a brown purse, credit cards and chocolate milk, this was all that was taken from the home of Leno and Rosemary LaBianca, both victims of Charlie's madness and a killing spree intended to set off Helter Skelter.

PART III

DROP OUT

SPAHN'S MOVIE RANCH

23

THE WITCHES' BREW

A FEW DAYS AFTER LESLIE'S CREEPY-CRAWLY MISSION, CHARLIE ORdered Bruce Davis to drive me and one of the children to the little town of Olancha, a nowhere ranch town on the outskirts of Death Valley, where we would meet up with Tex, who'd driven out ahead of us. When I got word of our departure, my assumption was that Charlie was planning for us to escape to the desert because Helter Skelter was on the horizon. There had been whispers and people listening to the radio. His agitation was visible, so I grabbed my knapsack and followed his command, hoping he wasn't banishing me to Barker Ranch again.

As we drove out to Olancha, Bruce explained that we were meeting up with Tex at a friend's place. The others would meet up with us later, and we would all go up to Barker together. I nodded my head in agreement but didn't say much else. I didn't know what to say—I had no idea what was happening around me. All I could think about was Charlie's separating me from everyone again, probably because of my age. I stared through the mud-streaked windows as I faced exile at the base of the Sierra Nevada.

As promised, Tex was at the house of a cowboy friend of his, along with Juan Flynn, a Panamanian who worked for George Spahn who had become an associate of ours. He wasn't a full member, but he was someone Charlie trusted enough to have him drive out with Tex, bringing a dune buggy and some stolen motors in the back of a truck. Juan, Bruce, and Tex worked out a well-choreographed exchange of items, and I was left with Tex, the stolen goods, and the other young Family member.

Tex's friend's house turned out to be ramshackle, so he decided it would be just as well for us to camp out behind it near a water irrigation ditch. We seemed on our own out here, and I always found running water soothing, so that suited me just fine. We ended up all swimming naked in the water, and for the first time in months, things seemed normal—or at least our version of normal. Our sense of isolation turned out to be an illusion, because someone complained about the nude swimming and some local cops showed up. I never saw the kid again so I assume they took that underage child with them. The cops believed that I was older and let me stay with Tex.

After that, Tex went to run some errands, leaving me alone at our campsite. He told me not to go anywhere, but without any food, I started to get hungry. I couldn't sit still and wait. There was an old roadhouse restaurant with a hitching post in walking distance, and the smell of corn bread and beans was intoxicating. Since I didn't have any money, my first idea was to see if they had any Dumpsters outside. No luck. Next, I investigated behind a nearby gas station. It looked like the type of place where Gomer Pyle or Goober would walk out at any time to introduce me to Sheriff Andy. Then Aunt Bee would bring me home for some home-baked pie until they could find my folks.

As it turned out, that was almost what happened. As I was digging around in the trash, an Inyo County policeman drove up behind me to see what I was up to.

"Hey, young lady," the cop, more Barney Fife than Andy Taylor, yelled to me. I was startled and bumped myself when I pulled my head out of the trash. "What do you think you are doing in there?"

I froze. Charlie had taught us time and again that if you are stopped by a cop, be nice and don't mouth off. Always act innocent.

"Officer, I have been hitchhiking on my way to Big Sur and I don't have any money. I am sorry, but I was looking for something to eat."

He paused and looked me up and down. He studied my face as if to determine my age. "How old are you? Are you a runaway? Should I call your folks?"

"Oh, no, sir." I squinted, trying to create the illusion of age lines. It had fooled a carny at a guess-your-age booth at the Santa Monica Pier once, so I hoped it would work again. "I am twenty-one and hitchhiking to meet some friends."

"Let me see some ID." He held out his hand.

"I don't have any," I replied.

"Well, I have to take you in. We don't allow underage vagrants in our town. We can check it out when we get you to Independence." I didn't say anything as we drove the half hour to the Inyo County jail, which gave me time to think of a story to talk my way out of it.

When he walked me into the station I blurted out: "I was embarrassed to tell you this, but I am probably in the system. You can look me up. I got into a little trouble a while back in Ventura County, but there were no charges made. It was stupid." I was hoping he could find me but not the fact I was arrested for having a fake ID and being a naked hippie. The stars would have to align just right to get me out of this mess. The cop called in my name, Dianne Bluestein, and said he would have to keep me overnight but that they would take good care of me.

The next morning, he returned with an affirmative that my story checked out. I was indeed on record.

"That is you, all right. But what kind of town would we be if we allowed our weary travelers to starve to death?"

And with that, he took me home to his wife and a good home-cooked meal. I had the feeling he was prone to bringing home strays because his wife, a kind-looking woman in a shirtwaist dress, did not seem at all surprised. She had fried chicken ready to serve and a home-baked cake with chocolate frosting waiting on the countertop in a clear-glass dessert stand. She set another plate at the table, no questions asked.

Before dinner they invited me to use their shower and gave me some clean clothes. I know it was for my benefit, but I am sure it was also for theirs. My hygiene had certainly suffered with all the goings-on and the long drive from Spahn. The shower made me feel squeaky clean, an expression my mom used to use when we would all take our baths on Sunday night. She would run her hands through our hair to see if the soap was out and make it squeak. I felt a pang of homesickness.

The officer's wife gave me some salve for sunburn and some medicine for the impetigo that had been plaguing me since I first met the flies at Spahn Ranch. She didn't say a word about it, just treating me quietly, showing me more attention and kindness than I had experienced in a long time. Somewhere in the back of my mind I thought, *This is what family feels like.*

After dinner, the policeman and his wife insisted that I stay for the night. They promised he would return me to where he'd found me once I'd gotten some rest. As they both drove me back to Olancha the next day, I felt torn. They'd given me a sun hat, some money, and a bag of food for my trip, displaying an honest generosity unlike any I'd experienced in quite some time. Sitting in the back of the car, I wished I could tell him what I was facing. The way they'd treated me—with kindness, but also with respect—made me feel like they could help somehow. But there was no way to explain what I was really doing in Olancha without putting everyone, especially Charlie, at risk. So, I kept my mouth shut and waited to get out of the car.

"WHERE THE HELL HAVE YOU BEEN!"

Tex was sitting on his truck when I hiked back to our campsite from the road. I made sure to have the cop drop me off far away enough so he would think I was immediately going to thumb a ride to Big Sur. I didn't understand the look of hysteria and fury on Tex's face when he saw me sauntering back to where he had left me.

"Didn't I tell you to stay in the camp and wait?"

"Yes, but . . ."

"No *yes but*." He was starting to sound more like Charlie every day. All of the men sounded like him. They mimicked his intonation and his circular rap, and they now embodied his callous control over us women. I started to feel resentful until he explained why he was so upset. He motioned for me to sit next to him. He was holding a stack of newspapers.

"Take a look at this." He showed me the front page of the newspaper with a headline about seven people being brutally murdered in Los Angeles. I scanned the page as it depicted the horrible details of how the actress Sharon Tate, the eight months' pregnant wife of filmmaker Roman Polanski, her husband's friend Wojciech Frykowski, his girlfriend, coffee heiress Abigail Folger, her friend the celebrity hairstylist Jay Sebring, and another unrelated young man had been slaughtered at her home. A second paper revealed a headline that read that the day after, two more people, a middle-aged grocer, Leno LaBianca, and his wife, Rosemary, were also viciously slain in a similar way.

Confused, I stared at the papers and the headlines. I had no idea why Tex was showing me these sick stories except as a cautionary tale related to my wandering off. Perhaps there were killers on the loose, and he had been concerned.

He hit the newspapers with a balled-up fist and said: "I did this! Charlie told me to."

I was stunned into silence. Once Tex knew that I was aware of what he had done, he kept talking. He told me that Linda Kasabian drove Patty, Sadie, and him to a house they knew would be occupied by pigs. That is what Charlie called the establishment

and what the Beatles said in their White Album song "Piggies."
We had listened to the song over and over and the lyrics: "In their
eyes there's something lacking / What they need's a damn good
whacking." (What Tex did not say, and I only learned later, was
that the place they went to carry out Charlie's plan had been the
home of Terry Melcher, so Tex and Charlie were both familiar
with it.) Tex explained the plan was for him to lead the girls into
a murder spree with the full intention of viciously killing anyone
present in the home that night. They were to leave indications that
would point to the Black Panthers as the perpetrators of the savage
acts. That was the gist of what he told me, but I know I was barely
listening.

After hearing Tex's words, I was horrified, but I was also afraid.
This was not the act of self-defense in response to Helter Skelter.
This was something else entirely. I'd taken Charlie at his word that
he was training us to protect ourselves, but this awful crime made it
clear he'd had another plan all along. Violence wasn't a last resort—it
had become the point. And now I was alone and stuck with a man
capable of murder.

As I tried to remain calm, I stared at the headline about the
grocer and his wife. The date was meaningless but not the sequence
of events. Suddenly I realized that it was in the early morning after
their slaying that I'd seen Leslie burning her clothing. All at once
it became clear: The coins I was counting as my reward for hiding
Leslie had been taken from their home. There had been all sorts of
clues but now they had significance. I wanted to vomit, but I instead
dug my nails into my hand to divert the sensation. I couldn't look at
the photo of their faces in the paper.

Tex switched from bragging to unloading, but I still knew little
about what had happened those nights of August 9 and 10. Most
of my knowledge about how these murders had gone down would
come much later, as people pieced together the accounts through the

crime scenes, confessions, autopsy reports, and unreliable narrators. I thank God every day that I was not in any way present for the murders, and as a result, there are many details of the crimes that I've only learned from second- and thirdhand accounts.

However, I do know after looking at the various accounts that each of the victims was stabbed over and over. One horrifying detail that I discovered recently when looking at the autopsy reports chilled me to the bone. It was something that to me left Charlie's fingerprints on the crime almost as if he'd been at the scene. The autopsy reports show patterns of how the victims were stabbed. These seemed to match the instructions Charlie had given to us. Jab and thrust, pull up. That day that he'd handed me that large knife I'd wanted nothing to do with, we weren't being taught to defend ourselves, we were being trained to kill. And Tex, Sadie, and the rest of them were clearly following orders with a clear knowledge of what they were doing and how.

As Tex recounted the killings, he spewed Charlie-isms like how it was now "up to us to start Helter Skelter" to show "blackie" how it was done. All I could do was nod silently, my emotions moving quickly from terror to disgust to fear and back again. I had been with the Family from the start. I'd been there by everyone's side during the births, the garbage runs, the lovemaking, and the sermonizing. I'd been abused, I'd been raped, and I'd been forced to perform sexual acts at Charlie's command. I'd been through all of it. I may have been perceived as the kid sister or a mascot, but I was a witness to the changes that occurred from the first days at the Spiral Staircase House to our lives now as we searched in earnest for the entrance to the bottomless pit.

But after everything I'd seen, everything I'd lived through, I understood, brainwashed as I was, that this was the end of the Family as I knew it. While my prolonged indoctrination meant that even after learning about the horrendous criminal acts and senseless murders I still felt a loyalty to Charlie and the Family, a part of me could see clearly, and perhaps for the first time, that this was no longer the group I'd joined. Whatever I had been a part of, whatever I'd thought the Family was about, whatever shared vision we'd once held, was no longer there.

Just the night before, I'd slept in a real bed in a real home, and I'd been treated like a normal young woman. Those people had no idea that I was part of a family of murderers—and neither did I. For one night, I'd been safe from harm. For one night, I had the chance to tell someone what had been going on and the insanity that was growing by the minute. But that moment had passed. I had no idea what would happen next, but I understood that the bad situation I'd gotten myself into was about to get much worse.

WE WERE NOW OFFICIALLY ON THE RUN. WHEN EVERYONE JOINED US IN Olancha, I acted as if nothing had changed. I am sure that Tex let on to Charlie that I knew about the murders, but no one said anything further to me about them, at least not right away.

Once we arrived at Barker Ranch, we were so far out in the desert that if Helter Skelter had actually started, we would have had no trouble waiting it out until the bloodshed passed. Barker Ranch and the areas we were exploring were so far into Death Valley that it was clear Charlie did not want us to be found. Back then there were no clear roadways and it was rare for anyone, other than a few miners looking to strike a vein, to be out in this wilderness. We were in it for the long haul and Charlie kept us busy with the task of survival.

He organized us like troops. During the hottest hours of the day, we hid under camouflage army surplus parachutes. We did reconnaissance missions looking for strategic locations to place dune buggies. We took precautions with everything we did. Once the sun set, we built lookouts in caves, some hidden behind cactus or between rocks and brush. We covered some of our caves with scrap metal (I believe at least one of them still exists today). We searched for the opening to the bottomless pit, and before settling in for the day, the girls and I would take willow branches and wipe away any footprints or dune buggy tracks we might have made. Like animals burying their waste, we used our instincts to mask any trace of our presence.

Eventually, though, Charlie began to grow reckless. We didn't always wait for the nighttime to tear around the desert in the dune buggies. Perhaps the men needed to release pent-up agitation, since we had long ago stopped taking the time for sex, so they put it into crazy driving through the canyons. During one of these rides I sat on the back of one of the dune buggies until the speed and the canyon bumped me out of my seat. This did not feel like an accident; I held on to the tumble bar as I had once held on to the neck of the runaway horse at Spahn. Even when Charlie stopped and saw what was happening to me, he didn't say a word. It frightened me that no one was watching out for my safety, but worse, I worried they might want me gone. I hadn't done anything, and yet I knew enough to be dangerous to the Family. No wonder I no longer felt safe. I was shaking from head to toe but dismissed my anger as my need to toughen up, still vacillating between "This is insanity" and "There must be a reason for this."

During the latter parts of the day, as the sun moved closer to the horizon, we scouted the land for more hideouts and resources. Charlie also tried to keep up our morale, making sure we were busy and challenged so we wouldn't question him as much. One day he sent us out on a survival mission that was either going to toughen us up or kill us. We had nothing with us but a small amount of food and access to a gas tank that had been cleaned out and filled with water. The only problem was, you can't fully clean out a gas tank. The water tasted of gasoline and was not good for drinking. We were dropped off somewhere in the desert far enough away from

Barker Ranch that it took over twenty-four hours for us to find our way back.

Not long after this, Charlie figured out that there was a place about ten miles from Barker Ranch called Willow Springs that had some water. It was late September when Charlie went with a few of us to explore. A bloodred moon rose in the sky as we set out.

Patty, Leslie, and I were eating some watercress we found in the trickling water while we cleaned up a small house made of stones and wood that had likely once belonging to a miner; it would make a good hideaway if some of us needed to spread out from Barker. I went through the motions of cleaning and fixing up the house and finding food so I would appear busy and engaged. The girls started chattering with each other and then started talking to me. I tried to keep it to small talk because I was already coming undone. Leslie drew the conversation to the night of the slayings of Leno and Rosemary LaBianca.

"You know that night we went to the house near Griffith Park." Leslie looked to Patty and Sadie for affirmation.

As if the pump had been primed, Leslie's description of the night bubbled up in a gush. I didn't want to know any more than what I had read in the newspaper or than Tex had revealed, but it was too late. I remained silent as Leslie recounted the second night of murderous terror orchestrated by Charlie. Later accounts say that Charlie considered the first night too messy, so he would go along to show them how it should be done. Somewhere in the middle of this micromanaging of madness, Charlie left the rest of the job to Tex, Patty, and Leslie.

"Tex told me what to do," Leslie explained.

Leslie paused, but surprised me with her reaction. I thought she would say something about how awful it was. But instead she described how strange it was to stab someone but that after a while it was fun. Rosemary, whom Leslie referred to only as the woman, was still warm, and she may have already been dead when Leslie stabbed her. She couldn't really be sure. Then she was told to wipe the fingerprints off of everything—and she did, removing them from the refrigerator, the lamps, and the doors, even things that they hadn't touched.

She told me some other details like seeing a boat in the driveway, but by this time I had tuned her out. I wished I had not heard her say any of this. I flushed with fear and sadness for the victim as Leslie made it sound like the murder was no big deal. For something that was nothing it was later determined that Rosemary LaBianca, thirty-nine, had been stabbed forty-one times. Four days after his forty-fourth birthday, Leno LaBianca had been stabbed at least twenty-six times. He had no defensive wounds, a fatal wound to the carotid artery, and the word *war* carved into his stomach. A fork had been stabbed into his flesh as if he were a suckling pig.

Patty later claimed responsibility for those special touches as well as leaving the misspelled words *healter skelter* on the refrigerator door in Leno's blood. Patty and Leslie said they took some chocolate milk and hitchhiked home.

"Un-huh." I nodded my head but couldn't say anything more. I didn't have to, as Sadie took this as her opportunity to describe her important role in the first night's slaughter at Cielo Drive. Sadie explained her role in the killings, but also how she had contemplated saving Sharon Tate's unborn baby.

"The woman was pregnant and was begging for her life. I thought about saving the baby while I was stabbing her but decided against it," Sadie described as my blood ran cold.

In the years since this night when I was a reluctant audience for her words, Tex has also claimed responsibility for the murder of Sharon Tate and Sadie, at different points, has both recanted her confession and reiterated that it was indeed she who had killed Sharon Tate. Who really did what has remained a controversy. No matter what they've both said, there is no doubt in my mind that Susan Atkins was telling me the truth that night in the desert. She was not embellishing. She was not lying and there is nothing that would allow me to think of anyone other than Susan committing this unspeakable crime.

The girls continued to compare notes like teenage girls discussing makeup and the boys they liked at school. I slowed my breathing, so my face would not betray my emotions.

"Charlie told us to do something witchy and we did," Patty said proudly.

As if it was possible, she made things worse by describing the scene at the Tate house the first night. I listened to her talk about the blood and how she had dragged a woman, later determined to be Abigail Folger, from the bedroom to the living room. After she had stabbed her, the woman got up to run and Patty said she chased her out of the house and tackled her. She then stabbed her until she saw the life leave her eyes.

I stared at them, speechless and shocked but doing my best not to reveal my feelings. I remember looking up at that eerie moon, haunting with its presence, as a stray feather floated by in the sky. When Tex had told me about the crimes by pointing to the headline, it had been an abstraction—disturbing, of course—but the absence of detail had put distance into the story. These girls showed me just how real it was.

For some reason, I found myself thinking of that first step onto the bus almost two years earlier, looking around and really taking in Sadie and Patty's faces for the first time. I had no idea how we'd ended up here. How had we moved from that moment when it seemed so natural that we all belonged together on that bus to standing in the desert in the middle of the night as they spoke about cold-blooded murder? This wasn't supposed to be where our story led us. I thought back to even before I'd joined the Family, to the Oracle house, the human be-ins, the atmosphere of love and acceptance. I thought about the good times with Charlie at the

Topanga Canyon houses, when he seemed to be guiding us some-where special, and at Dennis Wilson's house, when there had been so much promise for the future. Those places all epitomized what drew me in to Charlie's ideas; they'd shaped and encouraged my vision of community and belonging. For some of that time, each of these women had been my confidante, lover, and friend, and now I was listening to them recount the events of those two awful nights on a blood-fueled high. They'd become a perversion of whatever I'd thought we believed.

As I struggled to keep my emotions in check, I found I was less surprised by how Sadie and Leslie gleefully described their roles in these murders. In the time I'd known them, I'd never fully believed in their ability to feel for others. Patty, however, was a different story. Learning both of her involvement and what she had become left me heartbroken.

Patty had joined Charlie because he made her feel loved in a way she had never felt before. Throughout my time with the family, she became the most loyal to him, as if her identity was only a re-flection of how he saw her. She didn't exist outside of his aura, and now to me she was forever lost. She'd become something I couldn't recognize. Her transformation spoke volumes about the power of Charlie's manipulation. As confused as I was with my own loyalty to Charlie, I could not understand how Patty could become a murderer for him.

It's hard to say why I didn't leave the moment I heard the girls speaking. Unlike others who tried to leave at different points, Char-lie actively wanted to get rid of me, since I was a liability. Somehow this only made me cling more tightly to him and his warped mis-sion. I tried to rationalize my loyalty to Charlie by holding tight to the idea that Charlie didn't actually do any killing. I also thought that if we were in the middle of a revolution leading to the end of the world through a black-white race war, Charlie had his reasons.

This nightmare was real—Helter Skelter was really happening. We were facing a war and we were now the ones who might have started it.

But in general, I was simply too confused, too programmed at this point, to stand my own emotional ground. I felt guilt by association and feared for my life. Months removed from escaping from their house and the alternative school, I had no idea where my parents were, or if they even cared about me. I am deeply ashamed that I believed this for even a minute, that I could not tell the difference between a false prophet and the God that I now know is real. But at the time, this all seemed real to me.

The girls also talked that night about Bobby Beausoleil. They wanted to draw attention away from him. He was in jail and charged with the killing of Gary Hinman. Until this moment I had no idea that Gary was dead. I felt tears begin to fall, so I turned away. I knew that Charlie had cut Gary's ear and that we were trying to raise bail money for Bobby, but until that day in Willow Springs I had never put the two things together. I also didn't see the larger picture of Bobby, Gary's killing, Helter Skelter, and now the murders at the Tate and LaBianca houses. These things were all connected in some kind of nefarious plan, and I was mired deeply in the middle of it with no exit strategy.

The girls must have figured out that I didn't know about Gary, so Sadie quickly explained that Gary wouldn't give us his money, and so Bobby killed him and Mary and Sadie helped because he just wouldn't die. She described almost with a sense of annoyance how she and Mary had to hold a pillow over his face to stop him from his silly Buddhist chanting so they could finally leave. They wrote something like "political piggies" on the wall, which is why they did the same witchy things at the other places.

This was more than I could handle. The thought of poor effeminate Gary being tortured to death over something as stupid as money was the saddest thing I could imagine. To me he would always be the kind man sharing a plate of Oreos and a peanut butter and jelly sandwich. As horrific as the thoughts of the other crimes were, Gary was someone I knew personally. The image haunted me.

It was obvious something was wrong when Charlie found me sitting outside the little house separate from the other girls. I couldn't hide my sobbing. Without warning he punched me in the mouth and told me to get it together. I remember the blood splattered from my mouth in a way that reminded me of that feather passing across the moon.

When we returned to Barker Ranch, Charlie spent every night after that preaching to us about what was now coming down in L.A. He also said people were going to be looking for us. I started to think I heard people walking behind me everywhere and imagined that under every bush was someone with a machine gun pointing at me. I couldn't sleep and we had very little to eat. We were living on brown rice, powdered milk, ketchup, and the occasional vegetation we found in the desert.

Charlie took us on a mission into the desert in a place north of Goler Wash. The place was in the Salinas Valley, close to a dry lake feature called the Racetrack in Death Valley National Park. The area was flat, with a hot springs running through it, and Charlie seemed excited that we might be getting closer to the opening to the bottomless pit. The springs looked like a small creek, which would have made sense if the bottomless pit had water in it.

We were there for a couple of days, exploring and camping. When we came back to return to Barker Ranch, the road appeared blocked by rocks pushed there by a large Michigan Loader earthmoving machine. This was a huge imposing machine, with tires bigger than I was. With the rocks in the way, that we now had to move, Charlie grew pissed that the big inanimate machine had caused us such a hassle. He spoke to it as if it had consciously attempted to foil us by its presence.

While Charlie had already become careless with his actions,

what happened next was the impulsive act that led to his ultimate undoing. We had extra gasoline and they decided they were going to burn the thing. They poured the gasoline over it and stepped away to light a match. The only thing that burned were the tires. Still, it was terrifying to see how out of control and irrational he'd become. Somehow in Charlie's mind the burning of this Michigan Loader was something he had to do. It was part of the quest.

It was getting late in the day. I looked up and saw a big star above the horizon. I was in awe of how bright it was. I thought to myself that this was what the star of Bethlehem must have looked like. To me it felt like a sign from God—the real one, not the one that Charlie had made himself into. Seeing this star reconnected me to something higher than myself. It made me feel that everything would be okay. It was a reassurance of another reality beyond Charlie, and I needed that reassurance because I was floundering and on the verge of losing my grip.

I tried to remember that bright star every day, but my sadness and despair was becoming debilitating. During one of his lectures that followed, Charlie was either impatient or generally agitated or he thought my attention had wandered. He stopped everything and told me to stand up.

"Snake, I am going to hang you upside down and skin you alive." Everyone gasped and I did not for a minute think he was kidding. "Get out of my sight!" he yelled at me. Not only did Charlie not care about me, but apparently he wanted me gone for good.

Some time after Charlie threatened me, I remember going to the toolshed next to the house at Barker Ranch. I wandered aimlessly inside, and as I looked around, my mind started to attack me with thoughts like *You are not going to survive. Your life is a mess. It is all your own fault. No one loves you and you have nowhere to go.* I could not get these thoughts out of my mind because pushing them away just took too much energy.

I saw a hammer on the floor and picked it up. I felt the coolness of the claw against my hands and put it up to my forehead. I closed my eyes and felt tears on my face. It would only take a minute if I hit my head just right. Then everything would stop. I would be free. I raised the hammer above my head and closed my eyes. I was about to strike when my hand fell still. I felt a rush of warmth and heard a voice say "*Stop!*" I opened my eyes. There was no one around. No one had seen me go into the toolshed. This voice drowned out all the bad thoughts.

Suddenly I felt okay. The moment had passed. I wasn't sure what had changed, but I knew I needed to survive. There was a reason for me to continue and somehow things would work out.

I WASN'T THE ONLY ONE WHO WAS LOOKING TO ESCAPE FROM CHARLIE and what was happening to us. Some girls had joined us shortly before the murders took place. One had been a favorite of Charlie's for a little while. She was a pretty girl named Stephanie Schram. The other girl was Kitty. I have no idea how they did it, but they managed to escape from the middle of nowhere to walk away from us. They escaped during the night through miles of wilderness and desert. It is impossible to convey how remote this part of Death Valley truly is. In 1969 people didn't go to Death Valley as tourists or hikers the way they do now. The only people we ever saw were the old miners or hermits who didn't want to be found. Once you enter Death Valley National Park, it takes three to four hours by vehicle to get to the ranch. If you are on foot at night, the terrain is impassable and it is treacherous.

Death Valley and Goler Wash are surrounded by mountains, and there's very little around but tumbleweeds and brush. Hiking through the wash at night by yourself is something done only out of desperation and the will to survive. This part of Death Valley is also not close to Los Angeles. It is at least a four-hour drive. Charlie clearly planned that we would not be discovered by anyone and that none of us could easily leave his side.

After Charlie discovered Stephanie and Kitty were missing, he changed our mission into finding them. We looked under bushes, through the canyons, and in the caves and hideaways we built. I looked but hoped that they were long gone. I would never have had the heart to turn them in. I know that if he had found them, he would have killed them or had them killed without hesitation. I knew that they would show no mercy even to one of our own. What I didn't know was Charlie, Tex, Bruce Davis, Clem, and some bikers had already brutally stabbed ranch hand Donald "Shorty" Shea to death because Charlie believed he was a snitch.

Luckily for the other two girls and for me, fate intervened in the form of the errant earthmoving machine. The Michigan Loader debacle was discovered and reported, so the Inyo County sheriff's department now had probable cause to see what we were up to. On October 10, 1969, Barker Ranch was raided. The cops descended on us with guns ablazing. For some reason, Charlie was not there that day. I hid under a bush while everyone was being taken away in handcuffs, waiting until the last of them was gone before I moved from my hideout.

When I emerged from my hiding place, I had a major problem I had not anticipated: I was completely alone in the desert with no one around and the possibility that no one would be coming back for me. I was panic-stricken. As I wandered between Barker Ranch and Myers Ranch, every stick became a snake and every bush a machine gun. I eventually wandered back to the bus, which now was permanently parked in its final resting place. The terrain was too much for it, so it became a satellite sleeping area and clothing repository.

The night was closing in and it was becoming cold. I went into the bus and covered myself with clothing, inhaling the familiar scent of my friends, who were now long gone. The next thing I felt were hands around my throat. I pictured my death and prepared myself for what was to come. It turned out it was Cathy Gillies, who had also escaped capture and was hiding out in the bus as well. We were so grateful to see each other that we hugged and I am sure I cried. At least together we could figure something out.

The next morning, Charlie came back and found us there, but no one else. He knew what had happened but told us not to worry. He thought the cops didn't have anything they could hold the others on. He seemed pretty confident. We went about our business for a few days, and then while I was washing my hair in the sink, I heard some people crash through the door.

"You are under arrest!" they shouted. The officers had guns pointed at me. I was shaking and crying.

Then they found Charlie hiding under a small cabinet in the bathroom. He must have folded himself in half, because it was a very small space. They noticed his hair sticking out.

A cop opened the cabinet and Charlie saw him and smiled. He was the picture of cool.

Charlie put up his hands and said, "I'm Charles Manson."

24

RECLAIMING MY NAME

THE POLICE WHO RAIDED US THIS SECOND DAY CLEARLY HAD NO IDEA who we were or what some of us had done. As far as anyone knew, we were a ragtag band of hippies who had vandalized a piece of government equipment. We might well have been suspected of other criminal behavior, but none outside the realm of what people typically thought hippies were up to. They certainly didn't connect us to the lurid murders that had taken place two months earlier and four hours away.

We were taken to the county jail in Independence, and Charlie and the men were put in one cell while Sadie, who'd also evaded capture during the first raid, Cathy, and I were reunited with the others, who were already in another cell. They were excited to see us and Squeaky quickly reminded us that Charlie had said, "You don't say nothing to nobody in authority."

"Snake, how did you not get picked up with the rest of us?" Nancy asked. Squeaky, Sandy, Lynette, Ruth, Leslie, Gypsy, and Sadie all laughed about that. For a minute, it didn't seem like we had just been arrested and horrible crimes had been committed. We were just us girls, together as we had been so many times.

"I hid under a bush." I liked having the attention as I described how I had almost stopped my breathing while I heard the cops rounding everyone up. Then Cathy shared center stage with me while we described both of us hiding out in the bus. "I thought she was going to kill me," I said while playfully smacking Cathy on her arm. They told me how Patty had been bailed out by her father after the first raid and was now in Alabama, possibly for good. While being bailed out would have been nice, I had to admit, I was glad to be with the other girls in this cell, which was set up like a dormitory. There were several bunk beds, a toilet, and a sink for us to share. At least I wasn't stuck in the desert in the middle of the night with nothing other than my fear.

Because we were out of our element, our groupthink became our tool for survival. One of the first tasks at hand was to help Sandy, who had just had her baby, keep her breast milk coming in. The baby had been taken away, and in our way of thinking, this was an affront to all of us, just another way for the pigs to keep us down. We helped Sandy by taking turns nursing at her breasts. It didn't seem unnatural to partake of her baby's food, because we were helping her maintain nourishment for one of our own.

From there, our groupthink took on new forms of rebellion as we looked for ways to stay connected to Charlie. We were being fed three meals a day at the jail, more food than we were used to on a regular basis. Instead of feeling grateful, Nancy and Squeaky became worried we were all going to get fat and Charlie would no longer like us that way. We all made a pact that we would throw up our food instead of being forced by our jailers to gain weight. Nancy made it a regular habit and showed all of us how to stick our fingers down our throats to rid ourselves of food. After a while, it became like a rush and a way to control the situation. I knew I would continue the habit even after I was released.

It wasn't long before some of us were let out of jail. They were holding us on the vandalism charge and it was clear that not all of us were present for that. I was one of the lucky ones who got to witness Charlie and Tex set fire to the Michigan Loader, so I got to stay. We found out that the way we were connected to the crime was by a simple red Ralphs supermarket matchbook. They found one on the scene and another at Barker Ranch. Something so small was the only real evidence they had against us, and the only reason they could hold us long enough for the truth to come out.

Some of the girls like Squeaky and Sandy got an apartment nearby while we were in jail. I have no idea how they paid for it, but they wanted to stay close to Charlie. Sadie was moved over to Sybil Brand women's prison in Los Angeles around November 1. Kitty, who was pregnant with Bobby Beausoleil's child, and Stephanie, the other of the two girls who had escaped with their lives, had been picked up by the Inyo County police either during or right after the raids. They had come out of hiding and told what they knew to the police, particularly about the Gary Hinman murder. For some reason, the two didn't discuss the other crimes except in general terms that would connect only later on in the investigative process.

As far as Inyo County was concerned, that was as far as it went. We were going to be stuck in jail until we could be tried for our crime against government property. I tried to pretend that was all there was. But my anxiety levels were almost unbearable because I knew at any moment something could change. The girls and I passed the time playing gin rummy. Gypsy, who also used another alias, Minon Minette, spent her time writing letters to author Robert Heinlein to see if he would help bail us out, since we were only acting in defiance of the establishment. He wrote her back a nice letter admitting he had done some pranks in his youth, but unlike the character in his book *Stranger in a Strange Land*, he was unable to offer any other type of legal or financial support. He was, however, very sympathetic, and we used the paper upon which he wrote his letter to keep score for an ongoing gin rummy game. Gypsy, Ouisch, and I were trying to pacify our boredom.

I found a book in the jail's small collection that changed my life. It sounds like a cliché, but it is true. By escaping into the thousand-page book called *The Sun Is My Undoing* by Marguerite Steen, I was able to rise above my surroundings. This historical novel about the

British slave trade opened my eyes and restored my reality. I had now been off LSD for several weeks, and the book gave my life purpose as I followed the travails of the characters.

Another turning point for me was overhearing two of the matrons talking about us. "I feel so sorry for those girls," one of the women said. She was a plain but sturdy woman in her fifties. She must have been responding to intuition because at this time she couldn't have known the half of who she had sitting in her jail. She just saw us as drifters who had turned our back on normal society for a literal pipe dream.

"Why do you feel sorry for them?" the other, a younger but equally plain woman, asked.

"Look at them, they are so young and yet their lives are over. They will never be able to make something of themselves."

I was sixteen years old, and according to her, my life was over. That is not what I wanted. That is not who I was before this mess.

I AM NOT SURE IF THE CRIMES WOULD EVER HAVE BEEN TRACKED BACK to Charlie and the Family if Sadie's need for attention had not revealed itself while she was in prison. Our indoctrination was such that when we did not have one another, reality could come crashing in at any point. At the first opportunity Sadie tried to proselytize her prison roommates with the glory of Charlie and then told them of her part in the crimes. And with that she provided the missing puzzle piece that allowed the detectives to realize they had the main conspirator already in prison in the little jail in Independence, California. They would also have to move quickly because they only had him on a vandalism charge. Unless there was a way to get him under indictment for the murders, he would not only be out of jail it was likely he would disappear for good.

Now that they had a statement from Sadie that at least pointed to the Family, we were all taken to Sybil Brand women's prison in Los Angeles for questioning. Because they thought I was Dianne

Bluestein in my early twenties, I was treated just like everyone else. We were separated from one another and I was led into a small room to be interrogated by a very angry officer named Gutierrez. He didn't even try any small talk. He got right to the point.

"Miss Bluestein, someone is going to go to the gas chamber for these murders . . . These are the murders of the century. To protect yourself from getting indicted you're going to have to come up with some answers. You're going to have to think real hard about it."

I was shaking and sick, but I didn't tell him anything of any importance. I was ready to cry, but I knew that would be my undoing. Then not only would everything come pouring out, but I would then be put right back into the cell with the other girls—and they'd figure out that I'd snitched. And if Charlie found out that I'd talked, who knows what would happen. Charlie would find some way to fulfill his promise to hang me upside down to skin me alive even if he was stuck in a jail cell. I had no doubt about this.

Perhaps because of my obvious distress, Sergeant Gutierrez continued to press me, pounding his fist on the table for emphasis. "Somebody is going to get the pill in the gas chamber for these murders of which you are a part." He stared me down, getting so much in my face I could feel his hot breath on my cheeks. I closed my eyes as I had seen lizards do when they want to disappear unnoticed.

"Would you like to spend your life in prison?" His voice was loud and high-pitched. He was becoming frustrated. He took a deep breath and tried another tactic. "We're not interested in you. We're interested in the big guy, and you know who we're talking about, honey." I shrugged my shoulders and still said nothing, just like the good soldier I had been trained to be. My programming was deep and covered in many layers of fear. The thought of saving myself never entered into my mind. I didn't see any options but silence.

Not only had he accused me of the murders, he even offered me immunity. I found out later that he couldn't have given me that even if he had wanted to. He didn't have authority to do so. I was too terrified to separate from the group anyway, so it didn't matter.

Even though the police got nothing from me, I was still brought to the grand jury with the other girls to testify on the afternoon of Monday, December 8, 1969. I have no idea why they thought anything would be any different.

One by one, we were brought in to tell our stories. As I was being led into the hearing room, Charlie's admonition of silence played over in my head. Then the bailiff asked me my name. Even now, all these years later, I truly do not know what came over me in this moment that changed the course of my future.

"My real name is Dianne Lake," I said. "I am only sixteen years old and I want my mommy!"

For the first time, since my first arrest, I had given law enforcement my real information, but just because I'd admitted my age and who I was didn't mean I was honest when answering their questions. I was still far too scared of Charlie for that. I'd been away from the drugs while in jail for the past month and a half, but I was not away from his influence and that of the other girls. I could see his face when I closed my eyes and could hear his voice in my head telling me not to say a word and to remain loyal.

"They will see that this is coming down," I heard over and over. "Then it will be too late." Charlie may have been in jail, but if the girls succeeded in maintaining their silence, there was a strong likelihood he wouldn't stay there very long. He also had people who were now out of jail available to do what he needed to have done.

They led me in to testify right after Ruth Ann. I was to be the last witness before handing down indictments. They must have had enough probable cause already because I know I didn't give them anything useful. I was evasive and avoided telling them anything that could be used to implicate anyone in these crimes. I told them I wasn't at Spahn Ranch the nights of the murders and a pack of other lies so they wouldn't continue to probe. Charlie had drilled into us the advantages of playing dumb and I was going to be as dumb as I could be to get through this without raising anyone's ire, least of all Charlie's.

This was the first time I had seen attorney Vincent Bugliosi in action, but it would not be the last. He asked me all the right questions and I answered them as evasively as I could. I said on the stand that I never knew anything about anything and that I didn't even know the person who drove me to Inyo in the first place. I was going to cover every possible tie-in I could, even if I had no idea what information was important to the prosecutor's case. They must have figured they were not going to get anything useful from me, so they dismissed me from any further testimony.

After all the testimony, the court handed down the indictments. I knew I hadn't said anything to cause these, but I was still afraid of Charlie and the girls. I was going to be going back in the same cell with everyone else, and there was a strong possibility that we would each become paranoid that one of the others had broken our code of silence. They would have no way of knowing if the cops had gotten to me. I now really had nowhere to go that would be safe.

TELLING THE TRUTH ABOUT MY REAL NAME AND AGE PROVED TO BE THE first step toward reclaiming myself. Once the court discovered that I was underage, they took a drastically different approach with me.

When I was brought back to Inyo County I discovered, much to my relief, that they had decided to move me to a private cell. This could have been bad for me by raising others' suspicions, but soon after that, they made me a ward of the state, which further insulated me from the other girls. Perhaps most important, though, they changed their strategy of trying to get information from me, using a detective who knew how to get on my good side. Officer Phil Sartuchi gained my trust by gently interrogating me, offering candy instead of death threats. It didn't hurt that he was quite handsome. Like water on a dried-out plant, his attention brought me back to life and helped me feel safe enough to unburden myself.

My telling of the truth was incremental at first, and attorney Bugliosi also worked to gain my trust. Surprisingly, he was not a bulldozer. He was nice and intelligent, willing to listen to me at my own pace. His patience and real empathy were what allowed me to begin to provide him with the information he needed to piece his case together.

Another crucial change besides providing me with sympathetic ears was that, as a ward of the state, I was sent to the mental institution in San Bernardino called Patton State Hospital. Even now I am not exactly sure how it happened, because decisions were being made for me. My parents had been found, but they were determined not to be suitable for me as a stable home. In addition, at my intake, the psychiatrist determined that I was in a state of psychosis. He later changed his diagnosis to LSD-induced psychosis, which was an important distinction because he would be able to say that I was no longer considered legally crazy and therefore would be competent to testify at trial. At the time, I suspect that my prognosis was undeterminable. I was a true LSD-soaked, Charlie-programmed, traumatized mess. Patton State was definitely the right place for me.

It's also likely that I was put in Patton State for my own protection. Scared of Charlie as I was, I still didn't fully appreciate the danger I would be in as a witness for the prosecution. I was in the hospital, so I would be alive for the trial. This was a very real threat. Later on, I found out that Paul Watkins had tried to visit me at the hospital. If he knew where I was, then others did as well.

Regardless of why they sent me there, it was a blessing. Going to Patton State when I did is what saved my life and my sanity. The hospital was a locked facility, but it was modern as far as its mental health care. I now know that I was very sick when I went in, and they helped me find my way out of a nightmare.

When I arrived at Patton State Hospital, my senses were so heightened that I remembered every little detail. They brought me through the front door and locked it behind me with a loud clang. There was a nurse's station behind glass in the middle. It looked like they were trying to make the communal room look comfortable and homey. The walls were still painted an institutional puke color, but the floors were linoleum and fairly new compared to other parts of the hospital. I could see girls and women in varying states of distress. One woman appeared to be dead, but I realized later that she was catatonic.

The nurse took me to a dormitory with about six beds in it. There were bars on the windows, but it was not at all like a cell. This was not a jail. They did not strip me down and spray me with insecticide as they had when I was in juvenile hall. On the other side of the hallway from the nurse's station was a huge bathroom with rows of clean showers.

There was a separate bathroom with the toilets. There were dormitories on both wings, with the communal room in the middle. There was also a kitchen near the communal room. Beyond that were offices for the psychiatrists and therapists.

Patton State was a place for innovation when it came to any kind of substance abuse. Even though there were horror stories from its early days when mental health treatment was still in the dark ages, by 1970 it was the first institution to do a controlled study on alcoholism. The doctor who would work with me was Dr. Harvey W. Oshrin, which proved another fortunate connection that would help bring me back to myself. Dr. Oshrin had done work on problems stemming from LSD abuse, and I am sure he found me a fascinating case study, especially since my parents were the ones who had turned me on in the first place. Until Dr. Oshrin, I'd never made the connection between my parents' LSD use and my ending up with

Charlie. He helped me see that it was not okay for me to have been turned on to drugs at such a young age.

Each time I spoke to Dr. Oshrin, I was pretty truthful with him about what I believed at the time. I am sure that I sat there with the flattest affect as if I was a zombie or someone withdrawn from reality. In fact, I found out later from the transcript of my psychiatric report from the trial that at first I appeared almost autistic. I was clearly depressed and disconnected. I was frightened and disrupted. This was a completely new environment away from my "sisters." They assumed it was the long-term LSD use but I hadn't had any LSD since we moved to the desert in September and were on the run. Everything was real and crystal clear, disturbingly so.

I also kept hearing Charlie's voice in my head while Dr. Oshrin was talking to me. I could see Charlie's face staring sternly at me. "Don't give in to the establishment, Snake. Don't trust anyone in authority. I am just a reflection of you and you are me." This could have been interpreted as psychosis, which was his initial diagnosis, but it was also complete programming. I had no idea where I began or ended without Charlie telling me so.

Charlie-speak was so ingrained in me that I even sounded like him when I spoke. When Dr. Oshrin asked me to explain what life had been like for the past three years I had to explain it in metaphors and analogies like Charlie did. No wonder they said I was psychotic.

His assessment of me said: "Conservatorship is recommended for Dianne Elizabeth Lake, who is in my care." Then he added, "It has been determined that this person is gravely disabled as defined by the Welfare & Institutions Code, Section 5008(h) as a result of a mental disorder, and is incapable of accepting treatment voluntarily." He also came to the conclusion that I was schizophrenic and suffered from a major mental disorder of psychotic proportions. That meant that I was committed against my will. However, I was happy to be there. For the first time in years I truly felt safe. I couldn't get out, but better still, no one could get in.

One of the first things Dr. Oshrin did was to order some diagnostic testing. One of the therapists gave me this test called the Minnesota Multiphasic Personality Inventory (MMPI), which had over four hundred questions. I tried to answer as truthfully as I could, but the test was confusing. I knew that they were looking to see if I was crazy and my answers might have sounded crazy but they were what I believed at the time. The answers were true or false, with no allowances for anything in between or explanations of your answers.

One question asked if I had ever been in trouble with the law. Compared with Charlie and the others, I had to say "false." I had never been convicted of a crime. And I had gotten out of trouble many times and had the records to prove it.

Another statement was "I often feel as if things are not real." I had to answer "True" to that one. My reality of the past six months was hard to believe.

The most difficult statement to respond to was if I believe I am being plotted against. This had to be a definite "True," even though whoever was going to evaluate this would probably think I was paranoid. I didn't think people were plotting against me, I knew they were. That was one of the reasons I was so scared.

I WAS IN PATTON STATE HOSPITAL FOR OVER EIGHT MONTHS. AFTER THE first few weeks, Charlie's voice began to fade from my head. The nurses at the nurse's station were pretty in their starched white uniforms and caps. One of them, Lucille, let me sit and talk with her if I wasn't required to be in a class or in a group of some sort. She let me read the magazines before they went out into the ward. And she often made me hot cocoa. She honestly seemed to care about me.

Even though I was in a mental institution, I was required to attend classes as if I was in school. There were other young people on my ward who complained how unfair this was. They were too tired. They didn't like the teachers. For me it was a blessing. I loved my classes and I got straight As. Finally, there was some consistent structure to give me a lifeline. I couldn't get enough.

I buried my pain into learning to play the flute. Just like any kid in school, I was given music lessons by a private instructor who brought me along at my own speed. The more I practiced, the better I became. Music became a gift and the flute made me feel centered and alive. The music came from my soul. The empty space formerly occupied by Charlie was now filled with my own music.

I also learned to express myself through arts and crafts at the hospital. One of the nurses taught a class on crochet and I picked the skill up quickly and masterfully. It felt so good to create something beautiful just for its own sake.

"That is lovely, Dianne." I had made a collar out of little squares of crocheted lace. "Why don't we use some material and make dresses with what you have made." When I finished a yellow gauze dress with a lace collar, I started to cry. I had never made something so beautiful with my own hands.

The group therapy gave me a window into how sick other people were. I found myself feeling sorry for them. The therapists told me I didn't have to speak if I didn't want to, so I curled up on the couch with a crocheted afghan someone had made and stayed silent. I didn't want to talk about Charlie and the girls and no one pressured me to discuss it. In this place with the locked doors and grated windows, I was just Dianne. There was no Snake. There was no Charlie. There was no Family.

"Hey, wake up, Dianne," my roommate Anita said. She was standing over me. "You were talking in your sleep. You were scaring me and you were going to wake up the whole dorm."

I wasn't sure why Anita was in Patton State and whether she had volunteered to be there. She was in her early twenties, with long, full dark hair past her shoulders. She never seemed to do anything to it, yet it stayed nice and smooth. Although I tried not to look too closely, I did notice some faint lines on her wrists and some faint lines on her thighs as they peeked out from under her nightshirt.

Anita had the bunk next to mine. "Dianne, I don't know what you were saying, but you seemed really scared."

Now I was completely awake. "I don't really remember what I was dreaming. Sorry if I woke you up."

"I'm a light sleeper."

Falling asleep was hard for me too. Every time I would feel myself fully relaxing, I would see Charlie's face. Or worse yet, I would see the girls laughing and giggling as they had when they told me what they had done. This night I had a nightmare that I was back with Charlie and the girls. I had been having sex with Charlie, and everyone—including the prosecutors, Dr. Oshrin, and even Lucille the nurse—told me what a bad idea it was.

"Dianne, why are you here?"

"Oh, I used too many drugs. I think it made me sick."

She showed me her wrists as if she believed I had not already noticed.

"You don't have to tell me about it if you don't want to," I whispered. One of the other girls had started to stir. We were supposed to be in our beds, but so far no one had checked on us.

"You're the only person who has said that to me." She reached out and gave me a hug. It was the first time anyone had touched me since I left everyone at the courthouse.

I was starting to have fun at the hospital. I was eating well and at least three times a day. I was still throwing up on occasion but had met someone who was so anorexic that she looked like a skeleton with skin. I thought about how Charlie wanted us skinny and felt ashamed that I was doing something on purpose and that this girl couldn't help herself because she was too far gone in her disease. From that day I never threw up my food again. I also swore that I would find a way to get over my own fatal addiction.

When the hospital had a visiting day, the therapists thought it would be a good idea for me to spend time with my real family to see if it would strengthen my resolve to be my own person. They asked my parents to come, and I wore the yellow dress I'd made for their visit.

"Look at you," my mother said when she saw me for the first time.

She hadn't been allowed to see me when I was in jail, and since I was under conservatorship, my parents couldn't just come anytime. My father was there and he complimented me on my beautiful dress, too, but otherwise didn't have much to say. As I learned, my mother and father had a divorce ceremony, and she was now living someplace in Oregon with the man I met at the alternative school. But I didn't really care about all their changes; they'd come to see me at the hospital and that was all that mattered.

As we sat together in the community room, my mother took my face in her hands and started to cry. "You look so beautiful and healthy," she sobbed. "I am so sorry."

I didn't understand what she was talking about. "Why are you sorry, Mom?"

The therapist suggested we not talk about anything heavy but rather just enjoy the visit, so we left it there.

The visit went quickly and I didn't see them again while I was in the hospital. I didn't want to talk about them in therapy, even though Dr. Oshrin and my psychologist probed. My memories of them were so faint—if I probed them too much, it felt like they might slip away altogether.

On February 28, 1970, I turned seventeen at Patton State. As the day came closer, I was feeling very sad. No one mentioned anything to me, and the familiar feelings of being ignored and forgotten began to return. This was ironic because Charlie had always told us birthdays were just a sign of our egos. I think he even hit me one time when I asked about celebrating my birthday. But I was slowly thawing and wanted to have the attention of the one special day honoring my existence on earth.

Dr. Oshrin called me in for a session and kept asking me dumb questions that we had gone over before. As I was leaving, he gave me a note to bring to the therapist who was holding group in the community room. As I got closer I got confused. Everyone was gone. Even the catatonic sitting in the corner chair staring out the window was not in her usual place.

I went in anyway and looked around. Then Anita, who had been discharged, and the girls from my dorm jumped up from behind the couch and yelled, "Surprise!" The nurses brought out a cake from the kitchen and put on some music. Anita had planned the whole thing and had come back to the hospital just for my special day. I hadn't had a birthday party just for me since I had been a little girl in Minnesota. There were even presents.

"Dianne, open mine last." Anita put hers off to the side. It was a small package with a handmade paper bow.

One of the girls had crocheted me a hat. Another had drawn me a picture of a garden of flowers. I am sure I had mentioned the old greenhouse during a group meeting. Danielle, one of the nurses, gave me a beautiful gift book with inspirations. When I got to Anita's gift, she was so excited she helped me rip off the colorful wrapping paper.

"I love it so much!" It was a papier-mâché pin with a psychedelic picture with my favorite colors, and on the back it said *a lollipop*. This small token of our friendship is still one of my prized possessions. It reminded me of being a real person with a friend who liked me just for me.

WHEN I WAS FINALLY RELEASED FROM PATTON STATE, I FELT LIKE A WHOLE person, perhaps for the first time since I'd come of age. For the first time in years, I had been given structure and purpose. They treated me like a human being, not a piece of chattel to be toyed

with, abused, and passed around to old men with perverted fe-
tishes for young girls. They encouraged me to explore my own
voice and creative vision. When we were living with Charlie only
his reality held any importance. Now I was free to create my own
on *my* terms.

When it was time to leave Patton State, there was no way I was
going to be released into my parents' custody. The doctor might
have held some prejudice against my parents' lifestyle, taking into
consideration how their alternative ways might have led me down
the Manson family path. But it also had been years since I had lived
with them, and by this time my mother had a new baby with her
new husband. Even though my mother seemed perfectly happy, it
was too much for me to integrate.

Honestly though, I don't think the state wanted me anywhere
but under its control for my own safety and for the benefit of the
trial. With that in mind, Jack Gardiner, one of the arresting officers in Inyo County, became my foster parent. Jack and his wife,
Carol, had visited me at the hospital. What I remember about my
first meeting with Jack was his strong jaw and firm handshake. Aside
from his typical law enforcement demeanor, he was a father figure
that I sorely needed. I know there was partially a motive to his generosity, as he was assisting Bugliosi in figuring out the case, but Jack
was also a kind man who had fostered many children through their
difficult years. This was the second law enforcement family from
Inyo County to offer me their home, and this time I was going to
appreciate it to the fullest.

Jack and Carol took me into their home with their own children,
a younger boy and girl, but they made room in their hearts for me.
Carol made me feel welcome and never mentioned my past even
though I am sure she was not thrilled to have another teenager in the
mix. At seventeen years old and very much stunted in my maturity,
I was in desperate need of parenting. Their daughter, Cindy, was
four years younger than me and we immediately bonded like sisters.

We shared a clean and girlie room in their comfortable ranch-style home. We talked to each other at night and Cindy shared with me her growing interest in boys.

Patton State had done wonders to instigate my healing process, but the Gardiners' warmth was even more rejuvenating. This was the most normal I had felt in years, maybe ever. I am sure as any family they had their own issues, but to me they were like a television family, old-fashioned and real. Their values were homespun and they didn't put on airs. Carol was always dressed nicely whether she was headed to a ranch to ride or to the grocery store. Life with the Gardiners made sense. I arrived at their home the weekend before school was starting, so there wasn't much time to get acquainted before I had to face a completely new environment. All during Labor Day weekend we rushed to buy clothing appropriate for me to enter the school year as a teenager and not as a hippie escapee from a killer cult. This meant some disagreements over the clothing I was to wear, as I hadn't dressed so conservatively since elementary school in Minnesota. I kept choosing miniskirts, and Carol would return them to the racks for pants and skirts of appropriate lengths. Of course I relented. In a way, I was happy she cared enough about what I was wearing to argue with me.

I started school on Tuesday and immediately integrated back into teenage life. I was put into the tenth grade because I had missed so much school, but it didn't matter to me, at least at first. The school in Big Pine went from kindergarten to senior year, but since it was so small, different grades often shared the same classrooms. I could meet students my own age and no one made a fuss that I was in classes below my age group. Big Pine School was an old two-story brick building that contained the history of all the families whose children had passed through its hallways. I was the new kid in school, and when I began, I was viewed only as another one of Jack Gardiner's foster children. No one knew where I had come from, and no one bothered to ask.

School was such a welcome change. I got involved in my class-work and did all my assignments. My flute playing guaranteed me automatic acceptance in the school band. After school, I helped Carol around the house and did homework, and then we all had dinner together as a family. Each of us talked about our day and Jack and Carol showed genuine interest in what each of us had to contribute to the conversation. I didn't feel that I was struggling to be noticed or had to compete with anyone for the floor. It became very easy to live my life and to forget why I was in their home, where I had been and what I would be facing. I was accepted in the little community of Big Pine. The neighbors invited me to babysit for their children and I got a real driver's license after completing driver's education class. Carol was very nervous but still allowed me to use her Jeep Wagoneer for my road test. She had no idea how adept I was at driving. She thought I was overcautious, but it was because I still had the fear of my experience of driving in the wilds of the Death Valley canyons.

After I secured my place on the honor roll in the first report-ing period, I was invited to participate in the weekly school trips to Mammoth Mountain, where I learned how to ski. This is what I had dreamed that high school could be. But I had become too comfort-able, and with a simple phone call, my reality changed once again.

25

MY DAY IN COURT

THE STATE OF CALIFORNIA V. CHARLES MANSON, PATRICIA KRENWINKEL,
Leslie Van Houten, Linda Kasabian, and Susan Atkins had gotten under way right after the handing down of the indictments. While I'd been safely tucked away at Patton State, the legal system moved into high gear and Charlie made it his mission to control as much of the outcome as he possibly could, using his chameleon-like changeability and con-man charm to infiltrate every aspect of the proceedings.

I was present only for my own days of testimony, but as I read through some of the original transcripts, of which there were thousands of pages today, it's fascinating how from the start no one seemed to see Charlie for what he really was. From the very first day Charlie wanted to represent himself in court. Aside from his suspicion of the legal system and lawyers in particular, he wanted the platform to tell his story from his point of view. He had been able to convince us of his version of reality. I think he believed he could do the same in front of a jury.

Charlie argued vehemently in front of Judge William B. Keene, a distinguished silver-haired man in his late forties, who reluctantly gave him the benefit of the constitutional right for someone to waive counsel if they can show the capability of representing themselves. This was only after Judge Keene tried to show Charlie that representing himself would put him at a grave disadvantage. Charlie replied that "there is no attorney in the world that can represent me as a person. I have to do it myself." After extensive discussion in which

Charlie held his ground, Judge Keene recommended that Charlie discuss the matter with a lawyer who would not be representing him for neutral legal advice. Charlie agreed.

Looking back at what happened behind the scenes of the trial made me feel better about my own gullibility, because some great legal minds were easily fooled by Charlie. Charlie spent an hour with a top-notch criminal defense attorney recommended by the California Bar Association who at one time had been a prosecutor. Perhaps the lawyer had become too enmeshed with the "zealously represent your client" approach of overlooking guilt or innocence, but his report back to the judge reads as a clear sign that he had been Charlie-ized. Although the lawyer did not recommend Charlie represent himself due to the advantages a well-trained legal team could offer, he said he believed Charlie could handle it because he had a ready understanding of problems of law. In fact, the lawyer indicated he had a remarkable understanding and what he called a very fine brain. He believed Charlie had to have a high IQ to be able to converse as he had. He also described Charlie as an "able, intelligent young man, quiet-spoken and mild-mannered."

In the beginning the judges tried to treat this case as any other, in spite of their colorful defendant. Certainly, this was not the first capital crime in the courthouse. It had received more publicity than any other case, and the brutality combined with the celebrity status of some of the victims brought it into national attention, but the rules of law were the same. The judges were sincerely concerned that Charlie understand the implications of representing himself in court and that he could be giving up his constitutional right to a fair trial when facing legal complexities without the arsenal of education and experience possessed by the prosecutors. The judges, in their effort to strictly follow legal procedure, vastly underestimated Charlie, and the result was a trial that was more of a circus, with Charles Manson as the ringmaster. Thankfully, as the trial wore on, Charlie became his own enemy.

Charlie got away with quite a bit during most of the pretrial procedures until finally he pushed the envelope too far. He wanted privileges not afforded to attorneys but especially not to jailhouse lawyers accused of heinous crimes. Charlie played the mild-mannered victim of the unfairness of the system a little too long, filing absurd motions until they finally got under Judge Keene's skin and he revoked Charlie's privilege to represent himself. The end result was one that not surprisingly made Charlie very unhappy and caused him to lose his cool. No longer hiding behind the mild-mannered image he had created for the benefit of the court, Charlie changed his tactics to get what he wanted, creating months of additional delays as he fought unsuccessfully to represent himself.

After Charlie lost the right to be his own attorney, he seemed to have upped his game of crazy-making. What followed were months of additional pretrial motions in which the court seemed as if it was trying to work with a person who was reasonable and rational. In hindsight, it seems obvious what Charlie was trying to do, but he had become very good at manipulating the courtroom. After his loss of status, every little thing became an impossible argument where the judge could not get him to give a straight answer. Perhaps it was simple oppositional defiance, but it was likely calculated to at minimum drive the judge insane.

THE PRETRIAL MOTIONS FOR THE *STATE V. MANSON* AND THE OTHER defendants lasted so long and created such havoc in the game of attorney musical chairs that the trial itself didn't begin until July 1970.

By that point, I was still in Patton State unraveling my life with the Family and soon to be living in a stable life with Jack, Carol, and my foster siblings. This made it that much more difficult when the call came that I was to testify. Upon hearing the news, I found it hard not to retreat into the inner world I'd been trying to escape from for the last several months, but I understood that this was the price I had to pay to escape my past—for good.

Attorney Bugliosi prepared me for my testimony and warned me that I would be facing Leslie, Sadie, and Patty in the courtroom. I was aware that they had given Linda Kasabian, the driver on both nights of the murders, complete immunity, but they insisted they still needed my testimony. Linda was a key witness to the crimes, but she had been with us only a month. She was not present during the two years it took for Charlie to make us believe in him and his cause and to find willing accomplices to commit the worst crimes imaginable. There was no getting out of it. I would be seeing these women again and would be forced to recount what they had told me about what they had done.

Then Bugliosi reminded me that I would also be facing Charlie. Although I was not aware of the antics he had been pulling in the courtroom, Bugliosi certainly was. I was told that Charlie would try to rattle me and intimidate me. This almost made me laugh—as if I wasn't already terrified by him. I had been living with Charlie since I was fourteen years old and had watched him through most of his many phases. He had been angry at me, had beaten me, had raped me, and had threatened my life. And that was done when he still thought I was loyal and in love with him. I could only imagine what it would be like to confront him now.

Bugliosi knew this case was not going to be won easily. I would be the last key witness in a seven-month trial. The theme running through the pretrial motions and the testimony up to the day I was to step into court was that Charlie was going to use everything in his power to come out on top. He believed that he hadn't done anything wrong. He had also convinced his codefendants to parrot everything he said, and throughout the trial and in the aftermath, they eventually tried to bypass their own attorneys by insisting they were the only ones who could put on their own defense because no one else could explain their philosophy.

One of Charlie's maneuverings behind the scenes during the months of pretrial motions had been to join all the defendants under a team of Family-friendly defense attorneys. In doing this, Charlie had completely defused the impact of Susan Atkins's grand jury testimony, in which she had fully confessed to the crimes and explained a bit about Charlie's role. Because of two court cases called *People v. Aranda* and *Bruton v. United States,* and by joining all the accused as codefendants in a single trial, something that a non-Family attorney might have insisted was not in the best interests of his client, Charlie made sure the girls could not implicate one another or implicate him. If, for example, Patty, who was never going to testify anyway, wanted to testify to what Charlie might have told her, like "do something witchy," it would be inadmissible. If she had her own attorney and was separated from this trial, her testimony to this statement by Charlie would be allowed. That was really Charlie's main concern. That statement alone could prove conspiracy and support the prosecution. This was an interesting lockdown situation meant to protect defendants against each other, but it now served to protect Charlie by making it difficult for the prosecutor.

There were going to be problems with my testimony aside from the obvious fact that I had just been in a mental institution and had lied through my teeth during the grand jury testimony. The Aranda-Bruton Motion was going to limit how much I could share what I really knew about what had happened and what everyone had done. The case was tricky. If I knew something Patty said about what Leslie told her or what Charlie told her, it was inadmissible. It was as if a codefendant was giving the testimony himself even though it would come from me. The Aranda-Bruton Motion essentially limited all of our testimony to statements made directly to us or within our direct knowledge through observation. If Leslie told me something she had done, that was evidence. If I saw something circumstantial that could tie her to the crimes, that was evidence. The few things I did know that were admissible were keys to the puzzle Bugliosi was trying to piece together for the jury. I had the only admissible evidence that could directly link Leslie to the LaBianca murders. With this in mind, the defense lawyers were going to do everything they could to eliminate my testimony before I even got to the courtroom.

The first thing they were going to do was attack my credibility. Being in a mental institution is an immediate weakness on the witness stand, especially when you are diagnosed as psychotic and schizophrenic. Attorney Bugliosi made sure I was cleared by my psychiatrist, who determined that by the time I left Patton State I was no longer legally insane. He said I'd had a drug-induced psychosis through extensive LSD use. I didn't hold back when I was working with Dr. Oshrin about what the Family believed, and that would have made any doctor question my sanity. He was more focused on the trauma, dreams, and hallucinations.

In the fall, while I was at Jack's attending school, the lawyers had a hearing to determine if my testimony should be allowed. They were of course questioning my competency. From what I understand, the judge ruled that my detailed psychiatric records could not be read by the defense into the record, as they were not admissible. I believe the general report saying that I was no longer psychotic was permitted, but the defense wanted to use the entire file to impeach that finding. This way they could show that I was not competent, the first step toward eliminating my testimony altogether. In the end, there was a compromise ruling that I was to be examined by a court psychiatrist to determine my competency to testify.

When Jack got the call for me to appear in California for the psychiatric examination, I felt like my world collapsed. I had started to believe that I was a normal teenager living with a loving family who could forget her past. I was making friends, I was well liked, and I was working with the band to prepare for what would be our big end-of-the-year recital. The idea that now I would have to prove my sanity was crushing.

When I'd been in Patton State and living with the Gardiners, I didn't have to think about my own level of responsibility for having believed in Charlie. I didn't think about the consequences of having been involved with the Family. I'd been able to focus on getting better without diving too deeply into the pain I'd suffered. Now I was diving headfirst back into the current I fought so long and so painfully against.

AS JACK DROVE ME INTO LOS ANGELES FOR WHAT WOULD BE TWO EX-aminations by court-appointed psychiatrists, I tried to stay calm. I would be meeting Dr. Skrdla and Dr. Deering separately on October 26, 1970, to satisfy the court that I was competent to testify. I was feeling good about myself and not at all like the scared, withdrawn girl who was brought to Patton State the previous January. I might even enjoy telling these two men how much I progressed since then. It had become easier to tell my story to professional listeners.

Jack and I arrived in Los Angeles and checked into the hotel rooms we were given. The solitude was good for me and I made the most of having a full-size bed and a television all to myself. Jack had given me snacks and soda and told me to relax. Neither of us had any idea how long we would be staying in Los Angeles, so I ran a bath and soaked in it until my skin turned creased. Then I put on some clean pajamas, read a teen magazine, and fell asleep.

Dr. Skrdla talked to me for over two hours. He had the report from Patton State in front of him but only skimmed it. He said that the past was important, but he was more interested in who I am now and what I think about myself and what I had been through. Although I was eager to talk to him, it was obvious I was very reluctant and nervous about testifying.

"What are you feeling right now, Dianne?" he asked me in a typical psychiatrist tone. His presence was calming, but I had spent over eight months being asked that very same question.

"To be honest, I am really scared about facing everyone."

"Are you afraid something will happen to you?" he asked earnestly.

"I am not as afraid of that as I was. It is difficult to be reminded about how I felt back then when I first went to the hospital. I was so confused and depressed."

"Was it because you were in the hospital?" I was glad he didn't jump right into the reason I was really there and what had happened.

"I was depressed because everything had become so frightening and then when I was taken away from the girls and put into Patton State Hospital. It was a new environment and I missed everyone."

"Your records say you were very withdrawn when you first got there and seemed confused. They said you described things in ways that didn't make much sense." That made me giggle, even though I knew that could be considered an inappropriate response. I had been called on things like laughing to myself by my therapists, but they didn't understand the things that kept running through my head. How could my experiences have made sense to anyone? It was my first chance to separate reality from Charlie's fantasy.

Dr. Skrdla asked me a lot of questions about my family history. I could see him raise his eyebrows as I told him how even I didn't approve of how my parents gave me drugs at such a young age and dropped out of society. By the end of our session he smiled and said, "Dianne, I think you are really going to be okay."

Dr. Deering's session was a lot more of the same. Both doctors concluded that I was competent to testify and that I was no longer suffering from LSD-induced psychosis. They did, however, acknowledge that I was a very insecure, dependent girl who is very confused by the threatening world about her and by the chaotic and abnormal experiences during the last few years. This, they said, is what caused me to need to associate with either a family or a group. Of this, I would heartily agree.

WHEN THE DAY CAME FOR MY TESTIMONY, MY STOMACH CHURNED WITH nausea. Jack tried to reassure me and coach me on how to be on a witness stand. He avoided the substance of my testimony, as he had been careful not to overtly influence me or interfere with the attorney's role. He simply reminded me how to last through a trial without falling apart.

"Dianne, remember that less is more when you are on the witness stand."

"I shouldn't say very much?" I asked hopefully.

Jack explained how much the defense attorneys were going to try to confuse me and trip me up. *Kind of like Charlie,* I thought to myself. If that was the case I was already well trained. Jack admonished me to be on my best behavior, as Charlie had. Becoming sassy would make it look like I was not telling the truth. He also told me to listen carefully and answer only what I was asked. He said people tend to talk too much and volunteer information. Listening is your best tool. Where had I heard that before? Again, Charlie's tutelage would help me in testifying against him.

Above all, I needed to stay focused. If I allowed myself too much time to think about the reality of what I would be facing, I would relive the terror I felt in the desert. Even though I had been in the hospital for eight months, I had no idea that it would take almost a lifetime to unravel the web of trauma created during the two years I spent with Charlie and the Family. As much as I'd healed, I was still incredibly vulnerable.

Back then, as I faced giving my testimony against him, what I feared wasn't his intimidation or his threats. Those were easy enough to use to my advantage—after all, I was used to those. No, oddly enough, what I feared were the good times, the good memories, or the memories that at least back then still felt good. The love I believed I'd felt for him in the beginning. The way he looked that first night I met him at Spiral Staircase House when he'd taken me by the hand. Watching him play guitar with Dennis Wilson. I was the only one who knew it, but the good times were my weakness. They were more dangerous to me, as they were the only thing that could reignite my sick loyalty to this man and the women who had been my only family at a time when I had nobody. The good times were what made me think I belonged.

As we neared Los Angeles, I knew what I had to do. For years I hadn't belonged to anyone but myself. I'd stopped belonging to my family when we'd dropped out. I'd belonged to the Family only as part of the grander illusion of what we were for and what we represented. As much as they'd saved me, in my heart, I knew that I didn't belong with Jack and Carol; they cared deeply for me but weren't my real family either. The only constant through it all had been me. This was the only person I belonged to, the only person I was truly responsible for. It was time for me to put away the fantasy of anyone rescuing me and to realize that I would have to be there for myself. I would reclaim my own identity and my sense of purpose, and trust God that someday I would belong to a family of my own.

The first hearing was kind of a practice run, held in court but not in front of the jury. The lawyers had to see if I could testify without violating the Aranda-Bruton Motion. It didn't feel like practice to me. I made sure to dress nicely in the clothing Carol bought me when we were shopping for me to go back to school. I wore a white starched blouse and checked jumper. My hair was neatly styled in two braids. Charlie was in the room, and I could feel his presence before I even reached the courthouse. It was the Friday before Halloween. Before I could even get to Charlie, though, first I had to run the gauntlet. The girls were waiting behind a makeshift barrier in the hallway leading to the door to the courtroom. As I stared straight ahead, Squeaky and Ruth Ann were shouting at me as I was led in flanked by police guards. I didn't see them but I heard them shout to me, "You ain't plastic and you know it. You can't turn your back on your love."

I did my best to ignore them and smiled. The last thing I wanted was to be pulled back into their world. It represented nothing but pain for me. I inhaled deeply and looked straight ahead. I was vaguely aware of reporters all around me. Flashbulbs were popping and people were shouting at me to say things. The noise became an unrecognizable din as I pushed ahead.

My stomach jumped when I first eyed Charlie sitting at the defendant's table. I knew he couldn't touch me with his hands, but he could with his eyes. On some level, I believed he could still penetrate me with his mind. It didn't matter how much psychiatric therapy I'd had saying that was impossible. Charlie's glare telegraphed his disgust that I was in the courtroom, on the stand, and maybe even on the earth.

It was not surprising that the defense attorneys and Charlie tried to have me discredited and eliminated at this early stage so the jury would never hear what I had to say. The defense argued how improbable it was that I had entered the hospital with a diagnosis of schizophrenia and psychosis and was now fine to testify. They swore me in, but it took a while before I was to speak.

As the lawyers argued, my attention wandered to take in the scene. The courtroom in Los Angeles was much more impressive than the one in Inyo County. The grandeur of the wood paneling created a sense of awe in me and filled me with respect. As much as I'd been a part of the counterculture, I'd quickly adapted to life with a police officer, spending my days being surrounded by the prosecutors on the so-called establishment side of the case. I liked the structure of the courtroom. I discovered that rules made sense and I wanted to follow them.

Aside from simple tuning out, I wanted to avoid looking at Charlie, Patty, Leslie, or Susan. I imagine it is difficult for people to understand how it felt at this time to have been separated from a group who for almost two years had been closer than my blood family. Right up to the last moment, I wasn't sure I could do what was asked of me. Even as I walked into the courtroom the threads of connection had not yet been severed.

During this special hearing before only the defendants, the attorneys, and the judge, the lawyers planned to ask me everything I was planning to say. This would determine whether I would testify before the jury. I didn't realize until reading the transcripts much later that the defense was going to try to show that I was an accomplice with knowledge ahead of time of the criminal acts. This wasn't necessarily to charge me with a crime—although that was a real possibility—but was a ploy to eliminate my testimony. In California, the testimony of an accomplice is admissible against a defendant only if there is other corroboration. They tried to use this to eliminate Linda Kasabian's testimony, and now they were going to use it against me.

They didn't succeed with Linda Kasabian, but the loss of me as a witness might have had a more direct effect on the outcome of the case. There was corroborating evidence from other witnesses for things Linda said or they found other ways to get around it. If they knocked me off the witness list, there was little to tie Leslie to the crimes.

I avoided Charlie's gaze as I told what I knew in as much detail as I could. Charlie was seething. He has said more than once that he had only one law he lived by—he didn't snitch. I was breaking Charlie's law, but it could no longer be mine. When the lawyer asked me about Patty and what she had told me, I said that she'd proudly described how she dragged Abigail Folger from the bedroom to the living room. These were not the people I thought they were, and Patty was clearly acting for Charlie. What she did, she did for him and for what he believed. She believed it too. In that moment, I could admit that Charlie was the real evil behind these murders.

The attorneys asked me how I could remember anything after so many LSD trips, but they didn't understand how these experiences had been emblazoned in my memory, which unfortunately might even have been enhanced by my use of LSD.

After the attorneys were finished examining and cross-examining me, Charlie got my attention. He made full penetrating eye contact.

"Were you programmed to answer?" he shouted. I could see no love in his eyes. But I still felt a tinge of guilt. I quickly turned away and left when the judge said I was dismissed.

THE NIGHT BEFORE I HAD TO TESTIFY ON THE RECORD, I WAS GIVEN A court-appointed attorney named George Vaughn. There had already been a hearing about the grand jury testimony, so I knew that they would be asking about that. I knew I had lied to the grand jury and could have been charged with perjury. I said as little as I could and told them I wasn't anywhere near the Spahn Ranch the night of the murders so they would ask me as little as possible.

I don't think anyone realized how hard it was for me even to tell them my real name. They couldn't possibly expect me to tell them everything I knew. The girls were still in the jail cell that I would be going back to, and Charlie had made it clear not to say anything to anyone in authority. Telling the truth was not an option.

Attorney Vaughn had an expensive-looking leather-back chair that made him look very tall and official. He also had a small television set on the side of his L-shaped desk, along with a picture of his wife and neatly stacked newspapers. He had a bowl full of paper clips. His short dark hair was neatly combed, and he looked a little bit like what I remembered of John F. Kennedy. I was thinking I wanted to make a chain out of his paper clips when he said, "Dianne, you could be in some very serious trouble if you testify."

"I know that, Mr. Vaughn."

"Whatever you think you know, it is my duty as your court-appointed counsel to make sure that your needs are what are served in this proceeding, no matter the consequences for the case. I know that you want to do what is best, but you have to consider the outcome for you."

"I promised the people of the County of Los Angeles that I would testify." This sounded like a line, but it was the truth. Bugliosi represented the people, and I was not going to let him down. I knew that without my testimony, the state case against Leslie would have been weak and they all knew it. If one of the defendants was to be acquitted, it could have led to the falling of the legal house of cards. My testimony and a guilty verdict against Leslie would corroborate the conspiracy theory under which Charlie was being charged. In many ways, I hadn't felt like I'd mattered for years, but in this moment, in this case, I knew my voice counted. I was always the one being beaten, the one receiving Charlie's punishments. This was my opportunity to help make sure justice, if there could be such a thing for crimes like these, would be served.

"Dianne, you need to understand what the implications might be for you if you do this. I know that Mr. Bugliosi is a nice man and you want to do what you promised, but spending your life in jail or worse is not worth the risk."

"What do you mean?"

"For instance, there can be state charges brought against you. By testifying you are basically waiving your right against self-incrimination."

"That's okay. If I did something, then I did it."

"You could also be facing federal charges as someone participating in the so-called Manson plan. There could be potential conspiracy charges or whatever the court decides based upon your testimony."

"I wasn't part of the plan to kill anyone! I never thought they would kill anyone!" I was starting to hyperventilate, so Mr. Vaughn brought me a cup of water. "I am sure I want to testify, Mr. Vaughn. I really feel I have to do it. I don't care about what Charlie or the girls think about me anymore."

"That may be so, but with a case as complicated as this, anything can happen. It is my job to warn you about that and that bad things can happen to people even if they are not guilty. That is how this system works. If the court finds you were even somewhat responsible, they can bring charges. And this was such a horrific murder the public is looking for everyone who they could possibly blame."

I must have been in his office for two hours. I told him everything I knew and what I had seen. And when it was over, I felt the same as I did before. It wasn't the same for me as it was for Linda Kasabian. I wasn't indicted, and accusing me of complicity was a stretch. There was no immunity available. My biggest vulnerability was for perjury. It was a chance I was willing to take. My conscience was weighing too heavily on me to be passive in spite of what everyone, including the doctors, thought of me.

"I really appreciate everything that you are telling me, Mr. Vaughn. I am going to testify."

"Are you sure? There will be no going back. Once you get on the stand, the defense will try everything to make it look like you are a liar, or worse yet, that you are insane."

"Mr. Vaughn, both of those things might have been true in the past, but they are not now. I am going to testify because I believe in my heart that if I tell the truth the truth will protect me. I know if I tell the whole truth, that I have no reason to be afraid that anything bad will happen to me."

Attorney Vaughn explained that he was someone neutral and his role was to advise me without any emotional pressure that I might feel from people like Jack and Bugliosi. He knew I wanted to please them, but this was not about them, it was about me. No matter what, I was willing to take the risk because I needed my life back.

ON THURSDAY, NOVEMBER 5, 1970, AFTER A WEEK OF LAWYERS GRILL-ing me in front of Judge Older to determine if my testimony was admissible, I was led up the steps and back into the courtroom to face the jury. Out of the corner of my eye I saw some of the girls like Ruth Ann, Sandy, and Nancy Pitman sitting in a circle on the corner of the road as if they were having a vigil. They had shaved their heads and, I learned later, had a cross carved in their forehead.

This was a shock, but it didn't intimidate me, it made me feel sad. It showed me how caught up in Charlie they still were. They had mutilated themselves for him.

When I took the stand and was sworn in, I knew that this testimony would count. This time I had made a conscious decision to let my voice be heard. No one could talk me out of what I knew I had to do, not even Charlie. Even so, I didn't want to look at him. After eight months in the hospital, a new life, and a legal pep talk, I hoped that I was in remission from Charlie's influence. As expected, Charlie glared at me and tried to intimidate me by penetrating my thoughts as he had done in the past. He was so aware of my weak spots that he made it appear that he was in my head reading my thoughts and that he could influence them with a glance. At first my stomach jumped. I tried to avoid eye contact. He had a cross on his forehead as well. He said it was to X himself out of society, as he had already been condemned, but I knew otherwise. This mark was not to X himself out but to X himself in. This was the mark of the elect who would be saved during the apocalypse predicted in the Book of Revelation.

With Bugliosi's encouragement I began my testimony with inner strength. As far as I was concerned Charlie didn't have any power over me anymore. At least that is what I hoped.

I looked him right in the eyes when I stated and spelled my name. "I am Dianne Lake, D-i-a-n-n-e L-a-k-e."

When the prosecutor finished examining me, it was the defense attorney's turn. They cross-examined me for five days and were far more strident than when we were only in front of the judge. They tried to confuse me and intimidate me, but I felt as long as I avoided eye contact with Charlie or the girls, I would be okay. The attorneys tried to show that my testimony was coerced by the police department, who when they first interrogated me, threatened me with the gas chamber. This tactic was somewhat amusing, as they didn't realize that after I had spent two years with the Family, Sergeant Gutierrez, though a complete bully, could never be worse than Charlie. There was no proof that he had gotten anything from me under duress. In fact, I told Gutierrez less than nothing. It was Sergeant Sartuchi who figured out the way to get to me was with kindness, attention, and, in his case, candy.

Charlie, as expected, was disruptive during my testimony. When Ronald Hughes, Leslie's attorney, didn't have any questions for me, Charlie shouted out to him "Why don't you go home then if you're not going to ask any questions, lawyer?" Charlie didn't understand that by the limitations of the Aranda-Bruton Motion, there was nothing Ronald Hughes could ask me that would not violate that rule.

To cover himself, Ronald Hughes claimed censorship imposed by Judge Older.

Charlie then threatened the judge, saying, "One of these days you're going to be overruled, man." Then he added: "You've got your flunkies. It'd be a different story if it were just you and I."

I was holding up fine with Charlie's hostility permeating the courtroom. That strengthened my resolve. The real test came when it was attorney Irving Kanarek's turn to cross-examine me. He caught me completely off guard. I had made a commitment to the truth, but now I had to face my deepest fear with the same honesty. I was not afraid of Charlie, I was afraid of myself. The first question Kanarek asked me was if I had ever been intimate with Charlie. Images of the first time with him passed through my mind, how loved and cherished I felt. I said yes before the bad memories could erase my rose-colored nostalgia.

He then asked me if I had been jealous when Charlie was paying attention to other girls, especially toward the end of our time together. Again, I had to say yes. I didn't mind Charlie being with other women, but he had rejected me even before his latest recruits had come on board. I missed being the favorite even if it had been only in my mind. That was the truth, and the pangs of emotion were starting to weaken me.

Then he asked me what I truly wished he hadn't.

Are you in love with Mr. Manson now?

I looked over at Charlie, and for a moment his eyes seemed to soften—at least that is what I hoped. I weakly uttered in the affirmative: "I guess so."

I could hear rumblings in the courtroom and I felt defeated. Kanarek had started to ask another question when Charlie shouted out to me: "You loved everybody. Don't put it all on Mr. Manson."

The entire courtroom, including the judge, burst out in laughter. But before I could feel humiliated, I looked over at Charlie and saw through him, as if God had lifted the veil from my eyes. In this one moment Charlie showed me how little I really meant to him and how he was only out for himself. After all the physical beatings, the rape, and the knowledge of his responsibility for the horrifying murders, I have no idea why this bit of courtroom sarcasm was what broke the spell.

Perhaps it was because I was sitting in the safety of the witness stand rather than directly in his orbit or at his feet. I hadn't seen it before, how he could truly work a room. This man didn't mean to be funny. He wasn't being endearingly impish; he was deflecting responsibility from himself by humiliating me and dismissing my value as a human being. He had no idea how vulnerable I still was, how easy it would have been to reel me back. Instead he showed himself for what he really was and still is: a scruffy little man with an enormous ego who thought the rules didn't apply to him. He was no god, he was no son of man. He was a fake, a fraud, a pimp, and con artist. And now I was truly free of him.

I WAS THE FINAL WITNESS OF SUBSTANCE IN *THE STATE OF CALIFORNIA V. Charles Manson, Leslie Van Houten, Susan Atkins, and Patricia Kren-*

winkel trial. Over the course of twenty-three weeks, the longest trial at least to that date in California history, the prosecution presented eighty-three witnesses. At the end of the prosecution's case, the defense made a surprise decision to rest without calling one witness. When this decision was made, Patty, Leslie, and Sadie all stood up in the courtroom in front of the jury and demanded they get their day in court. What the jury didn't know is that the lawyers rested the case to protect them against themselves and Charlie's maneuverings. The girls had presented lists of questions to their attorneys that they insisted they be asked in open court. The lawyers refused even when faced with potential contempt of court because they were tantamount to full confessions that would exonerate Charlie completely.

As a compromise, on Friday, November 20, 1970, the judge allowed Charlie to make a statement on the witness stand, but not in front of the jury, to determine what of his testimony would be admissible. Charlie could finally say his piece and gave the court over an hour of a Charlie talk-to that has become part of American cultural history. The court and researchers since the trial have been able to experience the circular reasoning of Charlie's logic, which for some became the stuff of criminal psychology lore.

The verdict for the case came in on January 25, 1971. The jurors found Charles Manson, thirty-six, Patricia Krenwinkel, twenty-three, Susan Atkins, twenty-two, and Leslie Van Houten, twenty-one, guilty of what Bugliosi said in his closing argument was a "chilling, unearthly conspiracy" to commit this wanton orgy of murder. They had proven their case beyond a reasonable doubt, and all that was left was to determine the punishment for these crimes.

I was back at Jack's home when I heard the news. I know it was unnerving, but it was not unexpected. I knew what had happened and that this was the only just result. For a moment, I felt a twinge of sadness for the girls, who had been swept up into the madness of murder. Then I felt relief that I had escaped with my life and my sanity, and without blood on my hands.

In March 1971 it took ten hours for the jury to return the death penalty for all of the defendants. Charlie, Patty, Sadie, and Leslie would be facing the gas chamber. In February of 1977 these convictions were commuted to life in prison when the California death penalty was abolished. It was as if Charlie had an ultimate postulation, because in 1978 the California death penalty was restored and faced a great deal of controversy until being declared unconstitutional in recent years due to arbitrariness.

Charlie was convicted of the murders of Gary Hinman and Donald "Shorty" Shea in December of 1971.

THE TRIAL MAY HAVE DOMINATED THE LIVES OF A GENERATION TRANS-fixed by all things Manson, but for me the end of it represented a second chance. As soon as I gave my testimony I went with Jack back to Inyo County, my foster siblings, and the nice warm house where meals were served on time and life could be predictable.

I really believed that would be the end of it. The people in town had been so nice to me and I had been developing a life for myself like other kids my age. What I hadn't counted on was that my name had been in every paper in the country during the week of my testimony. Those articles followed a stream of publicity that had elucidated the gory details of the case that would now become my legacy. Now I was no longer Jack Gardiner's foster child from an underprivileged home. I was a member of the notorious Manson family who had said on the witness stand that I was in love with him.

There were also articles that discussed potential charges of perjury because I had lied in front of the grand jury. This label, liar, wouldn't come along with an asterisk and a footnote: "Read this to understand why." A liar is a liar. No one wanted to hear that I chose to lie to survive because there was a very real possibility a member of the Manson Family would kill me if I testified truthfully to the grand jury or that I was still frightened for my life. None of that mattered. When I realized that I could no longer be the new kid in school, I felt ostracized and dirty.

Jack and Carol were very well respected in the community, Jack especially. When I first got home, the phone kept ringing and I could hear Carol's or Jack's voice coming to my defense. "We believe in Dianne. She is a good kid who was caught up in a very bad situation." I also heard conversations condemning my parents, which hurt deeply. I didn't want to blame my parents. I wanted to believe it was my choice to live with Manson. I didn't want to think badly about my parents because it would only add to my pain and sense of isolation. And I had not unraveled what had really happened to me. It would take years to do that.

I held my head up as high as I could and returned to school. My friends still talked with me, but there were no more invitations to see them outside of the classroom. Their parents made me an untouchable. I can't say I blame them. Many of the parents were furious with Jack for bringing me into their community in the first place.

Of course there were no more babysitting jobs, and that made me sad. I loved taking care of the neighborhood children and feeling accomplished. The only nice thing about returning to school was my teachers, who were very supportive of me. They saw beyond where I'd come from to see what I could do. That made a tremendous difference far beyond what any of them would have imagined.

I continued to play the flute in the band, and the band teacher never mentioned anything about what I had been through. At the end of the year it was time for graduation. We had been practicing several songs, including "Pomp and Circumstance," to accompany the new graduates into their futures. As we began to play, I saw the first senior in cap and gown walk proudly at the front of the processional. Tears fell down my cheeks. I couldn't stop them. I tried not to sob aloud, but I was crying from a place inside that felt broken with grief.

At first I wasn't sure why I was crying. Then I looked around at all the families proudly watching their children take their first steps into adulthood. I should have been doing that too. These were young people my own age, and yet I was playing my best for them as my heart was breaking for me.

As the tears fell, I thought about all the things I had lost the minute I stepped inside the black bus. I realized the loss started long before that, as memories passed before me like photographs. I was crying for my lost youth and what I thought was my lost future. But I was also grieving for the senseless loss of the victims whose lives were taken from them at the behest of a madman. The last thought I had while wiping my tears with my sleeve was that I was also a victim. It was difficult to accept that.

Then I saw things differently. I had survived when others didn't. There were times when I could have lost my life or at least my sanity, but God was there. And now I would have to trust God that someday I could make sense of this experience and perhaps help others understand as well.

EPILOGUE

PEOPLE THINK THAT WHEN YOU GO THROUGH SOMETHING LIKE THIS, you're damaged goods, that the rest of your life is spent emotionally limping forward, forever trying to escape the gray area between atonement and denial. Perhaps that's true for some former cult members—it certainly could have been my story. Thankfully, though, it wasn't.

In 2008, after I received the call from Paul Dostie about his cadaver dog Buster exploring Barker Ranch, I knew there was a sense of urgency in sharing my story with my kids. Dostie had the go-ahead from CNN to film the dig, and even if nothing was discovered (which, as it turned out, was what happened), it was too much of a risk that my children would find out information distorted by the media. My husband, Todd, and I decided that they were old enough to know the truth, and that we owed it to them to hear it from our mouths and not through tabloid news or television reporting.

In truth, this was not the first time I'd been faced with the prospect of telling them. When my children were very young, in the mid-1990s, a man claiming to be a journalist knocked on my door when no one else was at home. Through some detective work, he had found my address and seemed quite proud to have located me. He asked me a lot of what I perceived as wild-goose chase questions to support his conspiracy theory obsession that Bruce Davis was the "Zodiac Killer." This self-proclaimed Manson expert raised my awareness of the danger of my real identity being revealed, but at the time my husband and I opted against telling our children anything about my past, because they were still far too young to understand and process the news. By 2008, waiting was no longer an option.

Still, I had my concerns. While I knew who I was, and what I'd made of my life, I was worried as any parent would be. Worried about their reactions, about their perceptions of me, about how their responses might cause me to relive the host of regrets I'd been carrying silently through the decades. But I also had faith in the people my children had become. Because they are such amazing kids, perhaps I shouldn't have been shocked when they handled the news with kindness and grace, but I was.

Since the clock was ticking, we started by calling our oldest son at college—we couldn't wait for him to come home.

"We have something to tell you," I mumbled. I could feel his anxiety rising so I quickly reassured him that no one had died. "I would prefer to tell you in person," I continued with more strength in my voice. I knew if I showed I was okay with it he would potentially respond in kind. He needed me to hold it together, or he would think it was worse than it really was.

"Mom, just tell me," he replied. "I can't get home just yet. You are worrying me."

"There is going to be a television show that could discuss some things about me that I have never told you and it could be very distorted."

"Okay," he said. I knew he wanted to blurt out "get to the point already," but he was being very patient as I gathered my thoughts.

"There is no way to say this so I will just tell you. Have you ever heard of Charles Manson?"

"Of course," he said.

"Well I was a member of the Manson Family from the time I was fourteen until I testified against them in 1971." The phone went dead but I could hear my son breathing. I quickly preempted the next natural question. "I was not there for the murders."

"How did this happen to you?" he demanded.

His tone sounded more protective than horrified. He had questions, but I figured the best thing would be for him to understand the big picture before I gave him the details. Maybe it was a bit of a cop-out, but I told him to read the book *Helter Skelter* by the prosecuting attorney, Vincent Bugliosi. I wasn't sure if it would be more information than he needed, but I thought it might give him a broader sense of the events, while also showing that the experience, tragically, was about much more than just what happened to me.

The next person we needed to tell was our daughter. She was visiting with us and was resting in her old room. When I knocked on her door, I found her sitting on the floor reading a book. She looked up and saw the expression on my face. Again, I reassured my child that no one had died. At least not on that particular day.

It was difficult for me to decide where to begin with my daughter. Her eyes puddled up even before I could speak. I told her how I was in foster care when I was a teenager and how I became a part of the Family, when I felt I had nowhere else to go. I could see the shock on her face. She was twenty-one at the time, but she was from a generation for whom Charles Manson was more legend than reality. She too was thankfully unfamiliar with the facts of the case and asked me a lot of questions that were surprisingly insightful. It is sometimes difficult to see our children as young adults capable of deep empathy. As Todd entered the room she looked up at him and said, "Thank you for loving Mommy."

We held each other and cried as she displayed her anger at Charlie for pulling me into his dark world. She never expressed any shame that I had been part of something so awful, but rather, gave me the kind of unconditional love that can only come from a child to a parent.

Todd and I didn't get a chance to tell our youngest son that day, but we figured there would be plenty of time. In the weeks and months that followed, our older son called frequently to ask pointed questions, eventually revealing that for the first few months after learning my secret he'd made sure to sleep with a baseball bat under his bed. Our daughter discussed it with her cousin, my brother's daughter, and it turned out to be very healing for them both. Of course, my brother had his own unusual life growing up in a commune with my parents, and while he obviously did not join a murderous cult, my niece said she gained new respect for me and a greater understanding of her father from learning about my past. For her part, my daughter had someone to confide in to help her process what I had shared.

In this way, bit by bit, we unraveled the pieces of my story together as a family, working in small increments without allowing it to become a focal point of our own life together. If friends and neighbors knew about my past, they did not ask too many questions. Our privacy was well respected and life continued as we had planned. I thanked God every day for my many blessings.

IT WASN'T A GIVEN THAT THINGS WOULD TURN OUT THIS WAY, THAT I would end up stronger for my scars and not weakened by them. There are no easy explanations for how this happened, but the truest one lies with my family, not the one I was born into, or the false one I joined, but the one that I helped build myself—a process that was started the moment Charlie and the others were convicted.

After the verdict in the Manson trial and aging out of foster care, it was time for me to move on from Jack Gardiner's home. I had grown attached to my surrogate family, but Jack was running for the office of undersheriff, and as much as he didn't say it directly to me, it was not going to be good for his image to have me living with him, Carol, and my foster siblings. That said, it wasn't as though he kicked me out or that there was any kind of falling-out. He was incredibly generous in somehow helping me bypass my lack of a high school diploma by signing me up for college courses and making sure I had a place to go.

During the summer after the trial, I met a young man named Jim who was an acquaintance of my mother and stepfather. We became friends and he invited me to spend the summer in Spokane at a Victorian rooming house so I could get a change of scenery from Los Angeles. He was a perfect gentleman, and I had a chance to recharge—it felt as if I slept for months. That summer was a welcome respite, with lazy bike rides through the town, naps on the sunporch, afternoon soaps with the spinster sisters who ran the house, and fresh fruits and vegetables from their garden. I caught up on fashion magazines and dreams for a future I'd thought I might never have.

As young people often do in idyllic settings, Jim and I fell in love and decided to save up money to backpack in Europe. We sailed to England on the *Queen Elizabeth II* for a much-needed change of venue. While we were in England we worked for a Christian Action group rehabilitating a church that had been bombed out in World War II. I learned to cook for twenty people at a time with real, fresh food purchased daily at the local open market. When the weather became too cold, we moved on to Spain where we stayed until our return to America in 1975. I wrote many letters home from Europe and found a noticeable absence of discussion about what I had been through. When I recently reconnected with Jim, he told me that during the time we were together, I spoke quite a bit about my time with Charlie and the girls, but always at a removed and superficial way, almost as if these things had happened to somebody else. That was how I wanted it. I needed to continue to process it in the way I had been taught at Patton State, by rejoining the world and learning new skills to take care of myself.

Although I can't remember why, Jim and I drifted apart after our return to the States, and a few years later, in July of 1978 as I was getting ready to participate in Leslie Van Houten's retrial, I met my husband, Todd, the man who would change my life. Todd and his brother asked a friend of mine to invite single women she knew to their Fourth of July party. As luck would have it, my friend and I were the only single women there, so I got to meet the host. From that day forward Todd and I never missed a weekend visiting each other and at Thanksgiving of that year he proposed to me.

We never looked back. We got married in a beautiful ceremony the following May in 1979 and shared a life together for thirty-five years. We had our ups and downs as all families do, but we raised three children together and created lives that we were proud of. After my children were in school I went back to college, and when my youngest was in high school, I went for my master's degree. I began as a paraprofessional in the school system but eventually was privileged to work with autistic children until my retirement.

While we were building our family, the church also became a central part of our lives, and eventually I became baptized and officially accepted Jesus Christ. I knew God was with me during those years when I was with the Family, but I wasn't fully aware of the power of that love and protection. I was grateful to surrender myself to the grace I had been given in the face of the horrific. Through the years, my pastors were some of the only people I shared my secret with and they were instrumental in helping me see the hand of God in how I made it through my time with the Family. My born-again experience was a gift and an acknowledgment that God is the center of my life and perhaps the greatest reason I survived to this day as well as I have.

My faith and perspective have given me the ability to look objectively at my parents and their role in how I wound up with Charlie. In the years after my marriage to Todd, I reestablished a relationship with my mother, who was by then happily married to my stepfather. I also reestablished a relationship with my father, Chance, who remarried as well, and in a twist of irony, became a mortgage holder for the second time. He never fully discussed his responsibility in my circumstances, but admitted that perhaps his resistance to the establishment could have been better thought out. He saw that his friends were now retiring while he still had twenty years left of a thirty-year mortgage.

The closest I got to an apology from my father was a statement in passing that they "might have thrown the baby out with the bathwater." That was all I needed from him because, although it is difficult at times for me to process my complicated feelings about him, I have a better understanding of the limitations of parents and of all human beings. I know that my parents were sincere in their seeking of a better life. Whatever misjudgments they might have made helped me become the person that I was meant to be. I love them in all their imperfection as I am also imperfect. I have a healthy respect for my parents and what they believed in, but I also have a healthy unrest with what they did. In remembering with adult eyes, I am no longer in denial about my parent's part in what happened to me, but more important, I am at peace with it.

Forgiving my parents and using my faith in God to help my journey, have been crucial to how I've come to terms with my past. In recent years, I've spent quite a bit of time trying to understand how I've been able to emerge from this experience with the life I've led. So many people want to believe that darkness must beget more darkness. But for me, the ultimate saving grace was the family that Todd and I made.

I know I'm not alone in my belief that *family* is a loaded word. It is the foundation of our lives, yet for so many of us, it's our undoing. In my case it has become both. While my family was part of the reason why I lost my way so many years ago, and why my search for surrogates brought me to unfathomable depths, family was also what drew me a new map and showed me what it really meant to be a part of something bigger than myself. Because of Todd and my kids, I discovered that one can belong to other people in a way that is real and dependable, and that discovery was profoundly healing.

The life that Todd and I created, the love that we had for each other and for our kids, was the fulfillment of what I'd been searching for but had never grasped. It's difficult to think about where my journey across the last several decades would have led me, if I hadn't found my way home to them. My family was a gift, one I appreciated every day because I helped build it with my own two hands.

*   *   *

ON MAY 19, 2013, TODD AND I CELEBRATED OUR THIRTY-FIFTH WEDDING anniversary together. We were incredibly happy, but as much as we didn't want to admit it, Todd had an intuition that something wasn't right.

It was November 2013 when Todd got the diagnosis. It was not only skin cancer, it was a rare, aggressive form called Merkel cell carcinoma. In January numbness formed in his jaw after chemotherapy, so we decided to double-check the symptom with expert oncologists. Perhaps it was nothing. All kinds of symptoms happen with chemo. After some tests, the doctor told us the unimaginable news: the cancer had spread to Todd's brain. Even with a cancer diagnosis, we thought he would have a few more years. Everything was happening so fast. We could see by the doctor's expression that the prognosis was grave. Todd went into hospice care almost immediately.

The hospice nurses arranged for a hospital bed in the living room of the house we had designed and decorated together. All the children came home and we each took turns sleeping on the couch next to Todd as we watched him fade from the vibrant head of our household to someone too weak to speak. When someone is in hospice, there are no further efforts made to prolong life. This is the time for winding down and for making someone as comfortable as possible.

As the end drew near, I slept on the couch next to him listening for his labored breathing. One night I fell asleep, and in the morning, there was silence.

The day after Todd died I was talking with my older son and my daughter about how I never got around to telling my youngest about my family secret. The mind takes you to the places of your deepest fear and anxiety in the moment of grief. With Todd gone I didn't know what to do and when. The decision was taken from me as my son overheard the nervous whisperings.

"What are you talking about in here?" he insisted. I was somewhat relieved to give my mind something to do other than experience the deep pain I was in.

My grief was unmasking the shame I had buried. Now I would be alone without the unconditional love of my husband and lifemate. I decided to tell my son what he needed to know or perhaps what I needed to share.

I watched his face for some sign of how he was taking the news. His eyes widened.

"You were with these people and you overcame it. Eventually it made you into a better person and you came out on top." This was how my son interpreted what I had said to him. I think he could see my confusion as if I was waiting for him to reject me. "Mom, you have always been a loving free spirit. We'll get through this."

This was the last hurdle in bringing my secret out in the open with the people who mattered the most to me. Todd had protected me from my past by helping me feel safe and loved. Now I had to learn to feel that within myself.

In the years since Todd's death, I've finally found the space to ask myself the necessary questions to tell this story, in particular, about just who, exactly, was the girl I'd been all those years ago. That person who'd been searching to belong, who'd been willing to sacrifice so much of herself for one man's gain, that person who had been lost as I'd moved on with my life.

I uncovered the strength to answer that question and others, not because I couldn't say these things when Todd was alive (believe me, Todd knew everything about me and was comfortable, even more than I was, with the person I'd been and where I'd come from), but because honestly, I was too busy living my life with him to have any interest in what those answers would be. In my husband and my family, I'd finally found the path to living in the now, to being fully present in my own life. For me, the ability to live in the moment did not lie with gurus, drugs, sex, or music (though I'm not sure anyone from the 1960s really found answers that way). Instead, living a seemingly ordinary life had led me to realize the promise of the countercultural searching that had defined my youth. Simply put, I'd been too busy enjoying my present to spend too much time dwelling on my past. In the end, those two years as a teenager were just that—nothing more. Aside from a brief run-in with Barbara Hoyt, I never saw anyone from the Family again. My life came to define itself, not by where I'd been but by where I was going.

I'm now entering a new phase of my life, a time without secrets. Difficult as it has been to unearth the trauma of the past, I understand, better than ever before, how my past has shaped my present, and just how lucky I've been to have the family that I have. Secrets are dangerous things. If you're not careful a secret can take on its own life, sitting in the corner feeding off your oxygen. A secret takes up space. Sharing it leaves more room for people to connect, or in my case, to belong.

ACKNOWLEDGMENTS

I WOULD LIKE TO ACKNOWLEDGE GOD, WHO LED ME TO FIND AND AC-
cept Jesus Christ as my Lord and Savior because I know he preserved
me and helped me survive.

In addition, I would like to acknowledge God's hand in bringing
me the following people:

My late husband, Todd, who gave me love, support, and acceptance.

My children, for bringing me joy and for their love and support
throughout the telling of my story and the process of my healing.

My pastor, Lyn, for his prayers and his support.

My therapist, Ricki, for her ability to mirror to me the perspective of healthy boundaries and forgiveness and for renewing my
sense of self-worth.

My life coach Joan for inspiring me to write every day and showing me that doing so would be worthwhile.

My collaborator, or as I like to refer to her, "my co-blabberator,"
Deborah Herman, who opened her own heart with nonjudgment,
understanding, perserverance, and talent, and who shared this journey in untethering my shame.

My literary agent Jeff Herman, who brought this book to the
team at HarperCollins and who went beyond the call of duty by es-
corting me and Deborah through the treacherous canyons of Death
Valley all in the name of research.

The entire team at HarperCollins and the William Morrow imprint: Lisa Sharkey, Anna Montague, Danielle Bartlett, Shelby Meiz-
lik, Alieza Schvimer, Andrea Molitor, and especially Matt Harper,
for his tireless dedication as editor to the quality of this book.

My fiancé, Jim, for his love and support.